Birding the Southwestern National Parks

NUMBER
THIRTY-FIVE:
W. L. MOODY, JR.,
NATURAL HISTORY
SERIES

ROLAND H. WAUER

Drawings by MIMI HOPPE WOLF

Texas A & M University Press

COLLEGE STATION

Birding the Southwestern National Parks

Library of Congress Cataloging-in-Publication Data

Wauer, Roland H.
    Birding the Southwestern national parks / by Roland H. Wauer ;
drawings by Mimi Hoppe Wolf.—1st ed.
        p.   cm.—(W.L. Moody, Jr., natural history series ; no. 35)
    ISBN 1-58544-286-0 (cloth : alk. paper)—ISBN 1-58544-287-9
(pbk. : alk. paper)
        1. Bird watching—Southwest, New. 2. Bird watching—Texas.
3. National parks and reserves—Southwest, New. 4. National
parks and reserves—Texas. I. Title. II. Series.
    QL683.S75 W38 2004
    598'.07'23479—dc21
                                                        2003014842

Contents

Birding
the
Southwestern
National
Parks

Preface

America's national parks possess the best examples of the continent's natural heritage, complete with the grandest scenery and most stable plant and animal communities still in existence. In a large sense, our national parks represent a microcosm of our last remaining wildlands.

Birding the Southwestern National Parks has a threefold purpose. First, it provides the reader with a fresh perspective on bird life in seventeen national park units within the Southwest. It is intended to introduce the park visitor to the most common and obvious birds as well as to the fascinating world of bird identification and behavior. It also can be used as a reference about each park and its bird life during a visit and as a valuable tool in preparing for that visit.

Second, the book provides detailed guidelines on how best to get started with the absorbing activity of birdwatching. It helps the reader to select the appropriate tools, offers insights into bird identification and field techniques, and includes guidance on birding ethics.

Third, and just as important, the chapter titled "Parks as Islands" contains a discussion of the status and value of our national parks. In sections about threats facing the parks, the effects of wildland fires on bird life, and the importance of the parks for the future, I offer my perspectives on the health and vitality of parks and of the national park system.

This book is not intended for use as a field guide or primarily for bird identification. Several excellent field guides are already available; they should be used in conjunction with this park guide. Nor have I aimed to help the birder find all of the rarities or out-of-the-way specialties. My purpose is to help the park visitor appreciate the parks and their range of bird life more fully. If, in making new acquaintances, visitors should become interested in birds and grow concerned about their well-being, so much the better.

The segment on each locale begins with a personal experience of the kind that anyone visiting the park might have. At Organ Pipe Cactus National Monument, for example, Phainopepla activities about the campground are routine and hard to miss. At Carlsbad Caverns, Cave Swallows whisk around the cave entrance most of the year. And at Big Bend, I made my first-ever observation of a Colima Warbler.

A description of the national park itself follows, including the plant and animal communities that exist there, visitor facilities available, interpretive activities, and how to learn more about the place by letter, telephone, or by visiting the park's Web site. The common names given for plants are those in local use in each area; scientific names are included at the back of the book. The bulk of the text for each park is then devoted to its bird life, providing the common birds within several of the park's most popular and accessible areas. Each park segment ends with a summary emphasizing characteristic bird species of the park. Birds common to more than one park are discussed in all relevant chapters. This way, the chapter for any park of particular interest is complete and may be read out of order.

Where to Begin

A visit to any of the national parks should begin with a stop at the visitor center or information station to obtain a park brochure and activity sheet. These will contain basic guidance about roads and trails, accommodations, campgrounds, and picnic sites; details of interpretive activities offered; descriptions of the park's key resources; and so on. The numerous sites mentioned in this book are best located by using the area map supplied in the brochure for the park concerned.

Common names used for birds are taken from the most recent checklist of birds published by the American Ornithologists' Union (AOU) and its supplements and used in current field guides. The references at the back include all the works I consulted. My hope is that readers will use those books, articles, and reports for fuller understanding of birds and of the habitats so essential to their survival. We may go out to wild places in search of beauty or peace, but the better we understand what we see during a park sojourn, the more rewarding our visits will be.

Roland H. Wauer

Acknowledgments

This book would not have been possible without the kind assistance of dozens of employees of the National Park Service: superintendents, rangers, naturalists, resource specialists, scientists, and a few other individuals. I especially want to thank the following people: Gary Johnston at the Washington, D.C. office; Eric Finkelstein and David Larson for assistance with Amistad National Recreational Area; Mark Flippo, Rick LoBello, Jeff Selleck, and Keith Yarborough for Big Bend; Fred Armstrong, Bobby Crisman, Bill Reid, Brent Wauer, and Steve West for Carlsbad Caverns and the Guadalupe Mountains; Suzanne Moody and Walt Saenger for Chiricahua National Monument; Richard Boland, Charles Callagan, Esy Fields, Glenn Gossard, Ross Hopkins, Dale Reynolds, Ed Rothfuss, Doug Threloff, and Greg Volkman for Death Valley; Greer Price and John Ray for Grand Canyon; Alta Blietz, Chris Collins, Jerry Freilich, Bill Truesdell, and Arthur Webster for Joshua Tree National Park; Nancy Bernard, Mike Boyles, Cathy Cook, Ross Haley, and Kay Rhodes for Lake Mead; Glen Henderson and Babs Monroe for Montezuma Castle; Jon Arnold, Jim Barnett, Bob Cook, Kathy Davis, and Tim Tibbitts for Organ Pipe Cactus National Monument; Linda Booth, Tom Danton, Art Eck, Jeff Kartheisser, Natasha Kline, Don Swann, Meg Weesner, and Loretta Wyatt for Saguaro National Park; Eddie Colyott, Shirley Hoh, Dessamae Lorrain, and Faye Morrison for Tonto National Monument; John Mangimeli for White Sands; and Bruce and Sam Henderson for Wupatki, Sunset Crater Volcano, and Walnut Canyon.

I also want to thank Mimi Hoppe Wolf for her wonderful pen-and-ink sketches scattered throughout. Her marvelous ability greatly enhances my highlighting of many bird species.

Last and certainly not least, I thank my wife Betty, who supported this project with editorial advice and assistance, calling herself my "RV slave" throughout our travels to gather firsthand and up-to-date information.

Rewards and Techniques of Birding

The bond between birds and man is older than recorded history. Birds have always been an integral part of human culture, a symbol of the affinity between mankind and the rest of the natural world, in religion, in folklore, in magic, in art—from early cave paintings to the albatross that haunted Coleridge's Ancient Mariner. Scientists today recognize them as sure indicators of the health of the environment. And as modern field guides make identification easier, millions of laymen watch them just for the joy of it.—PAUL BROOKS

*H*ow often I have wished I could fly. To soar high over the mountains and valleys, to explore secluded places impossible to reach any other way, to escape earthbound existence with the ease of a bird—these were among my secret desires as a youngster. How I envied the hawks and swallows and even the tiny hummingbirds. They were the masters of my universe.

Of all the warm-blooded creatures, only birds and bats can fly for more than a few yards. Only birds possess the combination of feathers, powerful wings, hollow bones, a remarkable respiratory system, and a large, strong heart. They are truly magnificent flying machines. The power of wing beats, due to the marvelous flight feathers, allows a bird to cruise at speeds of twenty to forty miles per hour while flying nonstop across the Gulf of Mexico or the arctic tundra. The tiny hummingbird has been clocked at fifty miles per hour. And the powerful Peregrine Falcon is thought to stoop (dive) at speeds in excess of a hundred miles per hour.

A Blue-winged Teal banded in Quebec, Canada, was killed by a hunter less than four weeks later in Guayana, South America, more than twenty-five hundred miles away. A Manx Shearwater taken from its burrow on Skokholm Island, Wales, and carried by airplane to Boston, Massachusetts, returned to its burrow on the thirteenth day, having flown three thousand miles across the Atlantic Ocean. And a Lesser Yellowlegs banded in Massachusetts was captured six days later on Martinique in the Lesser Antilles, nineteen hundred miles away. That bird had averaged 317 miles per day.

Migrating birds usually fly below 3,000 feet in elevation, but observers at 14,000 feet in the Himalayas reported storks and cranes flying so high overhead—at an estimated 20,000 feet—that they could barely be seen through binoculars.

Other marvelous features of birds are their bill shapes and sizes. Anyone who has watched birds for any time at all cannot help but notice the diversity of feeding methods. Hummingbirds, for example, have long thin bills that they use for probing in flowers to feed on nectar, sometimes deep inside tubular flowers. Their bills are especially adapted to this type of feeding. Many shorebirds, such as dowitchers and Common Snipes, also have long bills, but these are much heavier, for probing for food in mud. The Long-billed Curlew's bill can reach into deep burrows to extract its prey.

The many insect feeders have dainty bills for capturing tiny insects. Vireos and warblers are gleaners that forage on trees and shrubs, picking insects off leaves and bark. A careful examination of feeding warblers will further suggest the size of their preferred food on the basis of their bill size. Flycatcher and swallow bills are wider to enhance their ability to capture flying insects in midair. Woodpecker bills are specialized so they are able to drill into insect-infested trees and shrubs to retrieve the larvae there.

Finch bills are short and stout, most useful for cracking seeds or crushing armored insects. Crossbills are able to extract seeds from conifer cones. And grosbeaks are able to feed on much larger fruit, actually stripping away the husk from fleshy seeds. Many birds feed on fruit when it is abundant in late summer and fall and on insects at other times of the year.

Then there are the predators with their variety of bill shapes and sizes. Raptors possess short, stout bills with a specialized hook used for tearing apart their prey. Wading birds have large, heavy bills for capturing prey. And the bills of diving birds are hooked for catching fish and serrated on the edges for a better grip.

Feet are another fascinating feature of anatomy helpful to understanding a bird's requirements. Webbed feet suggest its adaptation to water for swimming, and flattened toes help birds walk on soft mud. Tiny, flexible toes suggest an ability to perch on small twigs and branches. Large, powerful feet with sharp talons are required to capture and grip prey.

There are approximately ninety-six hundred kinds of birds in the world; about nine hundred of those are found in North America. And every one has slightly different characteristics from the rest, allowing it to utilize a slightly different niche (the combination of its needs) from any other species. Whenever two species within the same area have the same needs, in all likelihood only one will persist and breed. Competition either drives the other away or seriously infringes upon its ability to perpetuate its kind.

A bird is thus a very specialized creature indeed, but its bill and feet are usually less obvious than its plumage, the sum total of its feathers. A bird's plumage is unquestionably its most obvious and usually its most attractive characteristic. This is especially the case for the more colorful and contrasting birds, such as warblers, hummingbirds, some waterfowl, and some finches. Birds are the most colorful of all vertebrates.

Feathers reveal every color in the rainbow. The colors we see are the product of pigments and of the reflection and refraction of light due to feather structure. The concentration of pigments produces the intensities of color, as in the vivid red of a male Vermilion Flycatcher and the diluted red of a female Northern Cardinal. The total lack of pigment production results in white plumage. Many colors we see are due to how feathers reflect or absorb light. The bright blues of Steller's Jays or bluebirds result from a particular arrangement of cells in the feathers, which reflects light in such a way as to produce an iridescent sheen. Dull colors or a velvety appearance result from feather structure that absorbs light.

Of all the aesthetically pleasing characteristics of birds, birdsong may be the most enduring. Louis Halle (1947, 217) wrote: "As music is the purest form of expression, so it seems to me that the singing of birds is the purest form for the expression of natural beauty and goodness in the larger sense, the least susceptible of explanation on ulterior practical grounds."

For many birders, birdsong not only helps with bird identification but is also a most important part of the outdoor experience. Bird identification is just as sure by sound as it is by sight. In fact, many species are so difficult to see in the high foliage that their calls and songs are used for identification more often than are actual sightings. While novice birders may feel uncertain about recognizing bird songs, it is often surprising how many songs one can recognize without a great deal of study. For instance, the songs of jays, chickadees, mockingbirds, robins, cardinals, ducks, geese, and gulls are probably already known. And how about the calls of crows, owls, and quail?

Birds use songs to identify their territory; such songs are usually directed by males at other males. They also use songs to attract a mate. Or the song may serve to convey a message. While some birds sing only at dusk and dawn, and others sing primarily during the morning, there are species that sing throughout the daylight hours and even, in the case of the Northern Mockingbird during the nesting season, throughout the night. Ornithologist Margaret Nice recorded 2,305 songs in a single May day for a Song Sparrow. But the North American winner is the Red-eyed Vireo, a bird of the eastern forests. Ornithologist Harold Mayfield recorded a Michigan Red-eyed Vireo that sang 22,197 songs in a day.

The more we learn about birds, the clearer it becomes that they possess additional values that are often ignored, perhaps because they are simply taken for granted. For instance, certain birds are extremely adept at catching and consuming large quantities of insects, many of which are considered pests. These include obnoxious insects as well as those that are a serious threat to various crops. Some birds, especially hummingbirds, provide a valuable service by helping to pollinate a diversity of wildflowers.

In addition, birds offer important clues to our changing environment. Long-term databases, such as the Christmas Bird Counts, provide insight into declines and increases in avian populations so valuable to conservationists.

Human beings have been interacting with birds since our earliest history. Birds were worshiped in many early civilizations. Cormorants were ringed for catching fish. Pigeons have carried our messages. Songbirds were taken into mines and brightened our homes with their wonderful songs. In literature, Samuel Coleridge has immortalized the albatross, Percy Shelley the lark, and Edgar Allan Poe the raven. The concept and development of human flight derive from our observations of birds. Every state and province has an official bird, many of these highlighting flags and seals. Most Canadian coins and paper money display common bird species. And the most powerful country in the world utilizes a bird as its symbol: America's Bald Eagle is one of the most visible symbols in the United States.

Birds truly are an intricate part of the human ecosystem, an important link to nature. More than any other creatures, birds are obvious and omnipresent companions to the human community.

Essential Equipment

There comes a time when those of us with a natural curiosity about and appreciation for the outdoors want to know the names of the various creatures we see around us. The spark to identify birds may be kindled by some exceptional happening or a special sighting. Watching a family of jays at a campground as they actively investigate you and your food supply or suddenly being mobbed by a flock of Cliff Swallows at a nest site is likely to foster interest in those species and what they are about.

But identifying those birds can be awkward unless you know where to begin. Although you may already be able to identify more birds than you realize, further precision requires some basics, just as in any other endeavor. The basics include two essential pieces of equipment: a field guide and a pair of binoculars.

There are several very good field guides available that use the bird identification technique Roger Tory Peterson developed. Peterson's field guides and those published by the National Geographic Society, Golden Press, and National Audubon Society are illustrated with bird paintings. These guides are preferred over those with photographs because the paintings highlight key features that are not always obvious in photographs. The most recent of these books, the National Audubon Society's *Sibley Guide to Birds,* has become the most helpful because it includes an assortment of illustrations of each bird, representing plumages at various ages and times of year and sexual differences when they occur. For additional information on field guides and other bird books, see the references section later in this chapter.

Binoculars are absolutely essential for identifying, watching, and enjoying most birds. They vary in power, illumination, and field of view as well as in price. All binoculars are two telescopes mounted side by side, providing the user with a magnified, stereoscopic view. Each telescope has an eyepiece, objective (or front) lens, and prisms that are located inside halfway between the eyepiece and objectve lens. A prism actually "folds" the light path so that the length of the telescope can be reduced. It also acts as a mirror to reverse an image and turn it right side up.

The most popular birding binocular has long been an 8×35 glass. The "8×" indicates the power or magnification; 8× binoculars magnify a bird eight times, 7× glasses magnify it seven times, and so on. The "35" is the aperture, the size of the objective in millimeters, and is an indication of illumination or brightness. The larger the objective lens, the more light that enters the binoculars and the brighter the image. But the larger the objective lens, the heavier the binoculars.

Binoculars with magnification of 9× and higher are often too large and powerful for users who are not adept at holding them perfectly still. Pocket-sized, lightweight binoculars (those with a small objective lens) are small, easy to carry, and good for occasional use. But the loss of brightness and field of vision are serious drawbacks, and continuous use of small binoculars can cause eye strain.

In addition, central-focus binoculars, those with a centrally mounted wheel, are a must. Focusing distance is also important. Binoculars with "close focus" capability allow the user to focus on a bird that may be as close as twelve to fifteen feet; some binoculars focus as close as five to six feet.

A birder who uses binoculars often and on a continuous basis should purchase the very best binoculars possible. Better binoculars are less likely to lose alignment, more water resistant, less inclined to fog, armored for rough use, and offer quality eyecups that accommodate those who wear eyeglasses.

Using binoculars usually requires some experimentation, but the skill is easy to learn. First make sure that the right ocular is set at "o" for 20-20 vision. Then, while looking directly at an object, bring the binoculars up into position without changing your position or looking elsewhere, and use the center wheel to focus on the object. A few tries will soon produce success.

A spotting scope also may be necessary for birders who become involved with long-distance viewing and need additional power. Binoculars are seldom adequate for identifying waterfowl or shorebirds at great distances. Like binoculars, scopes come in all types and at a wide range of prices. Also like binoculars, the diameter of the objective lens determines the amount of light that can enter the optical system. The aperture of the scope's objective lens normally ranges from fifty to ninety millimeters. Eyepieces for scopes usually come separate. They can be fixed or zoom and vary in magnification from 10 to 250×, but 20 to 60× is typical. An important additional factor to consider is whether you want an angled or straight-through viewing eyepiece. Most scopes come with an extendable sunshade, tripod mount, and case. The more expensive scopes are armored for greater protection and are waterproof. Also, a sturdy tripod is essential. Before deciding on what scope is best for you, visit with others about their preferences and experiment with their equipment.

The next step is to get acquainted with your field guide. Start by leafing through the entire guide and locating the first page of tyrant flycatchers, just beyond woodpeckers. Flycatchers and all the birds illustrated from that point onward are perching birds (songbirds). All the other categories of birds are "nonperching" birds and are located within the first portion of the book—seabirds, waders, waterfowl, raptors (birds of prey), shorebirds, gulls and terns, grouse, hummingbirds, woodpeckers, etc. Leafing through the guide several times not only helps you get to know the sequence of bird families but also helps you learn the species.

Next read the introductory section, especially the discussion about field marks. You will find a drawing of a typical bird showing basic field marks. Look these over so that you have a clear idea of what is meant by descriptive terms like crown, eyeline, eye ring, chin, upper and lower mandibles, flank, upper tail and under tail coverts, wrist, wing bar, and so on. Be ready to refer back to this illustration for help when necessary. Browsing through your field guide time and time again is likely to pay dividends at a later time in the field.

Now that you have discovered the value of a field guide, it is time to start identifying real birds. You should have an idea of what features to look for. The following suggestions provide an identification strategy of sorts:

1. *Size.* It can be useful to relate bird size to those species you already know. For instance, consider five categories: sparrow size, robin size, pigeon size, duck size, and heron size. With a few exceptions, such as the Com-

mon Raven, any bird the size of a duck or larger is a nonperching bird and will be found in the first half of the field guide. By thinking about size, you immediately know where to start your search. Also, one can often pick out odd-sized birds in a flock for further attention or to recognize different species that might be foraging together. For example, a tiny bird within a party of warblers will more than likely be a chickadee, kinglet, or Brown Creeper.

2. *Shape and behavior.* Does your bird possess any outstanding features? Is it a wader with long legs and an upright posture? Possibly a heron. Is it walking along the shoreline? Possibly a shorebird. Is it swimming on a lake or river? Probably one of the waterfowl or gulls. Is it soaring high in the sky? Possibly a Turkey Vulture or hawk. Is it perched on a wire or thin tree limb? More than likely a perching bird, although hawks occasionally perch on wires. Is it a perching bird eating seeds at a feeder? Probably a sparrow or finch. If it is smaller than a sparrow, is creeping up a tree trunk, and is all brown, it is sure to be a Brown Creeper.

3. *Color and pattern.* Many birds possess obvious plumage that is an immediate giveaway. Cardinals, crows, robins, Yellow Warblers, and Red-winged and Yellow-headed blackbirds are the first to come to mind. Their bold and obvious color or pattern, or both, stand out like a sore thumb. But many of their neighbors will require a little more study. Do the all-white underparts extend onto the back, or does the bird have only white wing bars? Does its white neck extend only to the lower mandible or onto the face? Does the reddish color extend onto the back, or is it limited to the tail and wings? Do the yellow underparts include the throat and belly or only the chest? Answering these questions will eventually become second nature to you.

Field Techniques

Bird-finding techniques are often personal ones, and you will establish your own methods. For example, I like to move very slowly through a particular habitat, trying to discover all the birds within that immediate area. I find that part of birding most enjoyable and challenging. Other birders prefer to move faster, stopping only to watch birds that become obvious. This method is based on the concept of finding more birds by covering more ground. That is certainly a good reason for visiting as many habitats as possible, but I believe that the largest number of species can be found by moving slowly through each habitat, making yourself part of the scene, both physically and mentally.

The idea of blending into the scene is not always understood. Some successful hunters use the concept to good effect in their stalking. Perhaps becoming part of the surroundings is more of a state of mind than a real circumstance, but I have found over the years that being unobtrusive results in more observations. It also allows for more close-up views. A related idea involves approaching prey by not looking directly at it; a bird often allows an intruder to approach much more closely if it thinks it has not been seen. And then, when you are close enough, it is a matter of slowly shifting your view toward the bird of interest.

Moving slowly and taking things in gradually also allows for more extended observation of bird behavior. It can be satisfying to find new birds to add to a personal checklist, but to focus on the list alone and ignore the activities of the birds is to miss a great deal of the thrill of birding. Bird behavior is truly fascinating. Eventually, your observations and questions may open new avenues for finding birds as your understanding of what they are doing deepens.

There are definite clues to bird finding that you can use to your advantage. First are bird sounds. During the breeding season, birdsong is the very best indicator of a bird's presence and location. Songbirds often sing throughout the day. They almost always sing at dawn and dusk, and a few species sing only at dawn. Serious birders like to get out at dawn to experience the dawn chorus while most of us are still asleep. The majority of birds, however, can usually be found throughout the day.

Rustling leaves in the underbrush can be another valuable clue. Leaf rustling can be caused by numerous creatures, but when the leaves seem to be thrown back as if being cleared away for finding food underneath, the rustler is likely to be a thrasher, White-crowned Sparrow, or Spotted Towhee.

Songbirds in particular tend to ignore intruders who are quiet and move slowly, unless they get too close to a nest or fledgling. You can get surprisingly close to songbirds by moving slowly and not making any sudden motions. Also, wearing dull clothing instead of bright and contrasting colors helps you to blend into the bird's environment, usually permitting closer viewing.

Some of the nonperching birds permit a slow, cautious approach, but the wading birds, ducks, and raptors are not as trusting. These birds will probably need to be observed from a distance, and you may want to use a spotting scope to see them well. Or you may be able to use one of the blinds installed at some bird-viewing sites.

During the nonbreeding portion of the year, birds often occur in flocks or in parties. Flocks of waterfowl or blackbirds can number in the hundreds or thousands and are readily visible from a considerable distance. But a party of songbirds moving through the forest requires quiet study for identifying all the members. It is possible to wander through the woods for some time before discovering a party of birds that may include a dozen or more species. Migrant songbirds often travel in parties that can include hundreds of individuals of two or three dozen species. If you find such a party, remain still and let the party continue its feeding activities without disturbing it.

In cases when a bird party is just beyond good viewing distance, you can sometimes attract a few of the closer individuals by "spishing"—making low, scratchy sounds with your teeth together and mouth slightly open—a few times. Attracting the closer individuals often entices the whole flock to move in your direction. However, I find that spishing within a bird party tends to frighten some species off or to move the party along faster than it might otherwise go.

At times, a bird party is concentrated at a choice feeding site, such as flowering or fruiting trees and shrubs. So long as they are not frightened or unduly agitated by noises or movement, they may remain and continue feeding for some time, once they overcome their initial concern over your presence. Also, their activities will tend to attract other birds, allowing you to see a broad spectrum of birds at one spot.

Generally, birding along a forest edge, often along the edge of a parking lot, can produce excellent results in the early morning. Bird parties prefer sunny areas at that time of day, to take advantage of greater insect activity. Within two or three hours, however, feeding birds tend to move into the cooler vegetation, especially on hot sunny days.

Birds may then need to be enticed into the open; many species respond well to some sounds. Spishing often works well. Squeaking sounds made with your lips against the back of your hand or finger may also work. Birds are naturally curious and will often come to investigate, though at times spishing or squeaking seems to frighten birds away. Some species will be attracted once but will be difficult to fool twice. So always be prepared to focus your binoculars on the bird immediately when it pops up from a shrub or out of a thicket.

As already noted, the best way to find a large number of birds is to visit a variety of bird habitats. All birds occur in preferred habitats, especially during their nesting season. But they tend to frequent a broader range of sites during migration and in winter. Learn where species can most likely be expected. For instance, Boreal Chickadees occur only in the northern coniferous forests; this species cannot be found at Big Bend National Park. And one cannot expect to find a roadrunner in the boreal forest. A new birder should learn to take advantage of the range map and habitat description given for each species included in the field guide. This can save time and considerable embarrassment.

Birding by song is often left to the experienced birder, although today it is simple for novices to be almost as well equipped to utilize bird songs as are many of the experts. For anyone with an ear for melody, many records, tapes, and CDs are available to help you learn to recognize the songs of different species. During spring and summer, there is no better method of bird identification. When tiny songbirds are singing from the upper canopy of the forest, finding and observing these individuals can be difficult. But their songs are an instant method of recognition that does not involve eye and neck strain from staring into the high canopy for hours on end. Getting a good view of marsh birds like rails can also be trying, if not outright dangerous. Fortunately, rails and other marsh birds also have distinctive calls that can usually be easily identified.

Much of the knowledge required to make quick bird identifications must come from field experience. An excellent shortcut is spending time with an experienced birder who is willing to share his or her knowledge. That person can pass on tidbits of information that otherwise might take years to acquire. Most national parks have staff naturalists who give bird talks and walks during the visitor season. This kind of assistance can be extremely worthwhile for bird finding and bird identification.

Closer to home, consider participating in Christmas Bird Counts and other surveys. Novices are welcomed and can often provide valuable assistance to more experienced birders and at the same time obtain good field experience. In addition, many cities have bird or nature clubs that offer talks and field trips. One can also subscribe to birding magazines or join various national and state birding organizations that offer literature and online information.

Birding Ethics

As with any other activity, there are certain rules of the game. Birding should be fun and fulfilling. It can be a challenge equal to that of any other outdoor endeavor, but it should never become so all-consuming as to threaten the bird's health and habitat. Any time we are in the field, we must realize that we are only visitors to the habitat on which a number of birds depend for their existence. We must not interfere with their way of life. Disturbing nests and nestlings, for whatever reason, cannot be tolerated. Tree whacking to entice woodpeckers and owls to peek outside is not acceptable.

Most national parks are adequately posted, but sometimes thoughtlessness can lead to severe impacts on the environment. Avoid taking shortcuts in a vehicle and driving over meadows. Respect closures in the park; they are there for good reason. The survival of nesting terns or Peregrine Falcons may depend upon keeping an area undisturbed.

One practice that is fairly commonplace in some instances, such as with tour groups intent on making sure that all participants see a particular bird, is playing taped bird songs or taping a particular song in the field and playing it back. This is not permitted within national parks; there are regulations against such activities. However, most tour guides and experienced birders are able to attract many birds by whistling certain owl calls. The call of a screech-owl, even at midday, will usually attract birds in the vicinity that will not come out of hiding for any other reason.

The hobby of birding can be a most enjoyable pastime. And it is one that costs little and can be launched without special training. It can be pursued alone or in a group, at any time of the day or night, and at any time of year. And there is nowhere on earth where birds are not an obvious part of the natural environment.

Early naturalist Frank Chapman, in his *Handbook of Birds of Eastern North America* (1966, 1), summarized the enjoyment of birds better than anyone else. Chapman wrote that birds "not only make life upon the globe possible, but they may add immeasurably to our enjoyment of it. Where in all animate nature shall we find so marvelous a combination of beauty of form and color, of grace and power of motion, of musical ability and intelligence, to delight our eyes, charm our ears and appeal to our imagination."

References

Since there is a huge variety of field guides and other bird-related books on the market, the beginning birder can be overwhelmed when trying to choose a book or two to get started. As noted, a field guide is an absolute necessity. In my opinion, the best one is the *Field Guide to the Birds of North America* published by the National Geographic Society, now in its fourth edition (2002). I find the descriptions excellent and the paintings effective. The National Audubon Society's *Sibley Guide to Birds* by David Allen Sibley, as mentioned earlier, is outstanding, including several paintings of each bird, but it may need to be employed as a secondary guide because it is rather large for carrying in the field. Two other field guides rate well above average in my estimation: *A Guide to Field Identification Birds of North America* by Chandler Robins, Bertel Bruun, and Herbert S. Zim (1966), and Roger Tory Peterson's *A Field Guide to Western Birds* (1990).

Besides these references, several other bird books are worth considering. I use the three-volume *Audubon Society Master Guide to Birding* (1961) often, especially for its description of bird songs. Kevin Zimmer's *The Western Bird Watcher: An Introduction to Birding in the American West* (1985) is most helpful. And there are three general bird books that can answer questions about almost anything to do with birds: The National Audubon Society's *Sibley Guide to Bird Life and Behavior* by David Allan Sibley (2000); *The Audubon Society Encyclopedia of North American Birds,* by John Terres (1987); and *The Birder's Handbook* by Paul Ehrlich, David S. Dobkin, and Darryl Wheye (1988).

In addition to these, there is an abundance of other books for specific bird families, such as Jon Dunn and Kimball Garrett's *Peterson Field Guide: Warblers,* and two on hummingbirds: Steven N. G. Howell's *Hummingbirds of North America,* and Sheri Williamson's *Peterson Field Guide: Hummingbirds of North America.* There also are many excellent regional bird guides. A few of these include Richard Taylor's *A Birder's Guide to Southeastern Arizona* (1995); Mark Lockwood and colleagues' *A Birder's Guide to Rio Grande Valley* (1999); my *A Field Guide to Birds of the Big Bend* (1994); and *Birding Texas* (1998) by Mark Elwonger and me.

Parks as Islands

All living things possess an intrinsic value which is beyond calculation. Humans as rational beings are responsible for safeguarding forms of life which we did not create but suddenly have the power to destroy. By knowingly causing extinction of these species and their habitats, we sacrifice a part of our humanity.—PHILLIP M. HOOSE, 1981

*W*hen crisis came for the Peregrine Falcon, its last viable populations anywhere in North America south of Alaska were those remaining in national parks in the Rocky Mountains, on the Colorado Plateau, and in West Texas. The discovery that populations of this species and several similar high-level predators were being decimated by DDT and other chlorinated hydrocarbons, and the eventual banning of DDT in the United States and Canada in 1972, came too late to save any of the eastern Peregrines. The last active aerie in the Appalachian Mountains was at Great Smoky Mountains National Park. The entire population of that subspecies became extinct in three decades. Fewer than thirty pairs were known in the United States by 1975. Peregrines in National Park Service units at Big Bend, Black Canyon, Dinosaur, Grand Canyon, Mesa Verde, and Zion, however, were well enough isolated and still present in sufficient numbers to ensure the survival of an adequate breeding population.

These examples demonstrate the value of national parks as natural refuges. The western parks provided last strongholds for Peregrine populations to withstand human-induced pollutants. In most cases, those Peregrines fed primarily on resident bird life that had not been subjected to DDT elsewhere. But in the case of the Great Smoky Mountains population, insufficient buffers existed, and the eastern Peregrine disappeared forever.

During the 1980s, when Peregrine restoration programs were being implemented, park sites in the Great Smoky Mountains and at Isle Royale, Yosemite, Sequoia, and Zion were among the first selected. Nearly twenty-five hundred Peregrines were released in the West, said James Enderson, leader of the Western Peregrine Recovery Team. By 1990, Peregrines once again began to frequent their old haunts and nesting pairs were recorded at several areas. The finding of fifty-eight active aeries at Grand Canyon in 1989 suggested that

Peregrine populations were recovering sufficiently for this species to be de-listed (Brown et al. 1990).

In spite of an apparent Peregrine "fix," many other bird populations continue to decline. The most serious losses are occurring in Neotropical species, long-distance migrants that nest in the United States and Canada and winter in the tropics, in the Greater Antilles, Mexico, Central America, and to a lesser extent in northern South America.

The reasons for the declines are varied. Neotropical migrants are less adaptable than most resident species. They have a shorter nesting season, with only enough time to produce one brood before they must depart on their southward journeys. Long-distance migrants tend to arrive on their breeding grounds later and to depart earlier. They also produce smaller clutches than the full-time residents. And most of the Neotropical species place their nests in the open, either on the ground or on shrubs or trees. Their nests, therefore, are more susceptible to predators and brood parasitism by cowbirds than are nests of the full-time residents, many of which are cavity nesters (woodpeckers, chickadees, titmice, wrens, and bluebirds). If a raccoon, skunk, or fox destroys the nest of a full-time resident, the bird can start again, but one episode of predation or parasitism can cancel an entire breeding season for a Neotropical bird.

Breeding bird studies in the fragmented environment of Rock Creek Park in Washington, D.C., from 1947 through 1978, revealed that six Neotropical species (Yellow-billed Cuckoo, Yellow-throated Vireo, Northern Parula, and Black-and-White, Hooded, and Kentucky warblers) could no longer be found to nest there. And several other species, including Acadian Flycatcher, Red-eyed Vireo, Wood Thrush, Ovenbird, and Scarlet Tanager, had declined by 50 percent. Conversely, at Great Smoky Mountains National Park, with its 494,000 acres of mature forest, breeding bird censuses conducted in the late 1940s and repeated in 1982 and 1983 "revealed no evidence of a widespread decline in Neotropical migrants within the large, relatively unfragmented forest" of the park, according to the National Fish and Wildlife Foundation (1990).

These divergent examples—Peregrine Falcons in Big Bend, Grand Canyon, and other western parks and Neotropical breeders in the Great Smoky Mountains—demonstrate the value of large natural parks as preserves for the perpetuation of wildlife resources.

Threats to the Parks

North America's national parks are not immune, however, to the abundant environmental threats. Every park has experienced impacts that threaten its ecological integrity. Although parks may appear unchanged, and visitors may think the scenery looks pretty much the same from year to year, a number of strands in the parks' fragile ecological webs have been damaged.

During the early years, most of the natural parks had sufficient buffers around them to insulate them from development and pollution outside their borders. But with continued population growth and increased adjacent land uses, park buffer zones have dwindled. Many parks are bordered by farmlands that are maintained with chemicals, by forests that are clear-cut, and by increasing numbers of industrial centers, malls, and housing developments. Widespread air pollution reaches great distances and affects even the most remote parkscapes.

Long-term monitoring of air quality values in several of the parks reveals that prevailing winds, especially in summer, carry pollutants from far-away urban and industrial areas. Plant and animal communities all over the globe are linked by the air that is moved around by weather systems. In a sense, our world is like a large room where everything shares the same recirculated air. This circulation has created pollution in over one-third of the national parks. Even at isolated and pristine Isle Royale, wind-borne chemicals have turned up in inland lakes. Birth defects in aquatic birds and cancerous tumors in fish have been linked to the toxins (National Park Service 1980).

Inside the parks, roadways, trails, campgrounds, and other facilities permit greater human use of the resources. Facilities are often poorly sited and designed, so that they increase fragmentation and stress resources already threatened by external perturbations. Habitat degradation within a park as a result of improper management can have serious consequences for the park's bird life. Any fragmentation reduces the integrity of the unit, lowering its value for wild species. Developing new sites increases access to the forest interior for predators that feed on birds and their eggs; for parasitic cowbirds that lay their eggs in other species' nests; for exotic House Sparrows, European Starlings, and other invaders that compete for nesting space and food; and for exotic plants that can drastically change the habitat.

A number of recent studies suggest that cowbird parasitism can affect songbirds even in large forest tracts and may be a major cause of the decline of many Neotropical migrants. As John Terborgh reports in the May 1992 issue of *Scientific American*, researchers have concluded that cowbirds "will commute up to seven kilometers [4.35 miles] from feeding areas to search for nests to parasitize." He notes that a seven-kilometer radius "describes a circle of 150 square kilometers [58 square miles], equal to 15,000 hectares [37,065 acres]. It is disturbing to think a forest that might offer at its center a haven from cowbird parasitism would have to be at least that size."

Cuts into the forest interior also increase populations of several more birds of open areas, such as American Crows, jays, magpies, and grackles, which prey on other birds and their eggs and hatchlings.

Once a park's natural ecosystem has been damaged by fragmentation and pollution, all the resources become more susceptible to impacts from natural disruptions like fires, floods, and diseases. Events like these, although part of a long-term natural cycle, can seriously affect bird populations that have already been reduced by pollution, predators, parasites, and competitors.

Wildland Fires and Their Effects on Bird Life

Environmental changes are part of every natural system. Wildland fires, which occur in most forest, shrub, and grassland communities, are one example. A healthy bird population is able to withstand such changes. Indeed, many plants and animals are fire dependent. Some pine cones must burn in order to open, drop their seeds, and regenerate. Woodpeckers frequent freshly burned sites to feed on various wood-boring beetles that are attracted to trees weakened by natural fires. Many raptors are attracted to prairie fires to feed off the displaced rodents and insects.

Wildland fires have received considerable scrutiny by the public and government officials since the highly visible Yellowstone National Park fire of 1988. Almost one million acres of Yellowstone's parklands were affected by that burn. Although park officials readily point out the negative affects of fire, largely in areas where the fuel loads built up in excess over too many years without burning, they also are eager to discuss the benefits of fire to the Yellowstone ecosystem. Fire is a natural part of the ecosystem. Old growth forests do not have the diversity of wildlife that occurs in the mixed-age forests created by fires. Fire opens the forest so that new vegetation—grasses, aspens, and a variety of shrubs that had been overcome by the older forest—can contribute to the mix of habitats. Terry Rich's "Forests, Fire and the Future" in *Birder's World* (1989) includes a good summary of the effects of the Yellowstone fire on the park's bird life.

My own research at Bandelier National Monument showed that the 1977 La Mesa fire initiated a series of changes that continued to be evident fifteen years later. All three of my study sites revealed increased numbers of bird species and populations following the fire. Significant population increases occurred almost immediately in woodpeckers, with minor increases in all the other insect feeders, such as Violet-green Swallows, nuthatches, and warblers. Seed feeders like sparrows, juncos, and finches initially declined in varying degrees but soon increased with the newly available grass seed. Once woodpeckers became established, other cavity nesters like Ash-throated Flycatchers, Violet-green Swallows, Mountain Chickadees, nuthatches, and bluebirds increased to take advantage of vacated nest holes. Predators also increased with the additional prey base and more open character of the landscape. A few lowland species, such as the Mourning Dove, Say's Phoebe, Western Scrub-Jay, and Spotted Towhee, moved in to utilize the open and warmer terrain. Snag-fall provided increased habitat for House Wrens. Although the initial influx of Downy, Hairy, and Three-toed woodpeckers and Northern Flickers tapered off by the fifth year, Lewis's Woodpeckers moved into some of the vacated nest holes. And vireos, Virginia's Warblers, Black-headed Grosbeaks, towhees, and Dark-eyed Juncos were soon able to take advantage of the young aspens and oak thickets.

The Future

Although extinction is part of the natural process, the rate of extinction has never been as swift as it is at present. The greatest losses are occurring within the tropical forests, where many of our songbirds spend the winter.

In North America, at least 480 kinds of plants and animals have become extinct since Europeans first arrived. Seven species have disappeared since 1972, when the U. S. Congress passed the Endangered Species Act. More than six hundred species have since been listed as "threatened" or "endangered." Endangered species are those in danger of becoming extinct; threatened species are those on the verge of becoming endangered.

Today, the concept of threatened and endangered species is an accepted part of our world. Significant decisions are based on whether a species is listed. The names of some threatened and endangered species have become household terms—who has not heard of the plight of the Peregrine Falcon, humpback whale, and snail darter?

The shortcoming of the Endangered Species Act is that it addresses individual species instead of communities of plants and animals. Attempts to restore species do not always give adequate attention to the natural processes on which they depend. And at a time of inadequate funding and moral support for restoration, only the more charismatic species receive attention. An Endangered Ecosystem Act would have much greater success in saving species by giving adequate protection to large tracts of intact landscape (at least 58 square miles) that contain several threatened and endangered species. These larger areas are the essence of the national parks.

The bottom line is that North American birds are losing their breeding grounds, winter habitats, and many of the stopover places in between.

What Is Being Done within the Parks?

Much has been written about the threats to park resources. The National Park Service itself has been at the forefront of expressing concern about those threats. A major "State of the Parks" initiative was undertaken in the early 1980s to identify the threats and to establish a program for preventing additional threats and mitigating impacts. A Natural Resource Management Program that placed specialists in all the natural park areas was the most significant product of that effort. That program coninues to this day. During the 1990s, several additional programs, such as a Service-wide Inventory and Monitoring Program, were established.

Many of the national parks also are participating in Partners in Flight activities, such as International Migratory Bird Day. Partners in Flight is a consortium of government agencies and private organizations conducting an international program to identify and conserve bird species and habitats that are in peril. Early emphasis has been placed on the development of a network of parks and protected areas in the Western Hemisphere that are linked by Neotropical migratory birds. Activities focusing on Neotropical migrants have begun in more than three dozen parks as another way to develop linkages between pertinent park units.

In addition, the Park Flight Program of the National Park Service, partnering with the National Park Foundation, the National Fish and Wildlife Foundation, and the U.S. Agency for International Development, is designed to protect shared migratory bird species and their habitats in both the United States and Mesoamerican (Mexico and Central America) national parks and protected areas.

The majority of the national parks, especially the natural areas, are involved in one way or another with avian research and monitoring activities. In the Southwest, examples of current and recent research studies include inventories of birds at Lake Mead, Saguaro, Carlsbad Caverns, Guadalupe Mountains, White Sands, Big Bend, and Amistad; assessment of avian communities in salt cedar at Lake Mead; a study of the reproductive success of forest songbirds at Grand Canyon; riparian bird populations at Carlsbad Caverns, Guadalupe Mountains, White Sands, and Big Bend; and a survey of wintering grassland birds at Guadalupe Mountains.

More specific studies include the ecology of the Northern Goshawk at Grand Canyon; Spotted Owl surveys at Organ Pipe Cactus, Saguaro, Chiricahua, and Grand Canyon; Elf Owl ecology and migration at Carlsbad Caverns; survey of Buff-breasted Flycatchers in the sky islands at Saguaro; analysis of the Plain Titmouse complex at Joshua Tree; House Wren taxonomy at Saguaro; and effects of Brown-headed Cowbirds on breeding birds at

Organ Pipe Cactus. In addition, this author recently completed a seven-year breeding bird population baseline for Big Bend (2001).

Monitoring projects in southwestern parks include an array of Christmas Bird Counts, numerous Breeding Bird Surveys, and several programs involving threatened or endangered species. Examples include long-term monitoring of bird populations at Organ Pipe Cactus; wintering Bald Eagles at Lake Mead and Grand Canyon; Peregrine Falcons at Lake Mead, Grand Canyon, Organ Pipe Cactus, Saguaro, Guadalupe Mountains, and Big Bend; Ferruginous Pygmy-Owls at Organ Pipe Cactus; Willow Flycatchers at Lake Mead and Grand Canyon; and Black-capped Vireos at Big Bend and Amistad.

Death Valley National Park, California and Nevada

Joshua Tree National Park, California

Except where noted, color photography by Roland H. Wauer.

Lake Mead National Recreation Area, Nevada

Grand Canyon National Park, Arizona

Sunset Crater Volcano National Monument, Arizona

Walnut Canyon National Monument, Arizona

Montezuma Castle National Monument, Arizona

Tonto National Monument, Arizona

Organ Pipe Cactus National Monument, Arizona

Saguaro National Park, Arizona

Chiricahua National Monument, Arizona

Carlsbad Caverns National Park, New Mexico

Guadalupe Mountains National Park, Texas

White Sands National Monument, New Mexico

Big Bend National Park, Texas

Amistad National Recreation Area, Texas. Photo by Joe Labadie, courtesy of the National Park Service.

The Southwestern National Parks

The more one becomes familiar with the desert parks, the more one can appreciate the value of wild nature. To walk through the desert vegetation during an early morning, when everything is bright and fresh, when bird songs dominate the scene, is pure ecstasy. Such an experience is not only therapeutic, allowing one to regain whatever sanity is lost elsewhere in our modern society, but pure joy as well. I find that I must return to the desert and its amazingly diverse bird life time and time again.

—ROLAND H. WAUER

*T*he national parks in the southwestern portion of the United States contain some of the least known and most poorly understood units of the national park system. Yet these varied areas possess some of our most beautiful and serene landscapes. Desert areas with their sky-island mountains offer the visitor a greater diversity of wildlife than can be found in the more northerly mountainous parks. The Southwest has a much higher number of birds, and they usually are available to the naturalist at all times of the year.

The common and uncommon bird life to be found in seventeen southwestern national parks and monuments is profiled in the pages that follow. Presented in a sequence going from west to east, the parks range from California's Death Valley and Joshua Tree National Park through Grand Canyon, Organ Pipe Cactus, and Saguaro in Arizona to the Guadalupe Mountains, Big Bend, and Amistad in Texas. More than five hundred bird species occur within these varied units, and the visiting birder can see many of these with a minimum of effort.

The park descriptions provide the novice bird-watcher as well as the avid birder with fresh insights into the bird life of these amazing areas. You are invited to join me on a birding excursion through America's marvelous southwestern parks.

Death Valley National Park

CALIFORNIA & NEVADA

 Common Ravens are far and away the most obvious of Death Valley's birds. Year-round residents, they are common from Badwater to the summit of Telescope Peak, the park's lowest and highest points, and everywhere in between. No other bird is so representative of this fascinating area.

One winter morning at Furnace Creek Ranch, Common Ravens were present wherever I looked. A dozen or so were flying about the campground, searching for food scraps that might have been missed by the night shift, the coyotes and kit foxes. Ravens also were abundant in the date orchard, perched on the date palms or on the ground. And on the golf course, I found flocks of twenty-six and forty-two individuals gathered to socialize; they looked as if they were discussing the new day.

Their vocalizations varied from typical hoarse "caaw" notes to "groo," "graa," and deep "growl" sounds. Every now and then one would utter a series of deep guttural, croaking notes, sounding more like an oversized frog than a bird. One raven flew over the visitor center carrying in its bill a kangaroo rat, which it had either found dead on the road or captured alive. Two other ravens gave chase, and for several minutes these three birds put on a marvelous exhibition of their flying dexterity: rolling, twisting, diving, tumbling, veering this way and that, flying almost straight upward and rolling again. Then, for no apparent reason, the pursuers suddenly gave up the chase, and the bird with the kangaroo rat flew off alone, apparently to dine in peace.

It is commonplace in Death Valley to see flocks of a few to a dozen or more Common Ravens soaring high overhead, especially in midmorning when the thermals are at their best. Sometimes the birds soar completely out of sight. Anyone driving into the valley during the early morning hours will certainly see Common Ravens flying along the highway. They perform daily maintenance chores of cleaning up roadkills from the previous night.

Death Valley's Common Ravens normally nest on inaccessible cliffs in late winter or very early spring. Young of the year may already be present by March, and the adults can often be seen teaching their offspring the art of hunting, the intricacies of flying, and whatever else they need to survive in the harsh Death Valley environment.

Once the young leave the nest they are next to impossible to separate from adults, at least by their physical features. They are the same general size and possess the same glossy black plumage, massive bill, and wedge-shaped tail. Only by watching the youngsters attempt to mimic their parents or occasionally beg for a handout can they be identified for sure. But by early summer, when even larger congregations of ravens often gather at Furnace Creek Ranch, only another raven can tell the young apart.

THE PARK ENVIRONMENT

Death Valley is a north-south trough four to sixteen miles in width and 135 miles long. The valley is flanked on the east by the Amargosa Range, which rises steeply to a height of 7,738 feet at the summit of Grapevine Peak. To the west are the higher, more impressive Panamint Mountains; the high point at Telescope Peak reaches 11,049 feet. It rises almost directly out of the valley floor where Badwater, the lowest point in the Western Hemisphere, is situated at 282 feet below sea level. The resultant 11,331-foot rise in elevation makes Telescope Peak the "tallest" peak in the continental United States. This huge park encompasses more than 3.3 million acres.

Death Valley once held a lake six hundred feet deep but today has only the salty remnants, like rings left on a dried-out basin of dirty water. The Death Valley salt pan, with its white, tan, and brown rings, covers more than 150

Common Ravens

square miles. The entire region lies within the greater Basin and Range Province and supports Mojave Desert flora and fauna. Death Valley's desert environment, however, contains elements of the higher Great Basin Desert to the north and the lower Sonoran Desert to the south.

The bottom of Death Valley is like an elongated concave playa, with vegetation such as pickleweed at a few saltwater sites and along the edges, where (somewhat saline) fresh water can be obtained from the alluvium. Iodine-bush grows in isolated bunches closest to the salt pan, and a line of saltgrass, arrowweed, and sacaton grass forms a ground cover at the few areas dominated by honey mesquite. Desert holly and honeysweet grow at the base of the alluvial fans, where creosote bush persists and extends into the canyons and higher flats. Desert holly, fourwing saltbush, and brittlebush dominate most mid-elevation washes and exposed flats.

The canyons, which start at 800 to 2,500 feet elevation, are characterized by steep slopes and washes with only a moderate growth of vegetation. Common woody plants in the lower canyons include fourwing saltbush, dalea, creosote bush, rock nettle, bladdersage, water molly, brittlebush, bursage, cheese-bush, and desert-fir. The higher canyons are often dominated by green-molly, rubber rabbitbrush, and creek senecio. And a line of springs at about 4,000 feet elevation in the Panamint Mountains often supports heavy growth of willows and a few Fremont cottonwoods. The open flats and valleys of the high desert are dominated by shadscale, cliffrose, desert mallow, bladdersage, desert sage, big sagebrush, and cottonthorn.

The pinyon-juniper woodland, which occurs from approximately 5,500 to 8,000 feet elevation, is dominated by singleleaf pinyon, California juniper, fernbush, cliffrose, desert grape, desert sage, big sagebrush, Mohave brickellia, and cottonthorn. The canyons at this same elevation and upward onto the high ridges of Roger's, Bennett, and Telescope peaks support a pine community with limber pine, water birch, mountain mahogany, fernbush, maple, buckbrush, and tansy. Above 9,500 feet is a boreal environment dominated by bristlecone pine, alumroot, gooseberry, ninebark, tansy bush, and hawks-beard.

Although Death Valley holds one of the world's highest official temperature records (134°F was recorded in 1913), typical winters in the valley offer warm days and pleasant nighttime temperatures. Furnace Creek Ranch, in about the geographic center of the valley and with about five square miles of grasslands, ponds, date orchard, tamarisk rows, and mesquite thickets, is the heart of the park's visitor activities. Here are accommodations, campgrounds, restaurants, stores, an eighteen-hole golf course, and the park's visitor center and headquarters.

The Furnace Creek Visitor Center contains an information desk, exhibits, an auditorium for orientation and evening programs, and an extensive sales outlet for books, postcards, slides, and such; bird field guides and a park checklist are available. Smaller ranger stations also exist at Grapevine, near Scotty's Castle in the north; at Stovepipe Wells and Wildrose in the western portion of the park; at Beatty, Nevada; and at Shoshone, California.

Additional park information can be obtained from the Superintendent, Death Valley National Park, Death Valley, CA 92328; (760) 786-2331; Web address: www.nps.gov/deva/.

BIRD LIFE

Although the **Common Raven** is the undisputed sovereign of Death Valley, five common wintering birds at Furnace Creek Ranch look somewhat alike: Common Raven, Great-tailed Grackle, Brewer's and Red-winged blackbirds, and European Starling. Each appears all black at first glance, but they are very different in size, shape, and personality. The Common Raven is the largest of these, but the **Great-tailed Grackle** can be just as noisy and may exhibit more obnoxious behavior. This is the long-tailed bird that often sits around the ranch and campgrounds, sometimes walking about the campsites or even on top of RVs and trailers, uttering extremely loud whistles, cackles, and hissing notes; such antics can be extremely aggravating in the early mornings. Males are all black with yellow-white eyes; females possess a dark brown back, olive-brown underparts, and pale yellow eyes. Both sexes have a long keeled tail.

Brewer's Blackbirds are generally present only in winter and during migration, nesting in mountain wetlands and sagebrush flats north of the park. At Death Valley, they often flock with the larger grackles and have a harsh "check" call. But they are never as noisy or obnoxious as their larger grackle cousins. Male Brewer's Blackbirds are shiny black with yellowish eyes; females are dark brown with dark eyes; they possess a moderately long tail that is not wedge-shaped. The slightly smaller Red-winged Blackbirds, with red wing patches, usually occur only at wet areas and adjacent to the golf course.

The **European Starling** is the most numerous of the five species, occurring in huge flocks during the winter months. Starlings are especially common in the date orchard and on the golf course, wheeling about in unison when approached by a walker or golfer. This nonnative bird is readily distinguishable from the other four species in that it has a short tail and yellow bill, and in good light its iridescent black plumage is covered with tiny whitish flecks. Introduced from Europe to New York's Central Park in 1890, it has since spread all across the country. It first appeared in Death Valley in December, 1950; I found a flock at Furnace Creek Ranch in November, 1957, and a lone bird stayed all summer in 1959; it may now be Death Valley's single most abundant year-round avian resident.

My winter bird walk around Furnace Creek Ranch produced several additional bird species: a few Pied-billed Grebes, a pair of Canada Geese accompanying a huge flock of Mallards, a pair of Cinnamon Teal, numerous American Coots, and a few Killdeer in and about the ponds on the golf course. Marsh Wrens were calling from the cattails growing along the irrigation ditches. A Red-tailed Hawk flew overhead. And I also saw a few Mourning Doves, Northern (red-shafted) Flickers, Black and Say's phoebes, Ruby-crowned Kinglets, American Pipits, Yellow-rumped Warblers, Song and White-crowned sparrows, a dozen Western Meadowlarks, several House Finches, and numerous House Sparrows.

House Finches are full-time residents in the valley, widespread about the ranch and in the surrounding desert. However, some of the valley residents move to higher, cooler habitats in late spring after nesting. House Finches are usually detected first by their constant singing, rapid and joyous ditties that are repeated over and over again, each time with a slightly different inflection. They even sing in flight. Male House Finches are easily identified by their bright red throat, eyebrows, and rump, but females are rather drab birds with a brownish back and boldly streaked underparts.

The shift to higher locations in late spring also occurs with the **Say's Phoebe,** another of the park's year-round residents. This graceful flycatcher nests on a wide variety of artificial structures and ledges from below sea level up into the pinyon-juniper woodlands. At Furnace Creek Ranch, watch for this buff-colored bird with a darker cap and tail flycatching about the golf course or from the numerous historic structures and objects. The phoebe's plaintive, sad "pee-ur" call is commonplace.

One winter day Betty and I also walked the Salt Creek Nature Trail and had a picnic at the Sand Dunes. The Salt Creek boardwalk circles a fascinating wetland, providing a wonderful opportunity to experience a habitat that has changed little since the Forty-niners passed through this area more than a hundred years ago. We did not find any of the unique desert pupfish from the boardwalk, but according to the park brochure, in winter when the water is cold, "the fish are dormant in the bottom mud and virtually impossible to find." We did, however, find a lone American Pipit and several Killdeer.

The **Killdeer** froze in place at our approach, and we were able to get reasonably close before they realized they were under observation and flew downstream out of sight. The Killdeer is one of our best known shorebirds because of its abundance throughout North America and its loud and distinct call, an energetic "kill-dee" or "dee-dee-dee" notes, often repeated several times. Larger than a robin in size, the Killdeer has two distinct black bands across its all-white chest, a black-and-white forehead, red eye rings, and long buff-colored legs. In flight, it also shows a rusty tail and rump and white wing stripes.

At the Sand Dunes, we found several dozen Mountain Bluebirds feeding over the surrounding flats. We watched as they flew from saltbush to saltbush and to the ground in their search for insects. The male's bright all-blue plumage was readily distinguished from the more subtle blue and gray of the female.

The most exciting bird of the Sand Dunes was the **Loggerhead Shrike,** a husky black-and-white bird with a black mask and a strongly hooked bill. In flight, it shows a white patch on each black wing and white edges on its black tail. But the shrike's most interesting characteristic is its predatory behavior, capturing insects, small mammals, and birds—some as large as mocking-birds—and impaling them on thorns or barbed wire. Dozens of prey species have been found impaled, usually with the head up, on a single shrub or cac-tus, almost like ornaments on a Christmas tree. This habit was initially con-sidered to be a method of killing and storing food, but studies have shown that the male also uses this behavior for attracting a mate into his territory.

The Sand Dunes shrike was perched at the top of a large mesquite, calling and singing a variety of melodic phrases. Its call was a grating series of shriek notes. Its song was varied and musical; I jotted down my interpretation: "tut tut triil, tuu, trice, tr-uill, tuu tuu triiiill." After several minutes of singing it suddenly took flight, and I watched it fly off with swift wing beats in a per-fectly straight line.

The scattered mesquite thickets in the valley, such as those at Furnace Creek Ranch, Mesquite Spring, Eagle Borax, and Saratoga Springs, usually support a fairly large number of wintering birds. In winter these locations are the best places to find Northern Mockingbirds, Le Conte's Thrashers, Cedar Waxwings, Dark-eyed Juncos, Brewer's and White-crowned sparrows, and Lesser Goldfinches.

Le Conte's Thrasher may be the most wanted of these birds; birders often spend considerable time in pursuit of this secretive thrasher. Although it is a fairly large, long-tailed songbird, and it often sits atop mesquites to sing, it is extremely shy. Individuals usually fly away if anyone approaches, even at a considerable distance. Then the bird drops to the ground and runs away un-til it is ready to fly up onto another perch to check for approaching danger. Le Conte's Thrasher songs, which it sings chiefly at dawn and dusk, are loud and melodius. These thrashers also give an ascending, whistled "twheep" note.

The great alluvial fans directly above the valley floor are mostly devoid of

Loggerhead Shrike

bird life in winter. Not until one reaches the higher flats that contain more extensive vegetation does the number of birds increase. A wintertime walk on the higher flats, such as those en route to Wildrose, will usually produce a few flocks of Sage Sparrows, flying or running ahead. And there is never a time when a Common Raven is not present, either perched on a distant high point or passing overhead. It is as if this bird has become the park's official watchdog, always present and monitoring one's activities.

The wooded slopes of the higher Panamint Mountains contain a moderate bird population throughout the winter, except when a particularly severe storm forces birds to the warmer lowlands. For example, Clark's Nutcracker, a breeding bird of the high Panamints, has been found at Furnace Creek Ranch following heavy snow in the high country.

A winter visit to the Charcoal Kilns in Wildrose Canyon, even with patches of snow on the ground, will likely produce a dozen or so of the more typical mountain species. On one late January visit I found Dark-eyed Juncos the most numerous, with smaller numbers of Northern Flickers, Western Scrub-Jays, Mountain Chickadees, Juniper Titmice, Bushtits, Red-breasted Nuthatches, and Spotted Towhees. A pair of Red-tailed Hawks was soaring over the broad valley, and seven or eight Common Ravens cruised over the high snow-covered ridges.

Dark-eyed (Oregon) Juncos also move up and down the slopes in winter; they usually are most numerous just below the snowline. During some winters they are fairly common in the valley at Furnace Creek Ranch. This little "snow-bird" is easily identified by its all-black hood, pinkish bill, chestnut-brown back, buff sides, and black tail with conspicuous white outer feathers on each side. While feeding, juncos twitter constantly, and during sunny spring mornings they may sing partial or full songs—a simple but musical trill with an occasional change of pitch—almost as vigorously as they do on the breeding grounds at higher elevations.

Valley temperatures increase dramatically by March, and the resident birds begin their breeding cycle. Only three species are known to nest on the valley's alluvial fans: Burrowing Owl, Say's Phoebe, and Rock Wren.

The **Rock Wren** is probably the most widespread breeding bird in the park. Nest sites have been reported among the jumbled rocky outcrops from below the canyons at sea level up to the boreal areas near the summit of Telescope Peak. This bird, too, may make seasonal movements up and down the mountains. During the winter it occurs below the snowline and down to the below-sea-level region of Death Valley. But by midsummer it moves upslope; I have not found it below about 2,000 feet elevation after early June.

Rock Wrens are small, all-grayish birds with whitish eyelines and patches at the corners of the tail. Their habit of bobbing up and down, especially when disturbed, helps one to identify them even at a distance. And their songs are also distinct. In his *Field Guide to Western Birds* (1990, 223), Roger Tory Peterson describes "a varied chant, *tew, tew, tew, tew,* or *chr-wee, chr-wee, chr-wee* or *chee-poo, che-poo,* etc. Call, a loud dry trill on one pitch; also a clear *ti-keer.*" Rock Wrens have the strange habit of placing small objects about the entrance to their nest; see Joshua Tree National Park for more about this odd behavior.

The canyons and washes, just above the alluvial fans, possess a surprisingly rich breeding bird population. The Red-tailed Hawk, Prairie Falcon, Great Horned Owl, Common Poorwill, White-throated Swift, and Common Raven nest on the cliffs or on the ground. The Greater Roadrunner, Costa's Hummingbird, Ash-throated Flycatcher, Northern Mockingbird, Black-throated Sparrow, and House Finch build their nests on shrubs in the washes. And California and Gambel's quail, Chukar, Mourning Dove, Western Kingbird,

Verdin, Blue-gray Gnatcatcher, Common Yellowthroat, Blue Grosbeak, Lazuli Bunting, Hooded and Bullock's orioles, House Finch, and Lesser Goldfinch nest at springs and seeps just below the pinyon-juniper woodland.

The **Red-tailed Hawk** is one of the area's most obvious birds because of its large size and its habit of soaring over the open slopes during the daylight hours. It is the park's only full-time resident hawk. Its broad wings and rust- to brick-red tail are usually conspicuous, and its loud piercing call, a descending "tseeer," often helps one to pinpoint its location.

The Golden Eagle, a larger all-dark bird with a golden sheen on its head, is also present in the highlands. This magnificent bird is most often seen hunting the open sage flats and valleys; black-tailed jackrabbits are favorite prey.

Breeding birds of the open sage flats and valleys are limited to eleven species: Chukar, Greater Roadrunner, Common Poorwill, Say's Phoebe, Horned Lark, Rock Wren, Northern Mockingbird, Le Conte's and Sage thrashers, Black-throated Sparrow, and House Finch. Horned Larks can be abundant, running about or flying off with high-pitched "tsee-titi" notes. A careful observer may find one standing upright on the ground; the male is easily identified by its buff back, black-and-white face and chest, and a double crest like tiny horns.

Almost four dozen bird species are known to nest within the pinyon-juniper woodlands. The more common nesting birds of this habitat include the Ash-throated and Gray flycatchers, Western Wood-Pewee, Violet-green Swallow, Western Scrub-Jay, Mountain Chickadee, Juniper Titmouse, Blue-gray Gnatcatcher, Black-throated Gray Warbler, Chipping Sparrow, and Brown-headed Cowbird. Less common pinyon-juniper nesters include the Common Poorwill, Broad-tailed Hummingbird, Gray Vireo, Pinyon Jay, Bushtit, White-breasted Nuthatch, Bewick's Wren, Hermit Thrush, Loggerhead Shrike, Western Tanager, Black-headed Grosbeak, Black-chinned Sparrow, and Scott's Oriole. Mountain Quail, Orange-crowned and Yellow warblers, Lazuli Bunting, and Lesser Goldfinch nest in riparian habitats at mountain springs.

Of all these woodland birds, the **Mountain Chickadee** is most numerous; I recorded sixteen pairs on one quarter-mile-square study plot below Mahogany Flat one June 9. Although this little tit can be rather shy when nesting, it is normally easy to see anywhere in the woodlands and higher forest. Its very distinct, hoarse "chick-a-dee" or "dee-dee-dee" notes are commonplace. And if it is not readily visible, low spishing sounds will usually attract it close enough for it to be clearly seen without the aid of binoculars. The Mountain Chickadee is the only chickadee with white eyebrows; all the other chickadee species possess a solid black cap.

Mountain Chickadees are cavity nesters that utilize natural or wood-pecker-excavated cavities, lining these with moss, feathers, fur, and shredded bark. Paul Ehrlich and colleagues note in their *Birder's Handbook* (1988, 428) that the female "is a close sitter on the nest; if disturbed, will lunge and emit explosive snakelike hiss. Young fed by regurgitation until 4 days old. Male collects more food for young than does female; female spends more time tending young at the nest."

Another typical pinyon-juniper bird is the **Juniper Titmouse,** another little tit but without the black-and-white plumage. It is a nondescript all-gray bird with a short crest. Most of the year the titmouse has a scratchy "te-wit tee-wit tee-wit" call, but during the breeding season it sings "tchick-a-dee-dee," not too different from the notes of the chickadee. The titmouse also gives a scolding "see-jert-jert" call when disturbed. It, too, is a cavity nester and seems to prefer the lower juniper-dominated portion of the woodlands at that time of year.

The higher Panamint Mountains contain communities of limber and bristlecone pines with scattered sagebrush flats. The Hairy Woodpecker, Mountain Chickadee, White-breasted Nuthatch, House Wren, Mountain Bluebird, Townsend's Solitaire, Hermit Thrush, American Robin, Black-throated Gray Warbler, Dark-eyed Junco, and Chipping Sparrow nest within the limber pine community.

The bristlecone pine community supports eight species of breeding birds: Northern Flicker, Clark's Nutcracker, Mountain Chickadee, Rock Wren, Western Bluebird, Yellow-rumped (Audubon's) Warbler, Dark-eyed Junco, and Cassin's Finch. And the highest tracts of sagebrush support a few additional birds: Mountain Quail, Chukar, Green-tailed Towhee, and Sage and Brewer's sparrows.

In addition, the White-throated Swift and Rock Wren occur in the vicinity of outcrops, and Violet-green Swallows nest in rocky crevices in the cliffs.

The summer months in Death Valley are truly unique. Although the desert landscape supports only those specially adapted plants that are able to survive temperatures daily reaching more than 110°F for five months or longer, the few valley oases can be alive with birds. Steinegar Spring, located adjacent to Scotty's Castle at the north end of the Valley, attracts a wide variety of birds. Chukars and Ladder-backed Woodpeckers occur here year-round, and in summer, watch for Bell's Vireos, Black-tailed Gnatcatchers, and Hooded Orioles.

Furnace Creek Ranch, however, supports the greatest bird population in summer. This is where the majority of the 235 or more species that have been found below sea level occur. On a three-hour field trip to the ranch in mid-July, I recorded 608 individuals of 46 species: Great Blue Heron 2; Black-crowned Night-Heron 4; Turkey Vulture 6; Mallard 12; Cinnamon Teal 8; Redhead 4; Ruddy Duck 2; Cooper's Hawk 1; Red-tailed Hawk 1; Ferruginous Hawk 1; Prairie Falcon 1; Gambel's Quail 8; American Coot 10; American Avocet 4; Killdeer 23; Solitary Sandpiper 1; Spotted Sandpiper 2; Least Sandpiper 18; Wilson's Phalarope 1; Mourning Dove 55; Greater Roadrunner 2; Great Horned Owl 1; Short-eared Owl 1; Black Phoebe 2; Say's Phoebe 3; Ash-throated Flycatcher 4; Western Kingbird 2; Warbling Vireo 2; Common Raven 22; Horned Lark 5; Northern Rough-winged Swallow 12; Bank Swallow 5; Cliff Swallow 8; Barn Swallow 65; Northern Mockingbird 5; Phainopepla 1; Yellow-breasted Chat 4; Savannah Sparrow 8; Blue Grosbeak 2; Red-winged

Blackbird 125 (3 flocks); Yellow-headed Blackbird 26; Brown-headed Cowbird 95; Hooded Oriole 5; Bullock's Oriole 9; House Finch 18; and House Sparrow 12.

Many of these species were southbound migrants from cooler northern environs. However, some of the migrants that follow this long north-south valley never reach one of the desert oases. Some individuals succumb to the hot and arid conditions along the way. Dehydration undoubtedly accounts for a high number of bird deaths in summer.

Many Northern Flickers are found dead each fall. Herons, warblers, and sparrows have a high death rate. During midsummer, robin-sized and smaller birds seldom decay when death occurs. They become dried carcasses within eight hours. I placed a dead Brown-headed Cowbird in the sun at 7:00 A.M. and by 6:00 P.M. it was mummified, dry enough to be stored outside a freezer. In late August, I found a Red-winged Blackbird attached to a shrub; its wings were open and it was mummified.

Even at the oasis, shade is at a minimum. At Furnace Creek Ranch, swallows can be found, mouths agape, among the foliage of a salt cedar or in small bunches on the moist ground. Yellow-headed Blackbirds and Brown-headed Cowbirds find shade wherever possible. The dabbling of the Cinnamon Teal or the occasional call of a Western Kingbird or Black Phoebe is audible. Only the shorebirds are found in the open, usually half-submerged in water and moving only as their source of food necessitates. Mourning Doves and House Finches prefer the shelter of the date orchard, or they may join the House Sparrows along the irrigated paddies beneath the trees. When the sun sets there is a dash for food. After a little exercise there is a need to rest once more, for even after the sun sets, the temperature drops only a little. Twenty-four-hour minimum temperatures in July may well range from 100 to 110°F.

But the winter months are very different, and that is when the highest numbers of people visit the valley. Also in winter, at about Christmastime, birders take an annual bird count at Furnace Creek Ranch during one twenty-four-hour period. The 2001–2002 Death Valley count tallied forty-four species. The dozen most numerous birds, in descending order of abundance, were White-crowned sparrow, Brewer's Blackbird, European Starling, Common Raven, Mallard, Mourning Dove, American Coot, Great-tailed Grackle, House Sparrow, House Finch, American Pipit, and Lewis's Woodpecker.

In summary, Death Valley's checklist of birds includes 346 species, of which ninety-three species are known to nest. Of those ninety-three species, only two are water birds (Mallard and Killdeer), ten are hawks and owls, and six are warblers.

BIRDS OF SPECIAL INTEREST

Red-tailed Hawk. The park's only full-time resident hawk, it can be expected anywhere and is best identified by its large size and rust- to brick-red tail.

Killdeer. This is the noisy shorebird at moist areas in the valley; it is easily recognized by the two black bands across its white chest.

Say's Phoebe. To be expected almost anywhere in the desert or at developed areas, it is recognizable by its buff body, dark cap and tail, and descending "pee-ur" call.

Common Raven. The park's most obvious and widespread bird, it is readily identified by its all-black plumage, heavy bill, and, in flight, its wedge-shaped tail.

Mountain Chickadee. In the mountain woodlands, watch for this little black-and-white bird with a black throat, bib, and cap and bold white eyelines.

Juniper Titmouse. Resident in the lower pinyon-juniper zone, it is a little all-gray bird with a short crest and noisy chatter.

Le Conte's Thrasher. Look for this drab, long-tailed bird sitting atop mesquites in the lowlands. It sometimes gives a call note: an ascending, whistled "twheep."

Loggerhead Shrike. This husky black-and-white bird with a black mask occurs from the desert flats up to the pinyon-juniper woodlands.

European Starling. Common at Furnace Creek Ranch, it occurs in large flocks in winter; it is an all-dark, short-tailed bird with a yellow bill.

Brewer's Blackbird. Watch for this all-black bird walking about near water in winter; males have white eyes.

Great-tailed Grackle. This is the long-tailed blackbird that frequents developed areas and campgrounds and has a wide variety of raucous calls.

Dark-eyed Junco. One of the park's most common forest birds, it possesses an all-dark hood, chestnut-brown back, and black tail with two white outer feathers on each side.

House Finch. Males sport a red throat, crown, eyebrows, and rump and heavily streaked underparts; they sing a lively song that is repeated over and over.

Joshua Tree National Park

CALIFORNIA

The avian songfest was already under way when I arrived at the Oasis Visitor Center. Cactus Wrens, House Finches, Bewick's Wrens, and Gambel's Quail, more or less in that order of prominence, greeted the morning. One of the several Cactus Wrens sat on the corner of the building singing a loud, rollicking song, "cora-cora-cora-cora," over and over. A second Cactus Wren, perhaps its mate, sat atop an adjacent yucca, singing a slightly lower "choo-choo-choo-choo" song. They looked exactly alike: chunky birds with a long bill, dark spots on a light background, a rusty cap, and bold white eyebrows. More Cactus Wren songs were evident from the adjacent desert.

The smaller House Finches were most numerous, and their songs carried a joyous aura. Each contained a series of rapid short phrases, providing continual and rhythmic melodies. Several male House Finches sat on top of nearby mesquites and acacias. The crimson to pinkish throat, forehead, eyebrows, and rump of the males stood out in the morning sunlight on their otherwise all-brown bodies with streaked underparts. Females were duller versions of the males, but they were still part of the early morning songfest. The ten or more House Finches scattered about provided a great chorus, overshadowed only by the bravado of the Cactus Wrens.

A pair of Bewick's Wrens was also present in one huge mesquite. The male sang a wonderful song, filled with many and varied notes and delivered forcefully. Only half the size of the Cactus Wren, Bewick's Wren possesses a long, seemingly loose tail, edged with white spots, and gray-brown plumage with whitish underparts and bold white eyelines.

Less assertive were the abundant calls of Gambel's Quail. Their rapid "chi-*ca*-go-go" notes were easily recognized. I watched a flock of a dozen individuals run across the far edge of the parking lot, their short legs pumping furiously to carry their plump bodies out of danger. Then I noticed a lone male perched atop a yucca, as if he were the lookout for the scampering flock. Through binoculars, his black teardrop plume, belly, and forehead and chestnut cap and sides were obvious. Then he put his head back and called again, "chi-*ca*-go-go," and immediately dropped to the ground and ran after the disappearing flock.

THE PARK ENVIRONMENT

Legend tells us that Joshua trees were named by Mormon pioneers, who claimed that the plants' gesturing arms were beckoning them across the desert to the promised land just as Joshua, leader of the "children of Israel," had waved them into the land of Canaan. Conversely, in 1844 John C. Fremont, perhaps the first European to see a Joshua tree, called it "the most repulsive tree in the vegetable kingdom" (Trimble 1979, 3). Biologists are now intrigued with Joshua trees and recognize them as the indicator species of the Mohave Desert, the southernmost high desert, which abuts the lower Sonoran Desert to the south.

Joshua Tree National Park, nearly 800,000 acres in size, is at the southern edge of the Mohave Desert and includes an area classified as Colorado Desert, a subdivision of the more extensive Sonoran Desert. This biogeographic position gives the park five distinct plant communities: woodland, yucca, blackbrush, creosote bush, and riparian.

The woodland community at the highest elevations is dominated by California juniper, singleleaf pinyon, scrub oak, Parry nolina, and mountain mahogany. Often blending into the woodlands, the yucca community is dominated by the Joshua tree and Mohave yucca, with considerable amounts of bursage, blackbrush, spiny hopsage, and grasses. The blackbrush community may contain pure stands of blackbrush or this plant may be mixed with Mohave yucca or junipers. Most common along the lower, southern slopes, the creosote bush community contains substantial amounts of Bigelow cactus, ocotillo, bursage, and brittlebush, and in open washes smoke trees are common. Finally, the riparian communities at oases and other wetlands are dominated by California fan palm, honey mesquite, Fremont cottonwood, slender willow, arrowweed, and rabbitbrush.

Park visitor centers are located at the historic Oasis of Mara within the town of Twentynine Palms in the north and at Cottonwood at the southeast entrance, and Black Rock Visitor Center is near Yucca Valley. Ranger stations also exist at the west entrance and Indian Cove. Each visitor center contains an information desk, exhibits, and a sales outlet; bird field guides and a checklist are available. Interpretive activities are scheduled throughout the winter season and include a variety of evening programs, walks, and auto tours. Bird walks at Barker Dam are also included. Schedules are posted at ranger stations and campgrounds or are available for the asking.

Additional park information is available from the Superintendent, Joshua Tree National Park, Twentynine Palms, CA 92277; (619) 367-7511; Web address: www.nps.gov/jotr/.

BIRD LIFE

Gambel's Quail is one of the park's most charismatic birds, present at all park developments and wherever else it can find water, food, and shelter. This quail is a distinctive representative of the American Southwest, with a range that is limited to the deserts from southeastern California to southwestern Texas, north to the southwestern corner of Utah, and south into Sonora, Mexico. Paul Ehrlich and colleagues (1988) consider this species the most

Gambel's Quail

arid-adapted of quail; they note that in summer it forages primarily early and late in the day, with long quiet periods during the hotter hours.

I found the greatest numbers of Gambel's Quail behind the Oasis Visitor Center along the paved loop trail. Dozens of quail scattered ahead of me as I walked around the elongated patch of vegetation. Northern Mockingbirds and nonnative European Starlings were also common that morning. The gray-and-white mockers and the all-dark starlings, which remained largely among the high palm fronds, sang a wide variety of songs. The starlings even included versions of other birdsongs; during the hour that I spent in the oasis I detected Killdeer, Bewick's Wren, and grackle notes coming from the high palms. Perhaps the birds were demonstrating their unique form of one-upmanship over the mockingbirds, which are renowned for mimicking other birds. I couldn't help but wonder which native cavity-nesting birds these nonnatives were replacing.

The loud clicking sound of a **Greater Roadrunner** snapping its bill in an-noyance attracted my attention to the saltbush flat beyond the oasis. It took me several minutes to find this large, long-tailed cuckoo sitting on a fallen cottonwood limb. As I watched, it moved its tail up and down several times, and then drooped its wings to expose its feathered back to the warm sun-shine. Then, as if on cue, farther along the trail another roadrunner gave a call like the bark of a small dog, and my sunbather jumped from its perch and ran off in that direction. I followed its jerky movement as the bird made its way toward its apparent mate, pausing now and then to look about and raise and lower its tail. At one point I was able to see the blue-and-red patch of bare skin behind its eye and could admire its bushy crest and streaked plumage.

Roadrunners were named for their "habit of running down roads ahead of horse-drawn vehicles," according to John Terres, in *The Audubon Society Encyclopedia of North American Birds* (1987, 147). Their strange behavior has provoked lore of epic proportions. Although it is unlikely that the roadrun-ner can always outsmart the wily coyote as it does in cartoons, roadrunners do run down and capture a variety of prey, including lizards, small rodents, and even snakes. The male roadrunner offers his mate a choice item such as a lizard prior to copulation. Wherever they occur, these birds are enjoyed for their odd behavior and personality; the pair at the Oasis center provided park visitors many hours of fascinating observations.

Another desert bird found during my morning walk was the tall-crested Phainopepla, a slender mockingbird-sized bird that frequents clusters of mistletoe. It not only feeds on the tiny fleshy berries but also sometimes builds its nest within large clumps. This bird is often detected first by its low-pitched "wurp" calls. Male Phainopeplas are striking birds with silky black plumage and ruby-red eyes, and in flight they show large white wing patches; females are duller versions of the males. Their name comes from Greek words meaning "shining robe." Wintering birds usually occur in small flocks, but individuals maintain separate feeding territories. For more about this bird's odd nesting strategy, see Organ Pipe Cactus National Monument.

Other birds found along the Oasis loop trail that spring morning included a pair of American Kestrels perched high on a palm; two Anna's Humming-birds and a much smaller Costa's Hummingbird male; a few passing Common Ravens and Mourning Doves; a Northern (red-shafted) Flicker; several White-crowned Sparrows with their boldly drawn black-and-white head markings; and numerous House Sparrows.

The tall palms along the Oasis loop trail also provide roosting sites for migratory Turkey Vultures in spring and fall. District naturalist Arthur Webster told me that as many as six hundred of these large scavengers have been reported there in early October, and smaller concentrations are seen in February and March.

Four additional oases occur within the park: Fortynine Palms Oasis, reached on a strenuous 1.5-mile trail at the end of Canyon Road; Barker Dam in the Hidden Valley area; the easily accessible Cottonwood Spring; and Lost Palms at the end of a four-mile trail in the southeastern corner of the park. The resident bird life at these four sites is somewhat different from that at the Oasis Visitor Center because of their more isolated character. Dominant species include more desert birds, such as the Verdin, Black-tailed Gnat-catcher, and Black-throated Sparrow.

The Barker Dam Nature Trail, a 1.1-mile loop route, passes through a jumble of tall granite boulders, skirts a small reservoir, and returns through a Joshua tree woodland. Listen along the trail for the distinct song of Canyon Wrens, a remarkable descending and decelerating series of liquid "*tew, tew, tew, tew,* tew tew tew tew tew" notes, sometimes ending with a lower "jeet." This is a little cinnamon bird with a snow-white throat and breast and a long black bill. It uses its long bill to capture insects in narrow crevices. Even at a distance it can be identified by its habit of jerking up and down, especially when disturbed. Rock climbers find this wren to be their constant companion.

A second little wren of rocky areas is the all-gray **Rock Wren.** It is most common in summer; some individuals move to lower warmer climes for winter. Although it does not have the bicolored appearance of the Canyon Wren, it has a truly unique song and personality. Terres (1987, 1030) described its song as "keree keree keree, chair chair chair, deedle deedle deedle, tur tur tur, keree keree trrrrr." During the nesting season it will carry on singing for hours. And when flying from one rocky perch to next, this bird often spreads its tail, bobs up and down, and calls sharp "tick-ear" notes from each new place. But what is most interesting about the Rock Wren is its habit of decorating its nest entrance with varied materials. Arthur Cleveland Bent, in *Life Histories of North American Nuthatches, Wrens, Thrashers, and Their Allies* (1964b), reported a nest entrance hole in the earth lined with no less than 1,665 items, including nesting materials, 492 small granite stones, and 769 bones of rabbits, fish, and birds. Park biologist Jerry Freilich told me that he once discovered a Rock Wren nest behind a wren-constructed rock wall two to three inches high and six inches long.

The Barker reservoir itself contained several American Coots, chunky all-black birds with a white bill; two pairs of Mallards, the males with characteristic deep green head and white neck line; and a Pied-billed Grebe that called with cuckoolike "cow-cow-cow" notes from the concealment of cattails. One of the park's few areas of open water, the reservoir attracts a wide variety of water birds during migration. Although it held no surprises during my February visit, chief park interpreter Bill Truesdell told me that herons, egrets, waterfowl, and rails are occasional visitors.

A few other birds were found along the trail: Western Scrub-Jays called screeching notes from hiding; several Ruby-crowned Kinglets scolded me with husky "did-it" notes; and a small flock of Dark-eyed Juncos, winter visitors from higher elevations, flew off with obvious white edges to their otherwise all-black tails. A Bewick's Wren sang a lively ditty from the center of an oak thicket; a Verdin called loud chips at a distance; a pair of California Towhees ran ahead of me, calling loud "chink" notes; several Common Ravens, evident by their all-black plumage, massive bill, and wedge-shaped tail, passed overhead; and a lone male Ladder-backed Woodpecker sat near the top of a high Joshua tree arm, allowing me an excellent look.

The **Ladder-backed Woodpecker** is one of the park's most characteristic birds. The male on the Barker Dam trail sat in the open for an unusually long time; Betty was able to take several minutes of videotape as we admired its the black-and-white barring or ladder on its back, black tail with barred outer feathers, spotted underparts, white cheeks with two bold black bands, and black-and-red crown. This is the smaller of two typical woodpeckers that live in the Joshua tree forest, taking insects from infected trees and excavating nest holes for themselves and a variety of other cavity nesters.

The larger, less numerous Northern Flicker excavates larger nest cavities but spends considerably more of its feeding time on the ground, where it hops and walks about, very unwoodpecker-like. Flickers eat more ants than do any other North American woodpeckers, but they also feed on insect larvae, acorns, nuts, and grain. This bird, too, nests in Joshua trees. It and the

Ladder-backed Woodpecker are important members of the community: cavity nesters such as the Western Screech-Owl, Ash-throated Flycatcher, Juniper Titmouse, and Bewick's Wren take advantage of deserted woodpecker nest sites.

The **Ash-throated Flycatcher,** unlike the other cavity nesters mentioned, is resident in the park only during the nesting season. However, at that time it can be surprisingly abundant, and its "ka-brick" and "ha-wheer" calls can be commonplace in the Joshua tree forest, especially in early mornings and evenings. The bird is rather nondescript, with an ashy gray throat and breast, yellowish belly, gray-brown back, and with rufous color on its wings and tail. Nests are built in cavities, even in unused Cactus Wren nests, and are constructed of a variety of materials. Terres (1987, 383) notes that contents of the nests are "principally hairs, weed stems, rootlets, grasses, bits of dry cow or horse dung, built on foundation of felted mass of fur of different animals, sometimes dried, shed skins of snakes and small lizards."

One of the most vivid and charismatic of the summer residents of the Joshua tree forest is the yellow and black **Scott's Oriole.** Males are especially striking, their coal-black hood, back, wings, and end of the tail contrasting with bright yellow belly, rump, and bold wing bars; females are gray to greenish with whitish wing bars. This oriole is present only from March to early September, utilizing springs and Joshua tree habitats. Nesting birds use yucca fibers in building their basket nests, according to Miller and Stebbins, and splits in the dead yucca leaves afford places where strands to anchor nests can be securely fastened. Scott's Oriole songs consist of high, clear, and rich whistled phrases not unlike those of the Western Meadowlark.

Two additional summer orioles occur in the park. Bullock's Orioles prefer cottonwoods; the male has black and orange plumage with large white wing patches. The smaller Hooded Oriole, males of which have an orange crown and black face and throat, nest under palm fronds.

The upper edge of the Joshua tree forest intergrades with the pinyon-juniper woodlands on the higher, cooler slopes. This habitat supports typical pinyon-juniper birds, such as the Western Scrub-Jay, Oak Titmouse, and Bushtit. Black Rock Canyon provides a good example of this interface. An early spring morning walk on the High View Nature Trail, a 1.3-mile loop route beginning just above the Black Rock Campground, produced more than twenty bird species. The more common birds found included the Ladder-backed Woodpecker, Western Scrub-Jay, Common Raven, Cactus and Bewick's wrens, Black-throated and White-crowned sparrows, and House Finch. Detected in smaller numbers were the Red-tailed Hawk, Mourning Dove, Great Horned Owl, Costa's and Anna's hummingbirds, Northern

Flicker, Pinyon Jay, Oak Titmouse, Bushtit, California and Le Conte's thrashers, Loggerhead Shrike, and Lesser Goldfinch.

Western Scrub-Jays were common at Black Rock Campground, flying here and there in tail-flopping fashion, all the time calling loud scratchy "shreeeep" notes. Those that came close to camp showed their deep blue crown, nape, and tail, blackish cheeks, whitish throat with dark streaks, and brown back. I found this adaptable bird everywhere but in the open desert.

At night we were treated to the low serenade of Great Horned Owls. This large owl is one of twenty-five bird species reported to nest on Joshua trees. Later in spring, Common Poorwills call their sad "poor-will" songs at dusk

Scott's Oriole

Western Scrub-Jay

and dawn. And the Say's Phoebe, an all-buff to brownish flycatcher with a dark cap and tail, is common after sunup.

My greatest surprise was finding the two thrasher species in such close proximity; Le Conte's Thrasher was found in the open sandy bottoms, while the California Thrasher was present on the higher slopes dominated by scrub oak and Parry nolina. The western half of the park apparently is the eastern edge of the California Thrasher's range; it is more typically found in West Coast chaparral. **Le Conte's Thrasher** is typically a bird of the saltbush flats in our hottest and driest deserts. Terres refers to Le Conte's Thrasher as "one of the least approachable of all birds," and Ehrlich and colleagues claim that it is "intolerant of habitat disruption by humans." It was indeed strange to find it at almost 4,000 feet elevation in the Joshua tree–juniper association. See Death Valley National Park for more about it in that area.

Truesdell told me that Le Conte's Thrashers reach their greatest abundance along the park's lower mountain slopes amid the cholla, creosote bush, and blackbrush and in the smoke tree washes. There they build bulky, rather deep nests of thorny twigs and lined with plant parts. Ehrlich and colleagues indicate that the nests are "uniquely double-lined with inner lining of plant down (derived from seeds, leaves, etc.)" (1988, 476). Such nest insulation undoubtedly helps protect the eggs and nestlings from the extreme temperatures that characterize these low desert sites. And the adult's pale gray, almost whitish plumage has also evolved to help protect this denizen of the hot lowlands.

An early morning walk in the low desert community will not produce the number of birds one can find in the higher desert. But four species are especially well adapted to these arid slopes: Costa's Hummingbird, Verdin, Black-tailed Gnatcatcher, and Black-throated Sparrow. **Costa's Hummingbirds** nest as early as February, once bladderpod and a few other early bloomers are in flower. The smallest of our hummingbirds and one of the most colorful, the male Costa's possesses deep purple gorgets that extend beyond the throat like a great handlebar mustache. Courtship includes deep U-shaped flights from a hundred feet above the ground, accompanied by a shrill continual whistle. These displays can often be detected at a considerable distance. But once incubation begins, males desert their breeding grounds, leaving the females with the rest of the family chores.

Verdins are barely larger than the tiny Costa's Hummingbird, and the two species often feed side by side on early flowering shrubs. While the hummingbird's diet is chiefly pollen and spiders, the Verdin's diet consists primarily of insects and fruit. Although usually detected by a rapid series of chips or whistled "tee tee tee" notes, Verdins are easily identified by their tiny size, overall gray plumage, bright yellow face, and a maroon patch at the bend of each wing. The male builds several nests in spring, of which one is chosen by the female for laying eggs; the other nests are maintained for later roost sites. Unlike among hummingbirds, Verdin family groups usually remain together until the following spring.

The Black-tailed Gnatcatcher is often detected first by its very scratchy "buzz-buzz-buzz" song. Its long black tail and solid black cap help to separate the Black-tailed from the Blue-gray Gnatcatcher, with its blue-gray back and obvious white edges on an otherwise black tail. Blue-grays occur at slightly higher elevations in the Joshua tree and chaparral communities.

But of all the birds found in the desert, none is as widespread as the little **Back-throated Sparrow**—formerly called the desert sparrow because of its affinity for hot arid lowlands. Miller and Stebbins (1964, 139) wrote that these birds represent "an extreme in desert adaptations for they are in large part seed-eaters, and yet they do not require drinking water and occupy the most exposed and hot, open brush areas" (1964). Yet Black-throated Sparrows also occur at higher elevations in the park year-round. This sparrow is easily identified by its pert manner, coal-black throat, white belly, and dark cheeks bordered by two bold snow-white stripes; its scientific name is *bilineata,* Latin for "two-striped."

Although more birds are present at Joshua Tree during the spring and fall migration than in summer and winter, the best long-term indication of the park's bird life is provided by Christmas Bird Counts made annually since 1966. More than 130 species have been reported. The January 2002 count tallied forty-five species. The dozen most common species in descending order of abundance were the Mourning Dove, Rock Dove, Black-throated Sparrow, Gambel's Quail, White-crowned Sparrow, Common Raven, European Starling, Western Scrub-Jay, Dark-eyed Junco, Northern Mockingbird, Phainopepla, and Yellow-rumped Warbler.

In summary, the park's bird checklist includes 239 species, of which sixty-three are known to nest. Of those sixty-three species, four are water birds, eight are hawks and owls, and none are warblers.

BIRDS OF SPECIAL INTEREST

Gambel's Quail. This plump bird with a teardrop plume, black-and-white face pattern, and black belly is common at all the park's developments and oases.

Greater Roadrunner. A bird of cartoon fame, it is easily identified by its long tail and legs, large bill, and bushy crest.

Costa's Hummingbird. This is a tiny desert hummingbird; males possess deep purple gorgets that stick out like handlebars.

Ladder-backed Woodpecker. Found on woody plants throughout the park, it can be identified by its small size and the black-and-white bars on its back.

Western Scrub-Jay. This long-tailed bird with a dark blue head and tail and whitish underparts can be found everywhere but in the lower desert.

Cactus Wren. Noted for a loud, rollicking call, this large wren builds a commensurately large football-shaped nest among the thorns of a cactus or shrub.

Rock Wren. Most common in summer at rocky places, it has all-gray plumage and a long bill; it often bobs up and down.

Le Conte's Thrasher. Watch for this pale gray bird with long tail and bill in the desert shrub communities on the lower mountain slopes.

Black-throated Sparrow. One of the park's most common birds, this sparrow sports a coal-black throat and cheeks with two bold white lines.

House Finch. This is the little songster that is usually seen in flocks; males possess a crimson to pinkish throat, forehead, crown, and rump and streaked underparts.

Scott's Oriole. Watch for this black and yellow bird in the Joshua tree forest; it sings high, clear, rich whistled phrases.

Lake Mead National Recreation Area

NEVADA & ARIZONA

 The little bay below my rocky perch that winter morning contained more than a thousand water birds. Northern Shovelers made up the largest contingent, scattered all across the open bay as well as in the grassy edges. The male shoveler is truly a gorgeous bird with its contrasting bright green head, snow-white chest, and cinnamon sides. The female is a dull brown. But both possess the large spatulate bill from which their name is derived.

The majority of the shovelers were feeding in the shallow bay by dipping below the surface, with their black-and-white rumps pointed skyward, typical behavior of dabbling ducks. Others were either swimming about—communicating with neighbors like the sociable creatures they are—or sleeping, head resting on a wing, exposing an all-white breast. At first glance the couple of dozen sleeping shovelers among the cattails on the far side of the bay looked like shiny white dots.

I could identify a number of Mallards by the metallic green head and neck, narrow white collar, and chestnut breast of the males; several Green-winged Teal, smaller ducks distinguishable by a chestnut head and deep green ear patches; and lesser numbers of Gadwalls and Ruddy Ducks.

American Coots, clearly identifiable by an all-black body and white bill, were also numerous. These "mud-hens," members of the rail family, were more aggressive than the ducks. I watched several coots chase others away from an apparently choice feeding territory. For no reason that I could see, one coot suddenly charged another with its head low to the water surface and its short legs splashing like the wake of a speeding motorboat. After a chase of about fifty feet or so, the aggressor suddenly turned its back to expose the fluffed-up, all-white underside of its tail, as if to broadcast a warning for others to pay heed to that individual's territory.

American Coots are one of Lake Mead's most common water birds, present along the entire shoreline. They establish permanent territories that they defend vigorously against any intruder. One of our most pugnacious and aggressive water birds, they fight one another with bill and claw. Paul Ehrlich and colleagues (1988, 105) wrote: "While fighting, a coot usually sits back on

American Coots

the water and grabs its opponent with one long-clawed foot while attempting to slap the contender with the free one and jab it with its bill. Apparently, the aim is to push the opponent onto its back and, in some cases, hold it underwater. Quite impressive, this sequence can be seen in coots four days old."

American Coots are able to adapt to the extremely hot temperatures that exist at Lake Mead in summer. Their lobed feet, when immersed in water, effectively cool the bird by conducting heat out of the body. They also are opportunistic feeders in that they can take advantage of almost any situation. They naturally feed on submerged vegetation, but they may "pirate" plants brought to the surface by diving ducks, and they take all sorts of other food when it is available.

THE PARK ENVIRONMENT

Lake Mead was the country's first officially designated national recreation area, established by Congress in 1964, twenty-nine years after the completion of Hoover Dam. The first dam built on the Colorado River, this impoundment backed water all the way up into the lower end of Grand Canyon. The Lake Mead National Recreation Area encompasses 1.5 million acres, also including the much higher and isolated Shivwits Plateau in Arizona. The heart of the recreation area, however, is the 110-mile-long Lake Mead and the 67-mile-long Lake Mohave, behind Davis Dam; the two water bodies jointly cover an area of 290 square miles.

Most of the park landscape consists of rocky slopes and broad washes interspersed with rugged volcanic ridges and mesas. Deep canyons occur here and there along the lakes; Black Canyon, below Hoover Dam, is the most accessible. The dominant vegetation type in the park is Mojave Desert, and the predominant plant throughout this arid environment is creosote bush, with its tiny, shiny green leaves on thin, hard branches. Other common Mohave Desert plants include bursage, Mohave yucca, and beavertail cactus on the open slopes and brittlebush, catclaw, and rabbitbrush in the washes. The riparian zones along the Colorado River and moist side canyons are dominated by honey mesquite, willows, arrowweed, and nonnative salt cedar.

The stark, quiet, and desolate beauty of untouched desert backcountry is punctuated by twisted rock in the ancient mountains of the Basin and Range Province. Colorful vertical-walled high plateaus have been carved by the rivers. Hoover Dam was a historic achievement when it was built; and although the dam has always had detractors, the big lakes have become a mecca for boaters and birders.

Visitor facilities are widely scattered, from Overton Beach on the northern arm of Lake Mead and Temple Bar on the lake's eastern arm to Katherine, at the southern end of Lake Mohave. Ranger stations and concession-operated marinas exist at nine separate sites. The park's principal information facility is the Alan Bible Visitor Center located along Highway 93 between Hoover Dam and Boulder City, Nevada. It has an auditorium for orientation programs, numerous exhibits, and a sales outlet offering bird field guides and a checklist. The other stations all provide information, while those at Echo Bay, Temple Bar, and Katherine include exhibits. Interpretive activities, provided year-round at various sites, range from evening programs and ranger-guided walks to bird walks.

Additional park information can be obtained from the superintendent, Lake Mead National Recreation Area, 601 Nevada Highway, Boulder City, NV 89005-2426; (702) 293-8907; Web address: www.nps.gov/lame/.

BIRD LIFE

A few Great Blue Herons, a lone Great Egret, several Pied-billed Grebes, and numerous Ring-billed Gulls and Western and Clark's grebes were also present in the upper end of Las Vegas Bay on the winter morning when I saw the shovelers. And by carefully searching the far shoreline, I located four Black-crowned Night-Herons perched at the edge of the vegetation.

Ring-billed Gulls, one of the lake's most widespread birds, were either flying low over the bay or perched in the center of the shallow outlet of Las Vegas Wash. Their distinguishing markings were obvious through binoculars: white head and chest, gray back and wings with black tips, and yellowish bill with a distinct black band. This was the only kind of gull present, although smaller numbers of several other gull species do occur here. California Gulls, somewhat larger and with a yellow bill with a touch of red on the lower mandible, are also regularly found along the lake.

One of the long-legged Great Blue Herons was standing near the gulls, frozen like a statue, waiting for a passing fish or frog that it would grab with a swift strike of its heavy, yellowish bill. The few Pied-billed Grebes, smaller even than the little Green-winged Teal, swam about in their search for aquatic vegetation. I watched one Pied-billed Grebe, when approached by an American Coot, submerge straight down to the point that only the top of its head and eyes were above water.

The two larger grebes—Western and Clark's—were mostly farther out in the bay, but both were audible from a considerable distance. **Western** and **Clark's grebes** look very much alike, and until the 1980s were considered a single species, the Western Grebe. But ornithologists began to realize that these

Western Grebe (left) and
Clark's Grebe (right)

birds were two different species; they possess somewhat different bill color, facial markings, and voice. The best descriptions of the two species are provided by Kenn Kaufman, in *Advanced Birding* (1990, 31–33). Kaufman points out that the Western Grebe's bill is "dull greenish yellow, with a broad and diffuse, blackish ridge on the upper mandible and some blackish suffusion on the lower mandible." The bill of the Clark's Grebe "is bright orange-yellow, with a very narrow and sharply designed dark ridge on the upper mandible."

The facial pattern, most reliable from April through July, is also subtly different. In Western Grebe, according to Kaufman, "the dark area of the crown extends down to the area below the eye," with no white on the lores, the area above the eyes. The lores on the Clark's Grebe "are almost always clear white, contrasting with the black crown." And the voice of the Western Grebe is a "far-carrying, reedy, two-noted *crik crick,* with the second note sounding a bit higher." The Clark's Grebe call "is very similar in tone quality, length, and pitch, but it is all one up-slurred note without a break: *criiiick.* Both species also give a variety of other notes" (1990, 33).

These two grebes are fairly large water birds characterized by a long, swan-like neck and an obvious two-toned pattern—black on the crest and back of the neck with a snow-white throat and foreneck. Both also possess large ruby-red eyes. I found that the best way to separate the two species from a distance was to locate the bright yellow bill of the Clark's Grebe with binoculars, and then use a scope to examine the facial pattern. Both species are common on Lake Mead in winter but less numerous the remainder of the year.

The dense vegetation in Las Vegas Wash, above the bay, contained a very different assortment of birds. The upper edge of this habitat is accessible from the Wetland Trail, located at the 1.2-mile mark on the Northshore Road (Highway 167). The most abundant bird there in winter was the **White-crowned Sparrow.** Adults are easily identified by their bold black-and-white striped head. First-year birds possess a similar head pattern of brown and tan, not black and white. This winter resident migrates in spring to the western mountains, where it nests along mountain streams and among the stunted conifers at the treeline. It is strange to find White-crowns sometimes still present in late May, singing their wheezy whistle songs in the desert, when others are already on their breeding grounds at the edge of mountain snowfields.

Other birds found along the Wetland Trail included the Red-tailed Hawk; Gambel's Quail; Black and Say's phoebes; Common Raven; Verdin; Rock, Canyon, and Marsh wrens; Blue-gray Gnatcatcher; Phainopepla; Orange-crowned and Yellow-rumped warblers; Abert's Towhee; Song and Lincoln's sparrows; and House Finch. Of all these birds, the **Abert's Towhee** may be the most interesting. Its entire range is limited to riparian thickets in the Colorado River drainage from southwestern Utah to extreme southeastern California and east to southwestern New Mexico. Las Vegas Wash may be one of the easiest places of all to find it. Abert's Towhees are the size of a large sparrow, all brownish birds with a blackish face. Rather secretive in their behavior, they usually fly or run away at the slightest hint of danger. However, a careful observer can get a good look at a singing bird, often perched at the top of a high shrub. Its song consists of a "staccato series of notes: *peek peek peek, peek peek peek,*" as described by Scott Terrill, in *The Audubon Society Master Guide to Birding* (1961, 222). When they fly away, they typically give a metallic, "eeeek" call. See Montezuma Castle National Monument for a description of this bird's interesting behavior.

Phainopeplas frequent mesquite with mistletoe, feeding on the berries and nesting among the larger clumps. I found Phainopeplas most numerous at Rogers Spring, although a few were present almost wherever mesquites occurred. For example, each patch of mesquite along the river at Willow Beach contained one Phainopepla or a pair. Often detected first by their short, mellow whistle, males are easily identified by their tall crest and shiny, all-black plumage, conspicuous white wing patches in flight, and—with binoculars—their ruby-red eyes. Females are dull gray. See Organ Pipe Cactus National Monument for this bird's odd nesting strategy.

The **House Finch** was the most common songbird about the lake, present in substantial numbers at all of the developed sites as well as in the desert washes. Winter birds occur in flocks of a few to several dozen individuals; they pair up in late winter to nest, only to join large flocks again soon afterward. Although female House Finches are rather nondescript little birds with streaked underparts, males possess a bright red throat, bib, eyebrows, and rump. And they are among our most vocal and enduring songbirds, singing during all hours of the day from spring through late summer and also during warm winter days.

Arthur Bent, in *Life Histories of North American Cardinals, Grosbeaks, Buntings, Towhees, Finches, Sparrows, and Allies,* quoted Myron and Jane Swenk's description of its song: "The House Finch is a joyous bird, and it expresses its joy in its rollicking, warbling song. The song itself is not long, but it is rapidly repeated many times, producing a long-continued flow of singing. The song has many variations, in fact; but rarely do you hear two songs that are exactly alike. Different individuals will sing slightly differently, and the same bird will vary his song from time to time, but the song always has the same basic structure, is rather consistently given in 6/8 time, and all of the songs share the same general quality" (1968, 309–10).

House Finches, White-crowned Sparrows, and Gambel's Quail were all roosting together among the palm fronds at Katherine. As I was walking about the campground at dawn, groups of quail and sparrows exploded from palm fronds with loud rattling noises when I approached. I don't remember when I have found so many **Gambel's Quail** in so small an area. Flocks of five to twenty or more quail were present everywhere I looked. And others were calling loud, emphatic "chi-*ca*-go-go" notes, songs heard so often in Western movies, or uttering low, melodic "wa-kuh" notes as they ran ahead of me. The park's only quail, they are readily identified by the male's black teardrop-shaped plume, face, and belly and chestnut cap and sides. See Joshua Tree National Park for additional information about this bird.

My stroll at Katherine produced about two dozen bird species. Common land birds included the Gambel's Quail, American Kestrel, Greater Roadrunner, Say's Phoebe, Common Raven, Verdin, Rock Wren, Ruby-crowned Kinglet, European Starling, Yellow-rumped Warbler, White-crowned Sparrow, Brewer's Blackbird, Great-tailed Grackle, House Finch, Lesser Goldfinch, and House Sparrow. Common water birds included Pied-billed Grebe, Double-crested Cormorant, Mallard, Common Merganser, American Coot, and Ring-billed Gull. Lesser numbers of the Western Grebe, Great Blue Heron, Inca Dove, Anna's Hummingbird, Ladder-backed Woodpecker, Northern (red-shafted) Flicker, Black Phoebe, Cactus Wren, Abert's Towhee, and Dark-eyed Junco were detected.

The **Greater Roadrunner** was surprisingly abundant at the parking areas, apparently waiting for vehicles to arrive with a fresh assemblage of road-killed insects to be gleaned from grills and windshields. Early in the cool morning the roadrunners stood around with their wings hanging and back and rump feathers fluffed out and exposed to the warm sunshine. I discovered that I could get reasonably close to such a sunbather before it would clack its bill at me or walk away to a safer distance. Park interpreter Cathy Cook later told me that a roadrunner faithfully came to the visitor center each winter afternoon to peck at a certain spot on the window. She decided that it was pecking at a postcard of a Gambel's Quail that it could see through the window.

The Greater Roadrunner is one of our best known desert birds, made famous as a cartoon character that continuously outwits the hungry coyote. Indeed in real life it dashes here and there on its long bare legs, lifting or wagging its long tail and chasing down lizards to grab them with its long heavy bill. Lizards are a favorite food and are utilized by the male to entice sexual favors from his mate. Given the roadrunner's propensity to frequent roads, parking lots, and campgrounds, most park visitors see this characteristic desert bird without searching too hard, and its ways are at least as winning in the flesh as on the screen.

I found a large number of **Common Mergansers** on the lake, mostly along the shoreline, where they were feeding on small fishes. Several of these fishing ducks were already paired, providing good comparisons between the sexes. Although both possess a long, slim bill (with serrated edges for capturing prey underwater), the male is far more colorful than his mate. He has a dark green head, thin red bill, white breast and sides, and black back. She has a brown head with a ragged crest, dull red bill, white breast, and grayish brown back. Lake Mead and Lake Mohave apparently provide important wintering grounds for this diving duck. Frank Bellrose (1976, 456–60) estimated that of some 165,000 Common Mergansers found on wintering grounds, 120,000 occurred in the interior of the United States, some 24,000 of those on Pacific Flyway. He found that the Colorado River supported more than a quarter of these Pacific Flyway wintering birds—some 3,900 in Arizona and 1,400 in Nevada.

Common Mergansers and several of the wintering waterfowl undoubtedly increased after the dams produced lakes and a greatly expanded shoreline. Black Canyon, below Hoover Dam, now contains water from Lake Mohave, and this twenty-four-mile-long canyon is popular for canoeing and for daylong slow-water raft trips, available by concession; private and commercial trips require permits. This area provides good opportunities for viewing Peregrine Falcons.

One of the world's fastest birds, the **Peregrine Falcon** specializes in cap-

Greater Roadrunner

turing prey in flight. According to park resource management specialist Ross Haley, six pairs of peregrines were nesting in Black Canyon annually in the 1990s, making this area the most likely place in the park to find and observe these marvelous creatures. Breeding birds can usually be heard before they are seen. By March their high-pitched whistle calls can often be heard high over the cliffs. A lucky observer can watch their fantastic courtship flights; they streak along the cliffs, diving and rolling, sometimes in unison with their mates and with amazing grace for so large a bird. Their pointed wings, whitish underparts, slate-gray back, and black mustachial stripes are their most obvious features.

As is now widely known, Peregrine populations experienced serious declines worldwide during the 1950s and 1960s, primarily because of use of DDT, a long-lived pesticide that accumulates in the tissues of raptors feeding on insect-eating animals. Although the birds rarely died outright, the toxins caused their eggshells to become so thin as to be unable to withstand the weight of an incubating adult bird. Peregrines declined by as much as 90 percent in the West and were totally eliminated from the East before 1972, when the species was placed on the endangered species list, and DDT was banned from use in the United States and Canada. By the late 1960s, only a few of the more isolated breeding populations persisted, including those along the Colorado River in Grand Canyon National Park and in Lake Mead's Black Canyon. For more about Peregrine recovery, see Grand Canyon National Park.

Another cliff nester common in Black Canyon is the **White-throated Swift.** This little black-and-white speedster, shaped like a cigar with stiff, swept-back wings, can fly at over one hundred miles per hour. It spends its entire life in the air or clinging to high cliffs. Swifts sometimes zoom by so close to river rafters or to hikers on the cliffs that air movement is felt. They build nests in high crevices using feathers and their own saliva, and during cold weather they may congregate in larger crevices like bees in a hive.

Rafters also are likely to hear the wonderful descending and decelerating songs of the Canyon Wren, a little bird with a snow-white throat and cinnamon to buff upperparts. It can be common along the cliffs, and its song will be forever etched into your memory of a Black Canyon raft trip. Watch also along the canyon for the Double-crested Cormorant—a large all-dark water bird that flies away from the oncoming raft with much paddling before take-off or that may be seen perched on the side of the canyon—and for Common Mergansers, Western and Clark's grebes, Mallards, and a variety of other ducks.

Spring and fall migration can produce interesting bird sightings. A huge flock of circling American White Pelicans may seem out of place, but these migrating birds follow the Colorado River between their wintering grounds on the Salton Sea or the Gulf of California and their breeding grounds to the north, perhaps Great Salt Lake or Yellowstone Lake. Even Canada and Snow geese can be seen along this ancient migratory route. And hawks use the corridor in spring and fall, especially Red-tailed, Swainson's, Cooper's, and Sharp-shinned hawks.

Red-tailed Hawks and Golden Eagles are year-round residents within the area, but wintering birds from the north expand their numbers. Red-tailed Hawks, best identified by their brick- to dull-red tail, are common and can be expected almost anywhere in the park. Golden Eagles, less numerous, are most often seen hunting over the desert. These birds are almost twice the size of a Red-tail and possess all-dark plumage. In the right light, the adult's head reflects a deep golden sheen.

Lake Mead also has a number of wintering **Bald Eagles.** As many as a hundred individuals are found along the lake in some years. The park service monitors the Bald Eagle population each year. The largest numbers occur in the Overton Arm, with good numbers also at Temple Bar and Cottonwood Cove. This great bird, with a snow-white head and tail, has increased throughout its range since DDT was banned.

Summertime can be extremely hot and dry on the desert, and birds normally seek shelter from the midday heat. But early mornings can be most productive for birders, even in midsummer. The most common sound of the open desert is the tinkling notes of **Black-throated Sparrows.** This little bird can be surprisingly common, and low spishing sounds will often attract it close enough for a good look at its coal-black throat and chin, white stripes on each side of its gray cheeks, and whitish underparts. This desert sparrow can be abundant; flocks of several family groups are commonplace during the nonbreeding season.

Watch in the desert for the Loggerhead Shrike, a heavyset black-and-white bird with a short hooked bill; Gambel's Quail; Say's Phoebes at rocky washes that contain ledges for nesting; the nondescript, grayish Rock Wren, which bobs up and down and calls sharp "tick-ear" notes; and the ever present Common Ravens and House Finches.

The riparian areas along the river and moist washes support an additional assortment of nesting birds in spring and summer: Mourning Dove, Lesser Nighthawk, Black-chinned and Costa's hummingbirds, Verdin, Northern Mockingbird, Lucy's Warbler, Common Yellowthroat, Blue Grosbeak, Abert's Towhee, and Brown-headed Cowbird. In places with large mesquite and willow trees, the Western Screech-Owl, Ladder-backed Woodpecker, Ash-throated Flycatcher, Crissal Thrasher, Phainopepla, Yellow-breasted Chat, and Bullock's Oriole may also be found.

Postnesting birds can appear along the river and drainages as early as July, already en route toward their southern winter grounds. In August and September, the mud flats at Overton and elsewhere can be alive with shorebirds. The more common species include the Killdeer, Greater Yellowlegs, Willet, Least Sandpiper, and Long-billed Dowitcher.

Winter bird populations are only a fraction of what passes through in migration. Every year at about Christmastime birds are censused within a fifteen-mile diameter circle during one twenty-four-hour period as part of the annual Christmas Bird Count. On December 15, 2001, counters of the Henderson, Nevada, circle tallied eighty-seven species. The dozen most numerous birds in descending order of abundance were European Starling, American Coot, Rock Dove, Mallard, White-crowned Sparrow, Northern Shoveler, Ring-billed Gull, Brewer's Blackbird, Ruddy Duck, Red-winged Blackbird, Mourning Dove, and Great-tailed Grackle.

In summary, the park's checklist of birds includes 314 species, of which 102 are listed for summer and assumed to nest; note that these numbers also include birds of the higher Shivwits Plateau. Of the 102 summer species, twenty-three are water birds (grebes, herons, waterfowl, rails, and shorebirds), ten are hawks and owls, and four are warblers.

BIRDS OF SPECIAL INTEREST

Western and Clark's grebes. Both of these long-necked water birds are common in winter; they are recognized by a snow-white throat and chest and black cap and back.

Northern Shoveler. Males of this common wintering duck have a deep green head, white chest, and cinnamon sides; both sexes possess a large spatulate bill.

Common Merganser. The male has a deep green head, while the female's head is reddish; both sexes have a red bill.

Bald Eagle. Watch for this large raptor at Overton Bay, Temple Bar, or Cottonwood Wash; adults are readily identifiable by an all-white head and tail contrasting with an all-dark body.

Red-tailed Hawk. This is the common hawk often seen soaring overhead, identified by its brick-red tail.

Peregrine Falcon. The fastest of all birds, this midsized raptor is most often seen in and around the canyons.

Gambel's Quail. The park's only quail, it has a teardrop-shaped head plume and loud "chi-*ca*-go-go" call.

American Coot. This plump water bird, usually found in large aggregations, is black except for its white bill.

Ring-billed Gull. Found anywhere along the lake, adults possess a yellow bill with a dark ring.

Greater Roadrunner. The long-legged, long-tailed bird of cartoon fame may occur anywhere in the desert or in campgrounds.

White-throated Swift. Most common along the high canyons, this swift is black and white with swept-back wings and a high twittering call.

Phainopepla. Watch for this slender, crested bird at patches of mesquite; males are shiny black with a large white patch on each wing.

Abert's Towhee. This large sparrow with a blackish face occurs only in riparian thickets along the lake and in side canyons.

Black-throated Sparrow. The common desert sparrow has a black throat and bib, white stripes above and below its dark cheeks, and a black tail.

White-crowned Sparrow. Common in winter, adults possess contrasting black-and-white head stripes.

House Finch. This little bird may be common throughout the lowlands; males possess a bright red throat, eyebrows, and rump.

Grand Canyon National Park

ARIZONA

 The South Rim's Yavapai Point offers a vast and magnificent sweeping vista of the Grand Canyon of the Colorado River. The multiple layers of rocky cliffs and terraces represent a gigantic display of the known ages of the earth, laid out within the canyon like the open pages of a great book. Geologists can point out each chapter of the earth's history, exposed in sequence, from the deepest inner canyon to the highest rimstone.

One day in May, I watched the morning light gradually crawl into the canyon, lighting the layers one by one, until it finally exposed the bright green vegetation fringing the river that has carved this stunning landscape. Phantom Ranch, at the bottom of Bright Angel Canyon, glowed like a distant emerald. Just upriver was the Kaibab Bridge, one of two footbridges over the mud-red Colorado River. And directly below my perch was the threadlike Bright Angel Trail, a connecting link from the South Rim.

My gaze into the depths was suddenly interrupted by a dozen or more White-throated Swifts careening along the cliffs so close to where I sat that I could actually feel air movement. Their expressive, high-pitched descending trill notes were almost explosive as they passed by. I turned my attention to a pair of these black-and-white creatures that had veered away from the flock, going almost straight up two or three hundred feet or more. And I watched them clinging together in copulation as they fell hundreds of feet in midair, wings out to control their speed but spinning them around like an airborne pinwheel. They were several hundred feet below the rim before they separated, leveled off, and ascended again into the blue sky. Another time those flying cigar-shaped birds came so close that I could see their white throats, bellies, and flanks contrasting with their otherwise all-black plumage. They put on an incredible show.

Violet-green Swallows were also present that morning, soaring along the cliff and over the pinyon-juniper woodlands behind me. These birds were flying much more slowly, without the all-out acceleration of the swifts. Through binoculars I could clearly see their slightly forked tails, violet-green backs, and the snow white of their underparts, cheeks, and the sides of their rumps. Each time one passed below me, its back gleamed velvety green in the morning sunlight. Their calls were little more than high-pitched "chip" notes, far less exciting than the conversation of the speedier swifts.

The much larger birds soaring along the rim, all black with wedge-shaped tails, were **Common Ravens.** There were five individuals in all, and I assumed that three of the five were young of the year, already fledged and accompanying the adults on their morning foray. Once fledged, juveniles are almost impossible to distinguish from adults. The adults had probably nested somewhere

White-throated Swift

along the cliffs, building a stick nest lined with bark and hair on some high, inaccessible ledge. They passed by with the customary swooshing sounds of their broad wings.

The loud descending and decelerating song of a **Canyon Wren** suddenly resounded from just below the rim, and a moment later I was watching a cinnamon-colored bird with an all-white throat less than thirty feet away. It moved in a jerky manner, probing a crack for food. I was totally ignored. Then it sang again, a loud, descending series of whistled notes: "*tew tew tew tew* tew tew tew tew tew." It gave a short metallic "jert" note and disappeared over the edge. What a lovely creature it was, and so fitting a bird at the Grand Canyon. All through the day, whenever I was close to the rim, I could hear Canyon Wren songs from the canyon below.

A melodic "flew" note attracted my attention to a brightly colored male **Western Bluebird** perched on a pinyon snag about fifty or sixty feet away. I realized that I had detected the stuttering "flew" notes earlier, but it had not registered until now. Less than a dozen feet from the bluebird was his mate, more subdued in color. The male stood out in sharp contrast: his hood and wings were deep blue, almost a purple-blue color; his back, breast, and flanks were deep chestnut; and his belly was white—a truly gorgeous bird. One of the most common year-round residents on both the South and the North Rim, this cavity nester utilizes deserted woodpecker nests and other cavities in pinyon and ponderosa pines.

The male bluebird suddenly shot out from his perch, flying almost directly upward, and I watched him snap his bill on a passing insect. But instead of returning to the original perch he landed next to the female and presented her with the insect catch. Its acceptance was an act of courtship that undoubtedly occurs often in spring but one that few human beings are privileged to observe.

THE PARK ENVIRONMENT

Grand Canyon National Park, of course, showcases one of the world's most glamorous and photogenic canyons, truly one of the greatest natural wonders on earth. According to park brochures, writer-historian John C. Van Dyke wrote that Grand Canyon is "more mysterious in its depth than the Himalayas in their height. The Grand Canyon remains not the eighth but the first wonder of the world. There is nothing like it." Similarly, Theodore Roosevelt wrote: "The Grand Canyon of Arizona fills me with awe. It is beyond comparison, beyond description, absolutely unparalleled throughout the wide world." When commercial interests attempted to dam the canyon for profit, Roosevelt pleaded to Congress: "I want to ask you to do one thing in connection with it in your own interest and in the interest of the country—

to keep this great wonder of nature as it is now. . . . Leave it as it is. You can not improve on it. The ages have been at work on it, and man can only mar it. What you can do is keep it for your children, your children's children, and for all who come after you, as the one great sight which every American . . . should see."

Congress designated the Grand Canyon as a national park in 1919, and the enlarged park now encompasses 1,217,403 acres, an area larger than the state of Rhode Island. The Grand Canyon extends for 277 miles along the Colorado River from Lees Ferry, at the southern end of Glen Canyon National Recreation Area, to Grand Wash Cliffs, the upper edge of Lake Mead National Recreation Area. The full length of the Grand Canyon is thus now protected within lands administered by the National Park Service. The canyon is approximately one mile deep (5,000–6,000 feet) and from slightly under a mile to eighteen miles in width; the average width is ten miles.

Grand Canyon National Park contains unparalleled scenery, a remarkable sequence of rock layers recording the greater part of North America's geologic history—one of the most spectacular examples of erosion anywhere in the world. It also includes more than four thousand years of human history and an assemblage of life zones that extends from arid desert lowlands to spruce-fir forests in the highlands. These significant values were given special recognition when Grand Canyon National Park was granted World Heritage Site status by the United Nations Educational, Scientific, and Cultural Organization (UNESCO) in 1979. World Heritage listing officially recognizes areas of "universal value" and warranting "international respect."

Five distinct vegetation zones occur within the park: desert and its associated desert scrub and grasslands; pinyon-juniper woodland and its associated mountain scrub and chaparral, sagebrush, and blackbrush flats; ponderosa pine forests and associated meadows and oaks; spruce-fir forests and aspen groves; and riparian zones along the Colorado River and moist streamsides at a variety of elevations.

All these zones possess their own plant life, although there is considerable overlap due to the microenvironments created by the steep canyons and the resultant northern and southern exposures. For example, desert scrub occurs on exposed southern slopes remarkably high along the North Rim, and pockets of spruce and fir occur on shaded northern slopes at mid-elevations below the South Rim.

Typical desert plants found in the lower canyons, generally below 4,000 feet elevation, include creosote bush, ocotillo, honey mesquite, acacias, and a variety of cacti. Pinyon-juniper woodlands occur at elevations from approximately 4,000 to 7,500 feet. Two-needle pinyon and Utah juniper are dominant, but mountain mahogany, cliffrose, serviceberry, skunkbush, and snowberry are common as well. In places New Mexico locust, fendler-bush, fernbush, and Gambel's oak are added to form mountain scrub thickets. Elsewhere, manzanita, scrub oak, silktassel, cliffrose, and mountain mahogany form chaparral associations.

The ponderosa pine forest areas, which occur from about 6,500 to 8,000 feet elevation consist of open stands of ponderosa pines with a scattering of Douglas-firs and white firs on the North Rim. Above approximately 8,000 feet can be found spruce-fir forest areas. These are diverse forests that can be dominated by a variety of boreal tree species: Engelmann and blue spruce, Douglas-fir, and white fir; aspens occur throughout, often in dense stands. And a special characteristic of the North Rim are the rather extensive meadows, filled with flowering perennials in summer. At the bottom of the canyon flows the Colorado River; it and its lower tributaries support a riparian habitat that is dominated by Fremont cottonwoods, willows, tamarisks, and seep-willows.

Grand Canyon National Park is made up of two distinct units; the South Rim is separated from the North Rims by the great chasm of the Grand Canyon and by two hundred miles of highway from one entrance to the other. The more popular South Rim lies along the northern edge of the Coconino Plateau and is accessible via Highways 64 and 180 from Williams, Flagstaff, and Cameron, Arizona. The North Rim, which is closed in winter, lies along the southern edge of the Kaibab Plateau and is accessible only via Highway 67 from Jacob Lake, Arizona. Campgrounds, overnight accommodations, and supplies are available on both sides.

National Park Service visitor centers or contact stations exist at the Grand Canyon Village complex, Desert View, and Yavapai Museum on the South Rim and near the Grand Canyon Lodge on the North Rim. Each contains an information desk, orientation program, exhibits, and a sales outlet. Bird field guides, a checklist, and the excellent book *Grand Canyon Birds,* by Bryan Brown, Steve Carothers, and Roy Johnson, are available. The visitor center at Grand Canyon Village is the heart of the South Rim's interpretive activities. Programs vary throughout the season and include evening presentations, daily talks and walks, and special tours. Museums at Yavapai Point (geology) and Tusayan (Anasazi life) also contain exhibits and sales outlets. North Rim interpretive activities include similar programs. Interpretive schedules are printed in the *Guide,* available at park entrance stations and information desks.

Additional information can be obtained from the Superintendent, Grand Canyon National Park, P.O. Box 129, Grand Canyon, AZ 86023; (602) 638-7888; Web address: www.nps.gov/grca/.

BIRD LIFE

Pinyon-juniper woodlands occupy the main visitor focal points along the South Rim, with stands of ponderosa pine occurring back from the rim on higher ridges and cooler slopes. The South Rim's bird life is thus largely dominated by pinyon-juniper species. Besides Western Bluebirds, other common nesting birds include the Mourning Doves, with their well-known mournful song; Broad-tailed Hummingbirds, usually detected first by the male's loud wing-trill; Northern Flickers, with their red-shafted wings; Hairy Woodpeckers, with their sharp, loud "keek" calls; and Ash-throated Flycatchers, slender, slightly crested birds that sing a "ka-brick" or "ka-wheer" song.

There are two kinds of jays: the long-tailed Western Scrub-Jay with its bluish head, tail, and wings and whitish underparts, and the shorter-tailed Pinyon Jay with all-blue plumage and noted for constant crowlike cries. Also among the species that nest here are the Mountain Chickadee, with its black bib, cap, and mask and white eyeline; Juniper Titmouse, a little gray-brown bird with a short crest; the tiny Bushtit, with its gray plumage and long, darker tail; White-breasted Nuthatch, with its snow-white breast and cheeks; American Robin, with its red breast and cheery song; Blue-gray Gnatcatcher, looking like a miniature long-tailed mockingbird; Black-throated Gray Warbler, all black and white except for a tiny patch of yellow in front of each eye; and Chipping Sparrow, with its reddish cap and a song consisting of a rapid, monotonous trill.

Other less obvious pinyon-juniper birds include Cooper's Hawks, Western Screech-Owls, Common Nighthawks, Common Poorwills, Western and Cassin's kingbirds, Gray Flycatchers, and Bewick's Wrens. And in places where Gambel's oaks or other deciduous vegetation is mixed into the woodlands, Downy Woodpeckers, Virginia's Warblers, and Black-headed Grosbeaks also occur.

In the lower, open, and warmer canyons is sparse pinyon-juniper woodland that contains many desert plant species. This environment supports a few additional breeding birds, including Greater Roadrunners, Black-chinned Hummingbirds, Ladder-backed Woodpeckers, Northern Mockingbirds, Loggerhead Shrikes, Gray Vireos, Scott's Orioles, and Rufous-crowned Sparrows.

Grand Canyon's riparian environment has undergone a major change since the Colorado River was dammed in 1964. Prior to the construction of Glen Canyon Dam, the floodplain experienced annual flooding that scoured out the canyons, leaving few patches of vegetation. Since 1963, however, the sediment load has declined by 80 percent and the floodplain has been colonized by a variety of plants. The new growth has led to an increased number of riparian birds. These include Willow Flycatchers, Bell's Vireos, Yellow and

Peregrine Falcon

Lucy's warblers, Yellow-breasted Chats, Hooded Orioles, Summer Tanagers, Blue Grosbeaks, Lazuli Buntings, and House Finches.

This increased avian food supply in the lower canyons has had an effect on the park's predators. Riparian nesters like Cooper's and Red-tailed hawks and cliff nesters like Golden Eagles, Prairie and Peregrine falcons, and American Kestrels have undoubtedly increased. Of these key raptors, none has received as much attention as the **Peregrine Falcon.** Because of this bird's dramatic decline during the 1950s and 1960s as a result of widespread use of DDT, the

Peregrine was placed on the endangered species list. Since DDT was banned in the United States and Canada in 1972, Peregrines and other birds atop the food chain have made a comeback. In the case of the Peregrine, recovery was aided by an aggressive restoration program throughout its range.

Surveys in the Grand Canyon by Bryan Brown and colleagues (1990) have provided some startling numbers. A twenty-one-day survey in 1989 resulted in locating at least fifty-eight pairs. The researchers wrote that the "average distances between pairs on the South Rim, North Rim, and Colorado River were 3.7 miles, 5.0 miles, and 4.2 miles, respectively." Extrapolation from the 1989 data "indicates that approximately 100 pairs of Peregrines could occur in those areas of the park." These data suggest that Grand Canyon's Peregrine population, which represents the core of a much larger Colorado Plateau population, may be the densest ever reported.

With such a high population of Peregrines scattered throughout the canyon, the likelihood of seeing one or a pair of these magnificent birds from one of the many park overlooks is excellent, especially in spring when courting birds are most vocal and are actively pursuing one another. Watch for a large, powerful, slate-gray bird with long, pointed wings and wide black mustachial markings against otherwise white cheeks. It may be detected first by thin "screeee" calls. If the opportunity arises to watch this falcon during courtship or hunting, you will not soon forget that experience.

The North Rim is very different from the South Rim. It not only averages 1,500 feet higher, but the greater rainfall and the southward-dipping strata feed almost twice as much runoff into the canyon. This results in deeply cut side canyons that set the North Rim back farther from the Colorado River and isolate greater numbers of erosional remnants. The higher Kaibab Plateau contains a variety of features that are unique, not the least of which is the Kaibab squirrel, a white-tailed, tassel-eared tree squirrel that occurs nowhere else.

One morning in late September, when the aspen leaves were rich yellow and gold, I walked the five-mile Widforss Trail. In a sense, this trail is a microcosm of the North Rim. It begins at Harvey Meadow, just north of the North Rim Store complex, skirts Transept Canyon, and ends above Haunted Canyon at a magnificent overview. The morning was chilly; frost covered the top of the brochure box when I pulled out a Widforss Trail folder. Pygmy Nuthatches called from all directions; their constant chirping calls resounded through the forest. Their only vocal competition came from Mountain Chickadees, tiny but vociferous creatures of the highland forest.

The trail climbs along a densely wooded canyon and onto the plateau, where ponderosa pines fully dominate the scene. **Pygmy Nuthatches** were obvious in the pines, crawling about the scaly trunks and all over the branches and foliage; a few were searching for breakfast on the foliage-strewn ground. It seemed to me that every individual was talking to another. I focused my binoculars on one of these stubby nuthatches that was walking straight down a tree trunk, searching every crack and cranny it came upon. Its short tail, buff underparts, white cheeks and throat, blackish cap, and grayish back were obvious. It was so involved in its morning foray that it seemed to ignore my presence totally. And all the while it continued its perpetual calls, which from up close sounded like crisp "pee-di" notes.

A light hammering behind me attracted my attention to another Pygmy Nuthatch that had found a pine seed and was trying to open it the old-fashioned way. I watched it pound the nut more than a dozen times with great blows from its stout bill before the rich, meaty nut was exposed and consumed.

As I moved along the trail it was readily apparent that the fall harvest was in full swing. During the next few hours among the ponderosa pines, Douglas-firs, and white firs, I found a variety of creatures hard at work collecting seeds, undoubtedly preparing for the coming winter. Although Pygmy Nuthatches were most numerous, Red-breasted and White-breasted nuthatches were also active. The little Red-breasts seemed to prefer Douglas-fir seeds and were working the bract-covered cones. All three nuthatches nest on the North Rim; Pygmy and White-breasted nuthatches utilize cavities in ponderosa pines, and Red-breasts prefer the denser spruce-fir associations. Suddenly a Brown Creeper, an even smaller bird, landed on the base of a Douglas-fir less than a dozen feet from me and began to move upward over the furrowed bark. Its brown back, with fine whitish spots, and buff rump were most obvious. Its behavior of creeping over the bark, with its fairly long tail pressed firmly against the trunk, was distinct. Then it called soft, high-pitched "see see" notes. I watched it continue up the trunk to the upper foliage, from where it suddenly flew to the base of another Douglas-fir. It began another ascent, foraging over the furrowed bark for insects.

Small flocks of Red Crossbills and Pine Siskins and a lone Clark's Nutcracker passed overhead as I continued along the trail. **Common Ravens,** ever present here just as in other southwestern parks, soared along the edge of the high cliffs with occasional "caugh" calls. And as the day progressed, their communications expanded to a surprisingly varied repertoire of calls: "augh, augh, augh"; "gruut"; and a grating "r-r-r-r" sound, as if the bird was trying to clear its throat. In spite of their abundance, I couldn't help but admire this large, gregarious species. From below, I could readily see the all-black body, wedge-shaped tail, and large head and bill that confirm its identity. Once I was treated to an amazing display of aerial acrobatics. For more about Common Ravens, see Death Valley National Park.

A Cooper's Hawk appeared over the rim, soaring toward the south. Suddenly, it turned back toward where I stood enjoying the antics of a pair of ravens. It was as if all three birds, the ravens and the hawk, decided on a whim to get acquainted; they conducted their meeting in midair, closing to less than ten feet apart. There was a sudden loud swoosh as all three birds turned upward. The Cooper's Hawk turned back toward the south and soared away. Both Ravens rolled two or three times, veered downward for seventy to a hundred feet, and then shot straight up again. It all happened so fast that in a second or two it was over.

Brown and colleagues note that by midwinter, "these flocks of ravens around the Canyon may contain over 200 birds each. A communal roost of ravens was found below Grandeur Point on the South Rim during the winter of 1982 and 1983 which contained an amazing 800 ravens" (1987, 221).

Aspen stands are scattered along the trail, about a hundred feet from the rim. Most of their summer resident birds had already gone south, but I could well imagine those same groves ringing with songs: Downy Woodpeckers, Western Wood-pewees, Violet-green Swallows, Mountain Chickadees, Red-breasted Nuthatches, House Wrens, American Robins, Western Bluebirds, Warbling Vireos, Orange-crowned Warblers, and Black-headed Grosbeaks.

The few open areas in the ponderosa pine forest were mostly filled with drying perennials, but some grasses and a few of the late flowers remained. I identified a low-growing lupine, Indian paintbrush, a yellow-centered aster, and a thistle. In one meadow I encountered a mixed flock of Chipping Sparrows and Dark-eyed Juncos searching for seeds amid the sparse ground cover. The chippers consisted of many immature birds without their deep red caps, but they all possessed the fine dark lines running from bill through eye onto the back of the head.

The **Dark-eyed Juncos** all belonged to the gray-headed form, with reddish back and black face patches. I was able to approach to within a dozen feet or so before they took flight. They flew away into the adjacent vegetation with a flick of the white edges of their tail feathers. This little finch is another of the park's year-round residents; it nests in the high spruce-fir community and moves to lower elevations below the snowline during winter. Juncos actually perform an altitudinal migration, and those that remain close to their breeding ground move back and forth along the slopes in accordance with the snowline.

Other common summer residents of the spruce-fir forests of the North Rim include the Northern Flicker, Hairy Woodpecker, Steller's Jay, Clark's

Nutcracker, Mountain Chickadee, American Robin, Hermit Thrush, Ruby-crowned Kinglet, Yellow-rumped Warbler, Western Tanager, and Cassin's Finch. Species occurring in this environment in lesser numbers are the Northern Goshawk, Cooper's Hawk, Blue Grouse, and Band-tailed Pigeon; Flammulated, Northern Pygmy-, and Northern Saw-whet owls; and the Yellow-bellied Sapsucker, Olive-sided Flycatcher, Golden-crowned Kinglet, and Pine Siskin. In places where this habitat occurs on steep slopes, such as on northern slopes below the high rims, Sharp-shinned Hawks and Townsend's Solitaires are also present.

In summer, the song of the **Hermit Thrush** echoes from the conifer stands; this can be one of the most appealing of all the highland birds. John Terres (1987, 921) describes its song as opening with a "clear flutelike note, followed by ethereal, bell-like tones, ascending and descending in no fixed order," rising until it reaches "dizzying vocal heights and notes fade away in silvery tinkle." The Hermit Thrush is often heard but seldom seen unless one visits the shadowy forest. Even then one must be quiet and patient and wait until the bird makes the first move. It often stays close to the forest floor, although it will sing its territorial songs from the very tips of the highest conifers. It may suddenly appear at the base of a tall tree or among heavy branches and sit like a sentinel until it is convinced you are not a threat. Even in the open, the colors of the thrush are subtle—a brownish back, white eye ring, reddish rump and tail, and whitish underparts with black spots.

Of all the high country birds to be found along Widforss Trail, none is as obvious as the **Steller's Jay,** a fairly large, royal blue bird with a tall, blackish crest. This full-time resident can be shy and retiring, or it can be loud and insistent. Its mood seems to depend upon elements known only to jays. Most of my sightings were of lone birds at a distance flying from the top of one tree to another, usually quick flights with crests depressed. Now and again I also detected the jays' scolding nasal "screeech" or "skreek" calls from the forest. But I knew that they, too, were in tune with the season and busy with their fall harvest. Perhaps their aloofness was because they were so occupied with seed-caching behavior.

Widforss Trail ends at an open, southern bench covered with dense vegetation, most of which is more typical of lower elevations. Pinyons and junipers, cliffrose, Gambel's oak, New Mexico locust, and a few Utah agaves, banana yuccas, and cacti dominate the area. I sat on the sandstone bench admiring the grand view and watching for birds. Mountain Chickadees and Pygmy Nuthatches were busy searching for pinyon nuts below me. A Spotted Towhee called from a thicket. A lone Blue-gray Gnatcatcher flew up after a passing insect. Responding to my low spishing calls, an immature White-

Steller's Jay

crowned Sparrow, undoubtedly a migrant, came to within a few feet before retreating. My spishing also attracted a Townsend's Warbler that landed on an adjacent pinyon before moving down the slope. Two Violet-green Swallows passed overhead, heading south across the canyon. I had to envy creatures thus able to ignore the great chasm; to them it is no barrier at all.

I was startled by a sudden "screeeee" call from along the rim to my right, and a second later a **Red-tailed Hawk** soared into view. It was a magnificent adult bird, and from my eye-to-eye perspective, its dark back and broad wings, whitish underparts, and brick-red tail provided outstanding contrast against the blue sky. This bird is far and away the most common raptor in the park, residing from the lowest to the highest elevations and nesting in trees or on cliffs. According to Brown and colleagues (1987, 172), its nesting cycle is "tied closely to the abundance of rainfall, which causes the preferred plant foods of the desert cottontail rabbit to grow in greater abundance. More winter rainfall means more rabbits in the spring. A high density of cottontail rabbits in spring results in higher red-tail nesting density and success rates."

Snow can arrive on the North Rim by October, closing that portion of the park. The South Rim remains open all winter, and except during storms, the canyon is usually clear but cold. Some years, birders take a Christmas Bird Count to tally all the species present during one twenty-four-hour period. In 1986, South Rim birders tallied 428 individuals of twenty-seven species. The dozen most numerous species in descending order of abundance were the Common Raven, Western Bluebird, Dark-eyed Junco, Mountain Chickadee, Pine Siskin, Lesser Goldfinch, Ruby-crowned Kinglet, Black-chinned Sparrow, Pinyon Jay, White-breasted and Pygmy nuthatches (tied), and Canyon Wren.

In summary, the park checklist includes 287 bird species, of which 121 are known to breed. Of the breeding species, only four are water birds (Snowy Egret, Mallard, Killdeer, and Spotted Sandpiper), fifteen are hawks and owls, and eight are warblers.

BIRDS OF SPECIAL INTEREST

Red-tailed Hawk. This is the common broad-winged hawk with whitish underparts and a brick-red tail.

Peregrine Falcon. Watch for it along the rims or along the inner canyon; it is best identified by its powerful build, pointed wings, slate-gray back, and black mustachial stripes (sideburns).

White-throated Swift. This is the common black-and-white bird with swept-back wings that zooms past the overlooks and gives a loud descending trill.

Violet-green Swallow. A common swallow occurring throughout the forested areas of the park, it has snow-white underparts and cheeks and a violet-green back.

Steller's Jay. The park's only all-blue, tall-crested bird, this jay is most numerous within the ponderosa and spruce-fir forests.

Western Scrub-Jay. The long-tailed, noncrested jay of the pinyon-juniper woodlands is blue above, except for a grayish back, with a whitish throat and grayish underparts.

Common Raven. Its all-black plumage, wedge-shaped tail, and heavy head and bill are the raven's distinguishing features.

Juniper Titmouse. This little all-grayish bird with a very short crest is common throughout the park's pinyon-juniper woodlands.

Pygmy Nuthatch. One of the park's smallest birds, it possesses a short tail, gray-brown back, darker cap, and white cheeks; seldom quiet, it calls with high and rapid piping notes.

Canyon Wren. This is the bird of the canyons that sings a series of descending and decelerating "tew" notes; it is cinnamon above and with a snow-white throat.

Western Bluebird. Males possess bright blue hoods and backs, chestnut breasts and flanks, and white bellies.

Hermit Thrush. This is a forest bird that is seldom seen, but its wonderful, clear, flutelike songs are commonplace along the forested rims.

Yellow-rumped Warbler. It is best identified by five yellow spots: its cap, throat, sides, and rump; it nests in the high spruce-fir forests.

Dark-eyed Junco. This is another spruce-fir nester, but can be found almost anywhere in migration and winter; this little "snowbird" has obvious white edges on its blackish tail.

Sunset Crater Volcano, Wupatki, and Walnut Canyon National Monuments

ARIZONA

 The ruins at Wupatki and the cliff dwellings in Walnut Canyon provide stark evidence of their pre-Columbian settlements. The Sinagua peoples lived in this region from about A.D. 600 until the mid-1200s and then departed, leaving behind only echoes of their past. Nature has since reclaimed the old farm plots, but the stone walls remain, utilized only by a few of the native creatures for shelter, foraging, or as singing posts.

On my midsummer visit, Rock Wrens and Canyon Wrens appeared to have first claim on the deserted ruins. It is difficult to visit either site without at least being aware of these two wrens. Rock Wrens sang extended renditions of their trilling songs from each cluster of ruins at Wupatki. And at Walnut Canyon, Canyon Wren songs resounded from secret places below the rim. The birds' loud, descending and decelerating songs rocked the canyon; probably the wrens were just as lively a component of the historic scene when the Sinagua peoples occupied the area.

The Rock Wren is the plainer of the two, sporting gray-brown upperparts with fine whitish spots, lighter underparts, buff flanks and tail, and a long, thin bill. It has a rather stocky build and a habit of bobbing up and down with quick jerking motions. When flying from one rocky perch to another, it often spreads its tail, bobs up and down, and calls its sharp "tick-ear" notes from each new place. It then commences probing into promising cracks, searching for insects among the ancient building stones. And in spring and summer, territorial birds sing a complete song that John Terres (1987, 1030) describes as "keree keree keree, chair chair chair, deedle deedle deedle, tur tur tur, keree keree trrrrrr." See Joshua Tree National Park for details about the Wren's peculiar nesting habits.

The Canyon Wren is a handsome bird with a cinnamon back and belly, grayish brown cap, snow-white throat and breast, and a bill even longer than the Rock Wren's. The most distinctive characteristic of the Canyon Wren is its wonderful silvery song consisting of ten or more clear "tew" notes, "*tew tew tew tew* tew tew tew tew tew tew," each note slightly lower in pitch than the last. The bird sometimes ends its descending song with a short "jeet" note. It often sings the full song time and time again in spring and summer, but by fall and in winter it sings only occasionally during early mornings. The rest of the time it can be located by a metallic "tschee" call, which it may also repeat many times.

Canyon wrens are full-time residents of the Southwest, and are largely restricted to rocky canyons and outcroppings. They use deserted cliff dwellings for nesting whenever the occasion permits. Their nests are constructed of a twig base with a "cup of moss, spider web, leaves, catkins . . . lined with fine materials," according to Paul Ehrlich and colleagues (1988, 444). Rock wrens, on the other hand, prefer open rocky slopes and outcroppings, and they are summer residents only, migrating to lower, warmer regions to the west and south for the winter months.

Rock Wren

THE PARK ENVIRONMENTS

The three disjunct national monuments are located at the southwestern corner of the greater Colorado Plateau at altitudes ranging from 4,800 feet at Wupatki to 8,029 feet at the summit of the thousand-foot-high Sunset Crater. Wupatki is the largest (36,253 acres) of the three park units and was established in 1924. Nearby Sunset Crater (3,040 acres) was designated a monument in 1930 to allow public access to the volcanic remains of periodic eruptions that took place during a two-hundred-year period starting about 1064. And the smallest of the three units is Walnut Canyon (2,249 acres), just south of Sunset Crater; it was established in 1915.

Vegetation zones extend from desert scrub habitat in the lower areas of Wupatki and pinyon-juniper woodlands at mid-elevations to ponderosa pine forests at higher elevations and small but significant patches of Douglas-fir and associated plants on the north-facing slopes of Walnut Canyon.

Steve Carothers and H. Goldberg (1976) refer to Wupatki's lowlands as Great Basin desert scrub habitat; the area is dominated by fourwing saltbush, sand sagebrush, broom snakeweed, Russian thistle, and Mormon tea. This desertlike condition is undoubtedly due to many decades of grazing. Since the monument was fenced and cattle were eliminated in 1989, the lowlands have begun to recover. A greater abundance of grasses and perennials have begun to appear.

The pinyon-juniper woodlands in the higher areas of Wupatki as well as along the rim of Walnut Canyon include extensive stands of pinyon pine and Utah juniper; moderate numbers of mountain mahogany, fernbush, and cliffrose; and lesser numbers of banana yucca, squawbush, Gambel's oak, and pricklypear cacti. Ponderosa pines increase with elevation and moisture and are most abundant at the base of Sunset Crater and along the three-mile entrance road to Walnut Canyon.

The interior of Walnut Canyon contains two additional habitats: the Douglas-fir-dominated associations already mentioned and a riparian environment in the moist canyon bottoms. It is for the black walnuts in the canyons that this national monument is named. Other common trees of the canyon include New Mexico locust, boxelder, aspen, common hoptree, narrowleaf cottonwood, and Gambel's oak.

One National Park Service visitor center exists in each unit: at Wupatki Ruin in Wupatki, at the western entrance to Sunset Crater, and on the rim at Walnut Canyon. Each center contains an information desk, exhibits, and a sales desk; bird field guides are available at all three sites, but a bird checklist is available only for Sunset Crater and Walnut Canyon. Each area contains a number of picnicking sites; camping is permitted at the U.S. Forest Service campground adjacent to Sunset Crater. Interpretive activities are limited to self-guiding trails, including two at Walnut Canyon that provide the visitor with an excellent understanding of past and present human use of the area's native plants and animals.

Additional information on the three monuments can be obtained from the area Superintendent, Wupatki, Sunset Crater Volcano, and Walnut Canyon National Monuments, 2717 N. Steves Blvd., Suite #3, Flagstaff, AZ 86004; (602) 527-7134; Web addresses: Wupatki—www.nps.gov/wupa/; Sunset Crater—www.nps.gov/sucr/; Walnut Canyon—www.nps.gov/waca/.

BIRD LIFE

Sinagua is a combination of the Spanish words *sin* and *agua,* meaning "without water," a term given to the early human inhabitants of this land with little water. The presence of water, at least during most of the year, was what made Walnut Canyon so valuable to the Sinagua peoples. The same factor enhances the bird life today. The moist soils and lush vegetation provide excellent birding opportunities, especially along the three-quarter-mile Island Trail that drops 185 feet into the canyon and circles a high limestone ridge. This trail provides excellent viewing of the canyon environment and its bird life.

In spring and summer, more than a dozen bird species can be found with little effort, among them Turkey Vultures, with their black plumage, bare red heads and V-shaped markings in flight, and Red-tailed Hawks, evident by their broad wings and brick-red tails. The Mourning Dove's familiar mournful call signals its presence; White-throated Swifts are the black-and-white speedsters that zip along the cliffs at breathtaking speed; Broad-tailed Hummingbirds are best identified by the male's green back and red throat; and there are red-shafted Northern Flickers and Acorn Woodpeckers, black-and-white birds with a bright red crown and yellow throat.

Perching birds include the slender Ash-throated Flycatcher, with its vigorous "ka-brick" or "ka-wheer" calls; the Violet-green Swallow, with snow-white underparts and cheeks and violet-green backs; the royal blue Steller's Jay with blackish crest; and the Common Raven of all-black plumage, wedge-shaped tail, and large head and bills. As noted, Canyon Wrens are much in evidence. Also to be seen are the American Robin, with its bright red breast and cheery song; Western Tanager, the males having a canary-yellow and black body and red head; Black-headed Grosbeak, with cinnamon to yellow underparts and a large bill; Spotted Towhee, with rufous sides and blood-red eyes, males having black hoods; and the little Lesser Goldfinch, in which males have a black back and bright yellow underparts.

Other canyon birds that are less numerous include the Cooper's Hawk,

Great Horned Owl, Mountain Chickadee, Bushtit, Plumbeous Vireo, Virginia's and Yellow-rumped warblers, and Bullock's Oriole.

The **Acorn Woodpecker** is one of the park's most obvious inhabitants because of its showy appearance and its habit of flying from snag to snag, constantly calling to its associates. Its call is a loud, raucous "ya-cup, ya-cup," often repeated numerous times. The bird's name comes from its use of acorns as a principal food; when acorns are ripe this woodpecker spends much of its time gathering them and storing them in holes it has drilled in ponderosa pines or other tall woody structures for that purpose. There are records of up to fifty thousand acorns stuffed into one tree, according to Ehrlich and colleagues (1988, 345). Acorn woodpeckers also hoard other nuts, such as walnuts. During the remainder of the year they utilize their caches as well as taking large numbers of insects. It is therefore not unusual to see an Acorn Woodpecker flycatching from a high perch, dashing out after a passing insect, grabbing it with a snap of the bill, and sailing back to a favorite snag. All of this activity goes on with little concern for the hundreds of onlookers who may be present along Island Trail.

Another obvious bird of Walnut Canyon, as well as in the Sunset Crater ponderosa pine forest, is the **Steller's Jay.** This is the crested jay of the West, very different from the Blue Jay of the eastern United States, although the two species hybridize in Colorado where their ranges overlap. Both can be belligerent and aggressive toward other birds. Steller's Jays are fond of bird eggs and nestling and will also rob the caches of other birds, such as acorns stored by the Acorn Woodpecker.

The pinyon-juniper woodlands support a different set of breeding birds, although there is some overlap with the canyon species. One of the most abundant of the small bird species in the forest is the **Juniper Titmouse.** All gray-brown, it has few distinguishing features beyond its short crest and black eyes and bill. But it more than makes up in personality for what it lacks in color. As Paul and Elsie Spangle note in their (out of print) booklet *Birds of Walnut Canyon:* "One of friendliest of the birds, the titmouse will closely examine anyone who will sit still long enough, and its cheery voice will accompany its sharp-eyed examination." The bird's song is a clear whistled "witt-y, witt-y, witt-y," and its call notes, common throughout the year, are "see-jert-jert."

The Juniper Titmouse is a cavity nester and one of the few songbirds that retains the same mate year after year. Individuals rarely occur in flocks, staying mainly in pairs or family groups. Watching one or several of these tits searching for insects among the foliage and branches of a pinyon can provide enough amusement to retain one's interest for a considerable time. It is not unusual to see a titmouse "crawling" through the foliage or hanging upside-down from one leg. And when the bird acquires a seed too large to swallow whole, it holds the seed against a branch or rock with one foot and hammers away at the prize with powerful strokes of its short but stout bill until the nut is cracked and the meat can be retrieved.

Other common pinyon-juniper birds include Hairy Woodpeckers, Gray Flycatchers, Pinyon Jays, Mountain Chickadees, White-breasted Nuthatches, Western Bluebirds, Black-throated Gray Warblers, and Western Tanagers. Less common birds of this community include the Common Poorwill, Black-chinned Hummingbird, Western Kingbird, Western Wood-Pewee, Mountain Bluebird, Plumbeous Vireo, and Hepatic Tanager.

The **House Finch** can be especially common in the arid lowlands, providing the Rock Wren company about Wupatki's ruins and rocky outcroppings. It is an active bird in spring, appearing in large flocks and serenading all and sundry with its lively and melodious songs. Both sexes sing, and it is not uncommon to have mated birds singing at the same time, almost as if each were intent upon outsinging the other. Males possess a red forehead, eyebrows, and throat; females lack the red color and are rather plain except for heavy streaking on their underparts, as on the males. The House Finch uses a variety of situations for nesting, building nests in cracks or on ledges of the ruins or natural outcroppings as well as on various plants, including cholla cacti.

Birds of the ponderosa pine forest include some of the same species that occur in the adjacent woodlands. But there are several additional birds that are more or less limited to the ponderosa pines, at least during the breeding season. The Pygmy Nuthatch and Grace's Warbler are the best examples. The **Pygmy Nuthatch** is one of the most abundant and gregarious birds in this community, constantly communicating with its neighbors and always flitting from tree to tree and from one feeding site to another. Besides being one of region's most active birds, it is also one of the smallest. It is a short-tailed bird with a dark cap that contrasts with its white cheeks, bluish gray back, and whitish to buff underparts. See Grand Canyon National Park for a description of its behavior.

Grace's Warbler, on the other hand, may be difficult to find because of its more solitary ways and preference for the high ponderosa foliage, where it usually forages. But this is a beautiful bird with a bright yellow throat and breast, streaked flanks, grayish back, and darker crown and cheeks with a bold yellow eyeline. It can best be located by its rather distinct song, which it sings off and on throughout the day: a rapid accelerating trill, like that of a Chipping Sparrow but sweeter. Scott Terrill, in the *Audubon Society Master Guide to Birding* (1961, 148), describes the song as a "rapid, staccato, musical

Pygmy Nuthatch

trill: chee-chee-che-che." Grace's Warbler is truly a bird of the American Southwest. Although it spends winters in northwestern Mexico and southward, it nests only in the pine forests of the southwestern United States and nearby Mexico.

All of the conifer areas can be extremely busy during the fall when seeds are ripe. The pinyon-juniper, ponderosa, and Douglas-fir communities experience a rush of seed gathering that may attract birds from other habitats and from considerable distances. A late September visit to Walnut Canyon's mixed forest produced a strange assortment of species. Townsend's Solitaires called high-pitched "eek" notes from high posts. I could see their slender, grayish brown bodies with buff wing patches and white outer tail feathers in flight. Western Bluebirds appeared in flocks of a few to a dozen or more individuals. Their mellow "flew" notes resounded from the forest, and their deep blue, chestnut, and white plumage was a lovely addition to the day.

Pygmy and White-breasted nuthatches were active among the pinyons and ponderosas. I watched one White-breast hammering away at a pinyon nut, holding it with one foot against a squared rock that looked as it had once been a building block for one of the many Sinagua dwellings. Mountain Chickadees made themselves known by their constant "chick-adee-adee-adee" songs. And a bright male Spotted Towhee called a loud "chreee" from atop a dense squawbush. Steller's Jays, Northern Flickers, and a lone Hairy Woodpecker were also evident.

Flocks of American Robins were present as well. Many were only passing by, calling to one another while in flight. I located several among the brushy junipers, feeding on the ripe purplish berries. And there, too, were three Evening Grosbeaks. I stopped to admire these lovely birds as they picked and ingested the ripe berries. All three were males, showing the characteristic bright yellow body and eyeline across the forehead, in wonderful contrast to their black and white wings and black-brown faces.

A flock of eight Brewer's Blackbirds passed overhead, migrants no doubt en route to their wintering grounds to the south. A lone Red Crossbill passed over, calling its harsh double notes. The ascending "scree" calls of Pine Siskins were evident. I located a flock of eight or ten Mountain Bluebirds passing overhead. And Yellow-rumped Warblers were present among the ponderosa pine foliage; I watched one individual dash out after a passing insect. Its five yellow spots were evident through binoculars: on its cap, throat, sides, and rump.

Suddenly a huge flock of American Crows appeared from the west, calling out with loud "cahs" and strange throaty grunts. There were at least seventy-five individuals, and I watched as they circled and then descended into the pinyon-dominated woodland just behind the visitor center. They, too, had come to harvest the pinyon nuts. For the next half hour I watched as they gathered nuts from the trees and on the ground; even these large birds seemed unable to crack the nuts without a few sharp blows of their bills. They used the same technique as the smaller nuthatches, holding the nut against a stone or branch with one foot and striking it with the bill. I imagine that the flock of crows visiting Walnut Canyon had come from the nearby fields and pastures and that it was a typical wintering flock. These can number in the hundreds, and flocks of up to 200,000 have been reported in the Midwest. Flocks regularly travel fifty miles from their roosts to choice feeding sites. It was good evidence of the coming winter.

The best perspective on the area's wintertime birds can be derived from the Christmas Bird Counts made annually in nearby Flagstaff, Arizona. The Flagstaff Christmas count from December 29, 2001, tallied fifty-seven species. The dozen most numerous birds in descending order of abundance were Dark-eyed Junco, Mallard, Common Raven, American Crow, European Starling, Pine Siskin, Rock Dove, Canada Goose, House Sparrow, Northern Shoveler, House Finch, and Red-winged Blackbird.

In summary, the combined checklists include 152 species, of which forty-five are known to breed. Of those forty-five species, none are water birds, seven are hawks and owls, and four are warblers.

BIRDS OF SPECIAL INTEREST

Acorn Woodpecker. This black-and-white bird with a red, white, and yellow head is common at Walnut Canyon.

Steller's Jay. This is the dark-crested jay of intense royal blue occurring throughout the ponderosa pine forests.

Juniper Titmouse. A pinyon-juniper species, the titmouse has all-gray plumage and a short crest.

Pygmy Nuthatch. The tiny, short-tailed nuthatch of the ponderosa pines has a dark cap and white cheeks.

Canyon Wren. At Walnut Canyon, this cinnamon bird with all-white throat and breast is most often detected by its wonderful descending song.

Rock Wren. Gray-brown with buff flanks and tail, this wren can be common about Wupatki's ruins and on rock outcroppings.

Grace's Warbler. This is the little yellow-throated bird that sings a melodic trill. It spends its summers among the high ponderosa pine foliage.

House Finch. Males possess a red breast, throat, and eyebrows and heavily streaked bellies; they are most numerous in spring and summer at Wupatki.

Montezuma Castle National Monument

ARIZONA

 I followed the self-guided trail one spring morning beyond the visitor center to the "castle," a pre-Columbian cliff dwelling nestled in a shallow cave a hundred feet high on an imposing limestone bluff. The morning was bright and calm, and bird songs permeated the air. The loudest songs that morning were those of House Finches singing from high points along the trail and from various outcroppings on the steep slope. Rock Wrens, all-grayish birds with long bills, called "treiill" notes from the rocky slopes, and one individual was searching for insects along the trail in front of me. Its jerky motions and stop-and-go behavior amused me. To my left, among the dense shrubbery of cat-claw and willows, a Bewick's Wren sang a rather complicated song of warbles, whistles, and trills. And farther on, among the sycamores, I detected the sweet whistle song of a Summer Tanager.

Then less than a dozen feet away, from the low foliage of a hackberry, a harsh "ti-she-she" call greeted me. At first it sounded like a loud Ruby-crowned Kinglet call, but I knew that bird should be far away by now, on its breeding grounds in the spruce-fir forests to the north. It took me several seconds to locate the perpetrator. Suddenly, there it was: a trim little Bridled Titmouse. Through binoculars, I watched it forage among the new foliage, searching each group of leaves in a rather nervous fashion. The bird seemed extremely shy, and I watched its progress from leaf to leaf.

What a handsome bird it was! Its high crest and black-and-white face pattern—reminiscent of a horse's bridle, hence its name—gave it a special appeal. Crossing the white cheeks of the Bridled Titmouse is a bold black line that runs from the bill through and beyond the eyes and then turns downward to the all-black throat. The overall plumage of the one I saw was a buff-gray color, but its back and wings contained a tinge of green.

A second bird appeared, probably the female, judging from its slightly faded features, and I tracked both individuals as they continued foraging. I followed them from eye level to the high foliage of an adjacent sycamore and then back down into the lower foliage and along the sycamore trunk. One individual poked into every crack and under every piece of loose bark imaginable, almost to ground level. Their nervous movements made them difficult

Bridled Titmouse

to follow, but their constant vocalizations, which sounded more like those of chickadees than titmice, helped me to track their constant movements.

Suddenly I realized that one of the birds was gathering nesting material, plant down and cobwebs. Soon it disappeared with a bill-full of nesting materials into a crevice in a broken sycamore limb about twenty feet high. Seconds later the bird reappeared without its load and immediately proceeded to search for more of the precious material.

Arthur C. Bent, in his *Life Histories of North American Jays, Crows and Titmice* (1964a, 425), includes a description of a Bridled Titmouse nest found in an oak stump: "The small entrance was six feet from the ground, and the cavity was a foot deep, and two and a half inches in diameter. It was lined on the bottom and well up on the sides with a mat composed of cottonwood down, shreds of decayed grasses, some hair from a rabbit, and many fragments of cotton-waste." My little Bridled Titmouse was right on target.

THE PARK ENVIRONMENT

Montezuma Castle and Montezuma Well are situated along Beaver Creek, a tributary of the Verde River in the Verde Valley of north-central Arizona. The twenty-room, five-story castle is a twelfth-century apartment house built by the Sinagua people in a cave on a high limestone bluff overlooking Beaver Creek. The "well," located seven miles northeast of the castle, is a large limestone sink containing a small lake. The Sinaguas built houses along the walls and on the rim and ditched water from the runoff to adjacent fields for their crops.

Beaver Creek flows south through a semidesert environment that is dominated by creosote bush, honey mesquite, catclaw acacia, Fremont barberry, fourwing saltbush, winterfat, and broom snakeweed. A few Utah junipers occur on the higher northern slopes. A rather lush riparian habitat exists along the creek, where the dominant trees are Arizona sycamore, Arizona walnut, netleaf hackberry, and willows. Common understory plants include catclaw acacia, velvet ash, Arizona baccharis, fourwing saltbush, and sacred datura.

The combined 842 acres, established as a national monument in 1906, includes a visitor center, picnic grounds at both units, and interpretive trails to the base of the castle and to the well and its outlet, the starting point of the irrigation system. The park's visitor center, located at the entrance to the castle trail, contains an information desk and exhibits. Bird guides and an area checklist are available.

Additional information can be obtained from the Superintendent, Montezuma Castle National Monument, P.O. Box 219, Camp Verde, AZ 86322; (602) 567-3322; Web address: www.nps.gov/moca/.

BIRD LIFE

Bridled Titmice, in spite of their diminutive size, are among the area's most charismatic birds. In early spring when the bright green new leaves appear, this little full-time resident can be almost anywhere within the riparian zone.

But it has considerable competition, for several colorful breeding birds are also present and actively involved with courtship and defending territories.

One of the most abundant of the spring-summer residents, and also one of the most vocal, is the **Western Kingbird.** It usually sings from a commanding perch among the high foliage or from the very top of a sycamore tree. Betty Jackson, once a permanent resident at the monument, described one individual that "shrieked from the top of his tree, 'I'm the best man, here! I'm the best man here!' Suddenly from three other trees came the answer, 'The hell you are! The hell you are!'" She continued that "they all flew up and met in the air a little way from the challenger's tree, and fought it out, violently and vociferously" (Jackson 1941, 5). Kingbirds can thoroughly dominate the area. But they also can be confusing because two species—Western and Cassin's—nest within the monument, and both possess gray chests and yellow bellies. Principal differences exist in their songs and plumage. Kevin Zimmer points out in *The Western Bird Watcher* (1985, 208) that "the Cassin's has a sharp 'chi-queer,' while the Western gives a 'whit' or series of the same, often strung together in an excited chatter." The Western Kingbird's gray chest fades gradually into its yellowish belly, and its black tail contains white outer feathers; it prefers the broadleaf vegetation along the creek. The Cassin's Kingbird, on the other hand, is a darker bird that shows distinct color patterns, including a white throat, and its black tail has a whitish tip; it generally prefers the adjacent juniper slopes.

The **Summer Tanager** also nests within the riparian vegetation along Beaver Creek, although it is usually less conspicuous than the Western Kingbird. The male Summer Tanager, however, is difficult to ignore when it does come close enough to be seen. During courtship it often dashes about the lower foliage in pursuit of its mate. Males are all-rosy-red birds with a blackish wash on their wings and large, pale bills. Females are dull yellow versions of the males. This seven-inch bird sings a song that sounds at first much like that of an American Robin, though it is more hurried and possesses a slight trill. During the breeding season this tanager sings all through the day, but it rarely sings after nesting. Then it can be located by its rather dry "kit-it-up" call notes.

Other riparian nesters to be expected include the Yellow-bellied Cuckoo, recognizable by a long, barred tail, reddish flight pattern, and "kuk-kuk-kuk" call; Gila Woodpecker, with black-and-white barred back and rolling "churr" call; little Yellow Warbler, its plumage all yellow except for the male's chestnut chest stripes; the larger Yellow-breasted Chat, with its variety of grunts, squeaks, chortles, and whistles; Hooded Oriole, males having an orange-yellow head and coal-black face and throat; and Bullock's Oriole, somewhat larger than the Hooded, and the male having a black cap, back, and wings and orange cheeks and underparts.

The thicket areas along the creekbed support an additional assortment of birds, although considerable overlap occurs throughout the floodplain. Phainopeplas, also of the thickets, are all-dark birds with a tall crest and blood-red eyes. The tiny Bell's Vireo sings songs asking and answering questions—"Wee cha chu we chachui chee? Wee cha chu we chachui chew!" The equally tiny Lucy's Warbler, all gray but for the male's rusty crown patch and rump, can be common as well. Other birds of this habitat are the bright red Northern Cardinal; Blue Grosbeaks, identified by the male's deep blue plumage, chestnut wing bars, black face, and stout bill; Lazuli Buntings, males with bright turquoise head, bluish back, cinnamon breast, and white belly; and Abert's Towhees.

The rather plain, brown **Abert's Towhee** is surprisingly abundant along Beaver Creek, although it is more often heard than seen. Like the similar Canyon Towhee, which occurs on the drier slopes above the riparian zone, Abert's Towhee is a skulker that runs along the ground and seldom exposes itself. The birds are gregarious in their behavior, however, greeting one another with loud and expressive "peep, peep, peep" calls, especially when welcoming a mate. Males sing a series of rapid notes: "chip, chip, chee-chee-chee." Allan Phillips and colleagues (1964, 191) describe the two species thus: "Abert's Towhee is a more cinnamon brown than the Canyon Towhee; it lacks the chest spot, but shows a light-colored bill framed in black feathers of the front part of the face."

I found the normally shy Abert's Towhee to be extremely curious; I was able to coax it into the open and to approach it reasonably closely by making a series of squeaks with my lips against the back of my hand. One flew directly toward me from a thicket, landing on a fallen log about thirty-five feet away, but it stayed there only a second or two before flying to the ground. Then it ran from one patch of grass to another with jerky motions. However, I could keep it fairly close with additional squeaks, although it never did expose itself fully again.

Another bird of the riparian area is the **Gambel's Quail,** which also occurs on the adjacent slopes. This is the park's only quail, easily identified by the male's black teardrop-shaped plume, face, and belly and chestnut cap and sides. Like the towhees, it is more often heard than seen. The song of the Gambel's Quail, however, is well known, even if the listener has never before seen the bird; it is the common birdsong of Western movies. The typical song is an emphatic, four-note "chi-*ca*-go-go," and its call notes are "wa-kuh," common among conversing birds in a covey. John Terres (1987, 693) notes that "members of covey utter low chuckles or grunt like young pigs—quoit, oit, woet" as well.

The Gambel's Quail is truly a bird of the American Southwest, with a range that extends from southeastern California to southwestern Texas, north to the southwestern corner of Utah, and south into Sonora, Mexico. Paul Ehrlich and colleagues (1988, 262) call it the "most arid-adapted of quail"; they also point out that in summer it forages primarily early and late in the day, with "long quiet periods" in the middle of the day.

Beaver Creek has a history of high water after heavy summer storms, but shallow pools and a quiet flow are more typical. Two little flycatchers frequent the creekbed, the Black Phoebe and Vermilion Flycatcher. The **Black Phoebe** is a permanent resident that usually can be found flycatching off rocks in the creekbed. Its all-black body and contrasting white belly make identification easy. It can usually be located by its rather distinct song, a high-pitched "pi-tsee, pi-tsee." I located one especially active bird one day in October and watched as it flew back and forth just inches over a particular section of the creek, snapping its bill time and again as it grabbed up flying insects. Black Phoebes build nests of tiny mud pellets placed low on cliffs and rocky banks near the water.

In summer, the little Vermilion Flycatcher should also be watched for, as it is one of the park's most beautiful creatures. The male Vermilion Flycatcher has a vermilion head and underparts, contrasting with its dark brown back,

Black Phoebe

wings, and tail. In the sunlight, the vermilion plumage can appear velvety. Females are drab by comparison but have their own subtle beauty of light pink, white, and tan.

Beaver Creek also provides good hunting grounds for swifts and swallows. White-throated Swifts and Northern Rough-winged and Cliff swallows nest along the cliffs and banks, and Violet-green and Barn swallows either nest nearby or are late migrants. The Swifts are easily identified by their swept-back wings, cigar shape, and black-and-white plumage; they also call loud twittering notes almost constantly. The Rough-wings and Cliff Swallows nest on the bluff near the castle and are common in their comings and goings. Rough-wings are rather drab with brown upperparts and gray-brown underparts. They build twig nests in crevices along the bluff.

The **Cliff Swallow** is strongly patterned with dark chestnut and blackish throat, whitish forehead, buff rump, and light underparts. This is the bird that builds upside-down gourdlike mud-pellet nests along the high bluff in April and May. Like their Black Phoebe neighbors, these swallows gather mud from the creek and paste together hundreds of tiny round mud pellets in shaping their nests. Henry Collins wrote in his little out-of-print booklet *Birds of Montezuma and Tuzigoot* (1951, 5): "Soon after nesting cares are over these swallows start their southward migration, often as early as July or August. One day they are here; the next they are gone—off on a flight that will take them as far as Brazil or Argentina—until the revolving seasons bring them back once more as heralds of another spring."

A number of other interesting birds are occasionally found within the riparian zone. Great Blue Herons come there to fish from a rookery on nearby Clear Creek, according to park interpreter Babs Monroe. Turkey Vultures, identified by all-dark plumage, a bare red head, and wings held in a shallow V shape, are reasonably common. Common Ravens usually are found soaring overhead; look for their broad, pointed wings, a wedge-shaped tail, and heavy head and bill. The Common Black-Hawk, with its very broad wings and short tail banded in black and white, is less numerous. And the smaller, reddish-backed American Kestrel occurs all year, being especially numerous in spring and summer.

Two large raptors are reasonably common: Great Horned Owl and Red-tailed Hawk. Babs told me that Great Horned Owls occasionally nest on the walls of Montezuma Well, but their presence is most often evident from their loud, hoarse calls, "who who who-who."

The **Red-tailed Hawk,** a broad-winged bird with a brick-red tail, can be especially obvious in early spring when courting. Red-tails can put on quite a show; pairs spend considerable time in flight, chasing one another and diving, spiraling, circling, and screaming loud "kreee-e-e-e" calls, like escaping steam. The smaller male will often dive at his mate from a considerable height, whereupon she may turn over in the air and present her claws to his in mock combat. He also feeds his mate during courtship, presenting her with a recently caught mouse or other prey animal.

The Red-tail's diet is extremely varied—one reason that this bird is so common throughout its range from Alaska to Central America and the West Indies. Rodents make up as much as 85 percent of its diet, but it also is known to capture and eat cottontails, weasels, skunks, porcupines, a wide variety of birds, rattlesnakes, turtles, lizards, frogs, carp and catfish, numerous insects, spiders, and earthworms.

The Montezuma Well lake and wetlands contain very different bird life. Although this habitat is small and supports only a few resident species, it is visited by an amazing diversity of other birds at various times of the year. Resident species one is likely to find include the Pied-billed Grebe, Mallard, Virginia Rail, Sora, Common Moorhen, American Coot, and Common Yellowthroat.

The adjacent desertscape, such as the area along the entrance roads to both park units, supports several more nesting birds, including Greater Roadrunners of cartoon fame; Common Poorwills, which are most vocal during the evenings and at dusk; and the little Ladder-backed Woodpeckers with black-and-white barred backs. Additional nesting species are the Ash-throated Flycatcher, distinguishable by its grayish throat, yellowish belly, and reddish tail; the tiny yellow-headed Verdin with its rapid, high-pitched "chip" notes; that great mimic, the Northern Mockingbird; the Crissal Thrasher with its long bill and rufous crissum (undertail covert); the Loggerhead Shrike, with large head and black-and-white plumage; the little Black-throated Sparrow, with its coal-black throat and tinkling song; and in grassy areas, the Western Meadowlark, evident by its yellow and black breast and wonderful song.

Wintertime produces many more northern species that come south and join flocks composed of full-time residents. Christmas Bird Counts provide one of the best indicators of the winter populations. The annual Camp Verde Christmas counts include a portion of the monument. On December 27, 2001, counters tallied 101 species. The dozen most numerous species in descending order of abundance were European Starling, Common Raven, Mallard, American Robin, Canada Goose, Pinyon Jay, Mourning Dove, White-crowned Sparrow, Red-winged Blackbird, Sage Thrasher and House Finch (tied), and Common Merganser.

In summary, the bird checklist for Montezuma Castle, including species found at Tuzigoot National Monument and adjacent Tavasci Marsh and

Peck's Lake, totals 211 species. Of those, forty are listed as permanent residents and an additional thirty-seven species are summer residents and probably nest there; five of the seventy-seven summer residents are waterbirds, five are hawks and owls, and five are warblers.

BIRDS OF SPECIAL INTEREST

Red-tailed Hawk. This large, broad-winged hawk with a brick-red tail often soars over the well and creek.

Gambel's Quail. Males of the park's only quail species sport black teardrop plumes, faces, throats, and bellies, and chestnut sides.

Western Kingbird. Most often seen among the sycamores, where it is noisy in spring, this kingbird has a gray head, yellowish belly, and black tail with white outer edges.

Black Phoebe. This little flycatcher hunts along the creek; it is identified by its coal-black plumage and white belly.

Cliff Swallow. This square-tailed swallow, with a chestnut throat and buff rump, builds mud-pellet nests on the bluff near the castle.

Bridled Titmouse. One of the park's smallest and most charismatic species, it sports a tall crest and black-and-white head pattern.

Abert's Towhee. This is the plump, dull brown bird along the creek that has a black face and calls with loud "peep" notes.

Tonto National Monument

 I tried to imagine how the pre-Columbian Salado people who occupied Tonto's cliff dwellings from about A.D. 1300 to 1450 might have perceived their natural environment. In order to survive in the arid landscape, they undoubtedly took advantage of every possible resource, plants and animals alike. Were those early inhabitants in awe of the scenic splendor of their canyon, wondering at the soaring vultures and hawks? Did they enjoy all the bird song rising from the slope below?

I gazed down that same slope early one spring morning, tracing the half-mile trail that zigzagged in a steep 350-foot ascent from the visitor center, and identified the numerous birds around me. The most obvious were the large Turkey Vultures that soared along the slope and over the cliffs. Their all-dark plumage, bare red heads, long wings held in a shallow V pattern, and the slight rocking of their bodies were clearly evident.

The other large black birds, somewhat smaller than the vultures, were Common Ravens, with their coal-black plumage, wedge-shaped tails, and large heads and bills. One pair of these noisy creatures had constructed a stick nest in a crevice above the cliff dwelling, and from the constant attention given the site, I could only assume that it contained nestlings. Before long these gregarious birds would be showing off their youngsters. Watching the adults teaching the young about finding food, harassing their neighbors, and the secrets of aerial acrobatics would provide considerable amusement to the human visitors along the trail.

Also diving and soaring along the cliffs—sometimes in wild plunges from high overhead, past hikers, and into the valley below—was a group of much smaller birds. These were White-throated Swifts, identified by their swept-back wings and black-and-white bodies. White-throated Swifts have been clocked at more than a hundred miles an hour in a dive, and one could feel air movement when they passed nearby. Although swifts are often mistaken for swallows, they are more closely related to hummingbirds. Both are members of the order Apodiformes, Latin for "without feet."

Tonto's White-throated Swifts are summer residents only and are among the birds returning earliest in the spring, a sure sign of the new season. They

Turkey Vulture

build their nests of feathers glued together with their saliva and placed inside crevices on the high cliffs. This swift is a colonial nester; a dozen or more individuals may utilize a single crevice. They winter to the south, from the southern border of the United States (see Big Bend National Park and Chiricahua National Monument) to Central America, utilizing crevices in cliffs like those at Tonto.

THE PARK ENVIRONMENT

Tonto National Monument encompasses 1,120 acres of rugged canyonlands above Roosevelt Lake in the Sierra Anchas Mountains of south-central Arizona. The monument was established in 1907 to protect the remains of Salado cliff dwellings built in natural caves. The Lower Cliff Dwelling consists of sixteen ground floor rooms, three of which had a second story, and the Upper Cliff Dwelling contains thirty-two ground floor rooms; eight had a second story. The cliff dwellings are situated on southeast-facing slopes approximately 700 and 1,100 feet above the Salt River at Roosevelt Lake. Park elevations range from 2,300 feet in the north to 4,000 feet in the southwest corner.

The area lies within the upper edge of the Sonoran Desert, where tall, stately saguaro cacti dominate the slopes and ridges. Other common plants include catclaw acacia, honey mesquite, paloverde, jojoba, and ocotillo. Less numerous are the century plant, fourwing saltbush, sotol, tomatillo, broom snakeweed, and a variety of cacti. A perennial spring in Cave Canyon supports a riparian zone where Arizona sycamore, Arizona walnut, netleaf hackberry, and mesquite are most numerous.

The park visitor center lies at the end of a one-mile entrance road off State Highway 88/188. There can be found an information desk, exhibits, a twelve-minute video program, and a sales outlet; bird field guides and a checklist are available. Interpretive activities include the self-guided Lower Cliff Dwelling Trail and guided tours to the Upper Cliff Dwelling in fall, winter, and spring, on a reservation-only basis. A small picnic area is available along the entrance road, but there is no camping inside the park.

Additional information can be obtained from the Superintendent, Tonto National Monument, HC 02, Box 4602, Roosevelt, AZ 85545; (602) 467-2241; Web address: www.nps.gov/tont/.

BIRD LIFE

Songbirds were active that morning along the slope, chasing one another about the abundant shrubs or singing from the top of saguaros or other high posts. The rolling songs of **Cactus Wrens** were most obvious, like a deep, throaty "chuh, chuh, chuh, chuh," with a number of variations. Their football-sized grass nests were abundantly evident along the slope, built on chollas and spiny shrubs. These birds keep even their old nests in repair, raising a new family in the newer one and using older nests for roosting sites. One especially vocal Cactus Wren was perched at the very top of a tall saguaro near the cave dwelling. I could clearly see its rust-brown cap, bold white eyebrow, streaked back, and whitish underparts with black spots. See White Sands National Monument for more about this large wren.

The smaller, red-breasted bird perched on another saguaro just down the slope was a male **House Finch.** This bird's song was far more melodious than the Cactus Wren's, and it seemed to continue indefinitely in a long series of scrambled phrases, like "swing, swing, swing, sweem, sweem, te swee," sung over and over again. His mate, all brownish with a heavily streaked breast and belly, was perched on a nearby catclaw, singing the same song. I wondered whether they were purposely dueting, as so many tropical wrens do. They suddenly took flight, passing overhead toward the top of the cliff; they were calling sweet "cheet" notes as they passed.

A **Gila Woodpecker** appeared out of a hole in a saguaro farther down the slope, flew up to one of the massive cactus arms, and called out a loud "churr" note. I focused my binoculars on this medium-sized bird and could see that it was a female, without the male's bright red cap but with fawn-colored underparts and a black back heavily barred with white lines. In flight, its bright white wing patches were evident. The smaller Ladder-backed Woodpecker, another resident of the park and the greater Southwest, also possesses a black-and-white back and head. But the Gila Woodpecker is restricted to the saguaro cactus forest of Arizona and adjacent Mexico. The bird and the saguaros reach the northeastern edge of their range near Tonto National Monument. This woodpecker bores nest holes in saguaros, and the holes provide nest sites for a series of other cavity nesters. See Saguaro National Park for further detail about this unique species.

One of these cavity nesters is the tiny **Elf Owl,** the world's smallest owl at less than two ounces. It is fairly common at the monument, although rarely seen because of its nocturnal habits. Elf Owls have a loud voice and utter "chucklings and yips like a puppy dog," according to Allan Phillips and colleagues (1964, 53). These observers note that "most of their calling is done at dusk from the entrance to the hole, and again at dawn, following the Cassin's Kingbird chorus. Also they call incessantly during moonlit nights in spring, after which they are hard to detect."

Most Elf Owl sightings are limited to flashlight observations of a head at the entrance to a nest hole high in a saguaro. The little owl's dark bill, whitish eyebrows, and bright yellow eyes give it quite a ferocious appearance. It is a deadly predator that takes a wide variety of tiny creatures, including insects caught on the wing or on the ground, such as moths, grasshoppers, and crickets, plus scorpions, lizards, and small snakes.

Several loud "ka-brick" calls of **Ash-throated Flycatchers** resounded around me, but it took several minutes to locate one of these rather plain, slender birds, perched on a paloverde down the slope. Through binoculars, its grayish throat and breast, yellowish belly, and brownish cap and rufous tail were obvious. The bird suddenly shot almost straight up for twenty feet or so, grabbed a passing insect with a snap of its bill, and returned to the same perch with a quick flip of its tail. Insects and spiders make up about 92 percent of its diet, with fleshy fruits accounting for the remainder.

Several other birds were present that morning: a Red-tailed Hawk, with its brick-red tail; White-winged Doves calling "who cooks for who, who cooks for you-all"; and Mourning Doves calling with low, mournful songs. The equally sorrowful song of a Say's Phoebe came from below, near the visitor center, where I later found the bird nesting under the roof overhang. Rock Wrens, all-grayish birds with jerky motions, were issuing loud trills; a Curve-billed Thrasher gave its loud snapping calls from a little wash nearby; the mellow whistles of a Scott's Oriole floated across the canyon; and a pair of Canyon Towhees greeted each other with loud screeching calls.

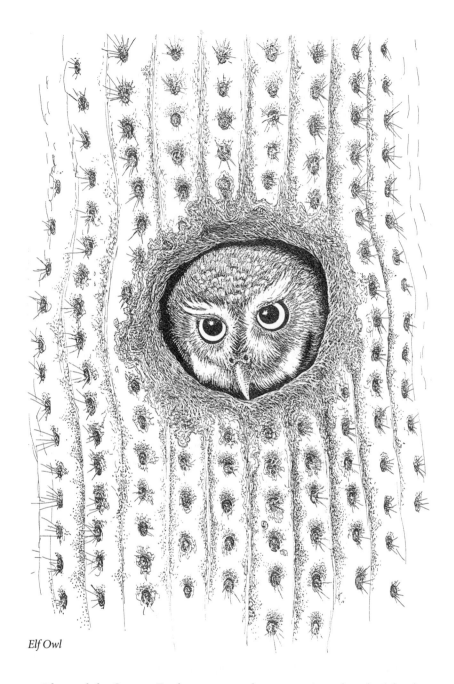

Elf Owl

I located the **Canyon Towhees** on a rock outcropping a hundred feet below me. I watched them through binoculars as they went about their strange
behavior, which I attributed to courtship: one individual, which I assume was
the male, was standing before the other with its wings drooped and quiver-
ing all over, like a leaf in a breeze. Both birds called loud and continuous

"pink" notes. Their rufous caps glowed in the morning light, contrasting with their rather drab bodies, all brown except for their cinnamon-colored crissums. These birds nest on the ground or on low shrubs amid grasses, where they make use of "mouse-runs" through the grass for escape routes. The male suddenly put his head back and sang a song that sounded like "chili-chili-chili-chili."

The Canyon Towhee was lumped with the California Towhee under the generic name of Brown Towhee until 1983, when the American Ornithologists' Union determined that the two should be considered separate species. Canyon Towhee range extends from eastern Arizona to the Texas Big Bend country and northward only to southeastern Colorado.

Two additional birds encountered on my walk back to the visitor center were Gambel's Quail and Black-throated Sparrow. I had detected distant calls of **Gambel's Quail** from the ruins, but their four-note "chi-*ca*-go-go" calls were most common near the canyon bottom. Then I discovered a lone male perched on a catclaw at the far corner of the visitor center parking lot. It was standing erect with its all-black plume and face, rufous cap, grayish chest and nape, and rusty wing patch highlighted by the bright sunlight. We watched each other for several minutes before the bird flew to the ground, where I could hear low clucking calls, probably from his mate.

Black-throated Sparrows were common in the lower canyon and even more numerous near the picnic area later in the day. This lovely little sparrow is one of the park's common year-round residents, distinguished by its coal-black throat and face, bold white eyebrows and slash between the throat and cheeks, grayish underparts, and gray-brown wings and tail. During the spring months, when birds are most active, its tinkling bell-like songs are abundant throughout the desert. This sparrow seems to be one of the area's most curious birds, responding almost immediately to low spishing notes.

Greater Roadrunners also occur in the park but are more common below the canyon in the open desert. This long-legged bird is one of the park's most asked-about birds. Roadrunners are members of the cuckoo family, and during their nesting season they often give deep "coo coo coo" notes, not unlike those of other family members. A courting male roadrunner performs outlandish displays, parading about with his head held high and stiff and his tail and wings drooped. Occasionally the male bows while spreading his tail and lifting and dropping his wings.

Roadrunner nests usually are placed in a low shrub or thicket. They are constructed of sticks and lined with feathers, leaves, and grass. Typically, four eggs are laid and incubated by both parents. Nestlings beg for food with strong buzzing notes. A roadrunner diet consists primarily of a variety of animals from lizards to insects, but the birds also consume fruit and seeds. Lizards seem to be their food of choice.

A few other desert species are more likely to be found in the lower canyon: little Common Ground-Doves, with their ascending "wah-up" calls; Lesser Nighthawks, flying during the evenings and at dusk; Northern Mockingbirds, with their aptitude for mimicking other bird songs; and blunt-headed, black-and-white Loggerhead Shrikes.

Cave Canyon's riparian habitat supports a very different assortment of birds, although there is some overlap with the adjacent desert environment. Many of the desert birds visit the spring for water, and many of the riparian species sing from high points or search for food in the adjacent desert. Common riparian species include the little Black-chinned Hummingbird; Western Wood-Pewees that sing descending "pe-eer" songs; and tiny Bell's Vireos, with their distinct question-and-answer songs, described by Phillips and colleagues (1964) as "Wee cha chu we chachui chee? Wee cha chu we chachui chew!" Also common in the riparian habitat are the equally tiny Lucy's Warbler, with an all-gray body, except for a rufous rump and the male's small rufous crown patch; the Summer Tanager and Northern Cardinal, both species in which the males are bright red; and the dark-backed Lesser Goldfinch, with its canary-yellow underparts.

Other birds found in the Cave Canyon riparian zone and adjacent thickets include Western Screech-Owls with their "bouncing ball" songs; Black-tailed Gnatcatchers with their distinct scratching calls; and black-and-white, crested Bridled Titmice. Commanding the high points are Western Kingbirds, with their yellow bellies and black tails with white edges on the outer feathers; white-bellied Black Phoebes frequent the creekbed. Also present are the Bewick's Wren, with long tail and white eyebrows; the Crissal Thrasher, a long-tailed bird named for its rufous crissum; the pert Phainopepla; the large-billed Black-headed Grosbeak; and Hooded and Bullock's orioles, both with orange-yellow and black markings.

Phainopeplas are fascinating birds for several reasons. They are North America's only representative of the silky-flycatcher family. They possess two breeding seasons; April and May breeders apparently move northward and nest again in June and July. Phainopeplas are also among the handsomest of birds. Each sex possesses a tall, somewhat shaggy crest and a slightly fanned tail. The males are coal black except for blood-red eyes and snow-white wing patches visible in flight. Females are duller versions of the charismatic males.

The scattering of juniper and pinyon trees along the cooler slopes supports a few additional bird species, including Cassin's Kingbird, Western Scrub-Jay,

Mountain Chickadee, Juniper Titmouse, Western Bluebird, Black-throated Gray Warbler, and Western Tanagers.

In winter, the riparian habitats and warm slopes of Tonto National Monument support surprisingly large populations of wintering birds. Most numerous are Blue-gray Gnatcatchers; tiny Ruby-crowned Kinglets, with their constant movement, white eye rings, and bright red (partially hidden) crown patches; nondescript, long-tailed House Wrens; secretive Hermit Thrushes; American Goldfinches, their characteristic yellow dulled in winter; and four kinds of sparrows. The reddish-capped Chipping Sparrow is tiny; the larger Lark Sparrows has a boldly marked head striped in chestnut and white; Lincoln's Sparrow, with its buff chest band, frequents the thickets; and White-crowned Sparrow adults are identifiable by distinctly marked black-and-white head stripes.

Other less common wintering birds include the Sharp-shinned Hawk, Northern Harrier, American Kestrel, Yellow-bellied Sapsucker, Mountain Bluebird, Yellow-rumped Warbler, Song Sparrow, Dark-eyed Junco, and Lawrence's Goldfinch.

In summary, the monument's bird checklist includes 143 species, of which sixty-three are listed as permanent or summer residents and assumed to nest. Of those sixty-three species, none are water birds, five are hawks and owls, and two are warblers.

BIRDS OF SPECIAL INTEREST

Turkey Vulture. This is the large soaring bird with a bare all-red heads; in flight, wings are held in a shallow V-shaped position and the bird rocks slightly from side to side.

Gambel's Quail. The park's only quail is easily identified by its plump body, black plume and throat, and loud calls of "chi-*ca*-go-go."

Greater Roadrunner. Watch for this long-legged cuckoo in the desert areas below the canyon.

Elf Owl. This tiny, yellow-eyed owl nests in unused woodpecker holes in saguaros; it is active only after dark.

White-throated Swift. From early spring through fall, these speedy black-and-white birds are common along the high cliffs.

Gila Woodpecker. This is the large woodpecker of the saguaros with a black-and-white barred back and loud "chuuur" calls.

Ash-throated Flycatcher. Often detected first by its loud "ka-brick" calls, it is a slender bird with a grayish throat, yellowish belly, and reddish tail.

Common Raven. All black with wedge-shaped tail and large head and bill, the raven can be common over the cliffs or visiting the picnic area and parking lots.

Cactus Wren. This is the large wren that builds grass nests on the chollas and sings loud, hoarse "chuh chuh chuh chuh" songs.

Black-throated Sparrow. A bird of the open, arid slopes, this sparrow sports a coal-black throat, two white face stripes, and a whitish belly.

House Finch. Males possess a bright red throat and forehead and heavily streaked belly; this is one of the park's most common and gregarious species.

Organ Pipe Cactus National Monument

ARIZONA

 Nowhere have I found Phainopeplas as abundant as they are at Organ Pipe Cactus National Monument in winter and spring. Especially in desert washes where mistletoe clumps are widespread on the mesquite, ironwood, and paloverde trees, this charismatic bird seemed to be present at almost every clump. It usually sits at the very top of a tree for a considerable time, then suddenly dashes out after a passing insect in a pursuit that may extend to sixty or eighty feet. At times its flitting is so graceful as to be reminiscent of a large butterfly. And during courtship, males perform fantastic display flights, circling and zigzagging high above their perspective mates. In mid-February, I watched groups of five to eight Phainopeplas fluttering together in a sort of cooperative display. After three or four minutes they returned to their respective perches among the mistletoe.

Phainopepla is Greek for "shining robe," referring to the male's shiny all-black plumage; females are duller. This bird is the only North American member and the only desert dweller of the silky-flycatcher family (Ptilogonatidae); three other species occur in the highlands of Mexico and south to western Panama. All possess a tall, shaggy crest, but the Phainopepla is distinctive in being all black with ruby-red eyes and snow-white wing patches (evident only in flight). Its abundant calls are discrete mellow notes, like a low "wurk" or liquid "quirt," which can be heard for a considerable distance. When disturbed they utter harsh "ca-ra-ack" cries. Their song is a short series of mellow notes that prompted Allan Phillips and colleagues, in *The Birds of Arizona* (1964), to describe it as "sweet gargling." Organ Pipe Cactus biologist Tim Tibbitts told me the Phainopepla's song is among the most complex and varied in the Sonoran Desert.

Phainopeplas nest in early spring, and young of the year are already out of the nest by early May, at about the same time that nesting is just beginning for the Neotropical species that have recently arrived from their wintering grounds south of the border. But unlike the Neotropical birds that go south after the breeding season, Phainopeplas move north to higher and somewhat cooler areas and nest a second time. This northward movement is largely completed by early June, leaving only a few individuals behind at Organ Pipe

Phainopeplas

Cactus. Phillips and colleagues suggest that southern Arizona Phainopeplas move northwest into the pinyon-juniper zones of California and central Arizona. By mid-October, however, the Organ Pipe Cactus birds have returned to their wintering grounds, again ready to welcome human visitors to the desert.

THE PARK ENVIRONMENT

Organ Pipe Cactus National Monument is a microcosm of the vast Sonoran Desert and is located at its geographic center. Although this 330,689-acre park is only a tiny part of the greater 120,000-square-mile Sonoran Desert, it contains a smorgasbord of Sonoran flora and fauna. A total of 312,600 acres is wilderness. Three large columnar cacti occur there: organ pipe, for which the national monument is named, saguaro, and senita. Several other Mexican plants reach the northern edge of their range here; a few examples include acuna cactus, dahlia-rooted cactus, ironwood, and elephant tree.

Five distinct habitat types are listed for the park by Kathleen Groschupf, Bryan Brown, and Roy Johnson, in *An Annotated Checklist of the Birds of Organ Pipe Cactus National Monument, Arizona* (1988): juniper-oak woodland/mixed mountain scrub, mixed Sonoran desert scrub, creosote bush, riparian, and marsh/open water. Although creosote bush occurs in nearly pure stands, it is also found in the mixed desert scrub community, along with paloverde, ocotillo, saguaro, organ pipe cactus, bursage, saltbush, and brittlebush. Riparian habitats occur along washes and at wetlands, such as the pond at Quitobaquito Springs. The washes are generally dominated by honey mesquite, acacias, and ironwood, and the pond edge by Fremont cottonwood, Goodding willow, arrowweed, and gray-leaved abrojo. Cattail and bulrush dominate the wetland sites. Finally, to be found above approximately 3,300 feet in the Ajo Mountains are scattered woodland species such as one-seed juniper, Ajo oak, oak-belt gooseberry, hoptree, hollyleaf buckthorn, desert olive, and jojoba.

The park's visitor center and campground are located along Highway 85, twenty-two miles south of Why, Arizona, and five miles north of the border with Sonora, Mexico. The visitor center contains exhibits, a bookstore, an information desk, and an auditorium for orientation programs; bird field guides and a checklist are available. The Visitor Center Nature Trail provides a good introduction to the desert plant life. The 1.2-mile Desert View Nature Trail runs between the visitor center and campground. And two self-guided scenic drives begin at the visitor center: the twenty-one-mile Ajo Mountain Drive and the fifty-three-mile Puerto Blanco Drive. Other interpretive activities include evening programs and nature walks during the winter season; programs vary and schedules are posted at the campground and visitor center.

Additional information can be obtained from the Superintendent, Organ Pipe Cactus National Monument, Rt. 1, Box 100, Ajo, AZ 85321; (602) 387-6849; Web address: www.nps.gov/orpi/.

BIRD LIFE

Although the **Phainopepla** is the park's most notable bird in winter and spring, several other species also are abundant in the desert community at that time of year. The most obvious of these include the Cactus Wren, Curve-billed Thrasher, Gila Woodpecker, Gilded Flicker, House Finch, Loggerhead Shrike, Black-throated Sparrow, Gambel's Quail, Verdin, and Black-tailed Gnatcatcher, more or less in that order.

The **Cactus Wren** is impossible to ignore because of its abundance and verbosity. These large wrens sit on top of saguaros at dawn, singing loud, rapid "choo-choo-choo-choo" or "cora-cora-cora-cora" songs for long periods. Campers in the park campground soon discover that the Cactus Wren provides them with excellent wake-up service.

Their name comes from their close association with cacti, not only as singing posts but also for nesting sites. The Cactus Wren usually chooses small to mid-sized cholla on which to build its flask-shaped, football-sized nest of grasses, small sticks, strips of bark, and other debris. The abundant spines of the cactus provide excellent protection for the birds. See White Sands National Monument for more about nest construction.

Cactus Wren diets vary. John Terres (1987, 1028) reports that this bird eats "beetles, ants, wasps, grasshoppers, bugs, some spiders and an occasional lizard and tree frog; also some cactus fruit, elderberries, cascara berries, some seeds, sometimes visits bird feeders for bread, pieces of raw apple, fried potatoes." Organ Pipe Resource Management Specialist Jon Arnold told me that a Cactus Wren came to a beehive wedged in the wall of a park residence every morning to eat bees: "I watched a Cactus Wren retrieve a bee from just outside the hive, fly to the ground with it, brush the bee's abdomen in the dirt to remove its stinger, then pop it down for breakfast. One morning I watched it consume twelve bees."

If the morning song of the Cactus Wren does not provide an adequate wake-up, surely the "snap-song" of the **Curve-billed Thrasher** will. Larger than Cactus Wrens, Curve-bills also commonly sit at the top of saguaros at the start of each day. They warm up with loud, almost explosive "whit-wheet" songs but before long shift into a more elaborate and melodic song that sounds very much like that of their close cousin the Northern Mockingbird. One February morning in the campground I timed several Curve-billed Thrasher songs that lasted from eight to a full thirty seconds each.

By the time the Curve-billed Thrashers are in full song, **Gila Woodpeckers** begin their calls, which can include a series of loud "eee eee eee eee" notes or a rolling "chuuur." They too may begin their day at the top of a saguaro, flying to other singing posts after a few calls to repeat their morning announcements. For these birds and their neighbors, the morning songfest has special meaning because its helps in the important business of maintaining territories, even if campers might prefer to sleep a little longer.

Gila Woodpeckers share their territories with another large woodpecker that may also perform its morning ritual from atop saguaros, the **Gilded Flicker.** During the winter months there are two forms of flickers present in the park: the resident Gilded Flicker, a yellow-shafted flicker, and the Northern Flicker, the red-shafted bird that is a winter visitor only. With three large woodpeckers present at the same time, identification can be confusing. But separating these three birds is fairly easy. The Gila Woodpecker is the smallest of the three and has clearly marked black-and-white barring on the back and rump and a buff-colored hood and underparts; males also sport a bright red cap. In flight Gilas show a single white patch on each wing. Flickers are boldly spotted below and possess a barred back and obvious white rump; males show a heavy red strip on each cheek. The resident Gilded Flicker has yellow underwing lining, while the visiting Northern Flicker shows red underwing linings.

A fourth woodpecker, the much smaller Ladder-backed Woodpecker, also has a black-and-white barred back. But this bird usually visits saguaros only when they are in fruit or flower, to eat the fruit or the insects attracted to the flowers. Nesting Ladder-backs rarely utilize saguaros; they prefer smaller trees and shrubs.

Another of the common morning songsters of the desert is the little **House Finch;** it, too, can be abundant about the campground. This is the sparrow-sized bird that sits atop saguaros or adjacent shrubs and delivers short, rapid songs that are repeated over and over. Several individuals singing together produce a lively and extensive chorus. Males show a bright red chest, crown, eyebrows, and rump; females are brownish birds with streaked underparts. See Joshua Tree National Park for more about this lively songster.

Watch also for a husky black-and-white bird with a black mask. This is the **Loggerhead Shrike,** often called the "butcher bird" because of its habit of capturing prey, sometimes as large as a mockingbird, and impaling it on a thorn or on barbed wire. This strange behavior was first believed to be a method of killing and storing prey, but recent research has shown that impaling prey is practiced only by the male and is used primarily to demonstrate his prowess to a prospective mate.

Perhaps the most abundant of all the park birds is the little **Black-throated Sparrow.** It is present in the hottest parts of the desert as well as on the higher mountain slopes and is usually detected first by its tinkling song, with sharp bell-like notes. Except while nesting, these sparrows occur in flocks of a few too many individuals, usually on the ground searching for seeds. If this bird is heard but not readily seen, it will often respond immediately to squeaking or spishing sounds and may come up to within a few feet to investigate. Up close it is one of our most attractive sparrows. It has a coal-black throat and tail, whitish underparts, and a black-and-white face: black cheeks bordered by bold white stripes.

Two of the smallest of the resident desert birds are the Verdin and Black-tailed Gnatcatcher. The **Verdin,** with its yellow head and a maroon patch at the bend of each wing, is an active little bird. Among the outer branches of a thorny shrub it builds softball-sized nests of interlaced thorny twigs, leaves, and grass, bound together with spider webbing. The nests are lined with feathers and soft down from various plants. The male Verdin builds several nests, from which his mate selects her favorite to raise a brood; the remaining nests are maintained as dummy nests and for roosting.

Black-tailed Gnatcatchers are slender, long-tailed birds, the tail being black with white outer feathers, and the breeding male has a black cap. They look a lot like the visiting Blue-gray Gnatcatchers, but the two can readily be separated by their distinct calls. Black-tails give a scratching call, very wren-like, compared with the querulous "pwee" note of the Blue-gray Gnatcatcher. The Black-tail builds its nest in the fork of a small shrubs, using "plant down and similar materials bound with insect and spider silk, lined with fine materials," according to Ehrlich and colleagues (1988, 452).

The birds mentioned are not the only full-time desert residents, although they are the ones most often encountered. Other reasonably common species include Gambel's Quail, with their loud "chi-*ca*-go-go" calls; Mourning Doves, usually seen in small flocks near watering holes or swiftly passing overhead; Greater Roadrunners, with long legs and tail; Say's Phoebes, all-brownish fly-catchers with a dark cap and tail and a sad "pee-ur" whistle call; Common Ravens, large all-black birds with a heavy bill, wedge-shaped tail, and deep "caw" calls; and Northern Mockingbirds, gray-and-white songsters with a long tail and a vast repertoire of songs.

Gambel's Quail are often found running across the roadway or trail, plump bodies atop short, pumping legs. Flocks of a dozen to sixty-five or more can be expected in fall and winter, but they pair up in spring and nest on the ground in the concealment of grasses or shrubs. The nest is little more than a shallow depression on the ground, in which are laid ten to twelve eggs; twenty-one to twenty-three days later their precocial chicks are already out of the nest and following dad, with mom trailing in the rear, in their never-ending search for food. For more about this quail, see Joshua Tree National Park.

Two other Organ Pipe habitats contain a few different birds: the wooded mountain canyons, such as in Alamo Canyon or along the upper trail to Bull Pasture, and Quitobaquito Springs. A morning walk into Alamo Canyon on the western slope of the Ajo Mountains cannot help but increase one's appreciation of the beauty and diversity of this fascinating national monument. One mid-February morning I found about three dozen bird species along the Alamo Canyon Trail. Although the majority of these were desert species already mentioned, I also found American Kestrels, Rock and Canyon wrens,

Canyon Towhees, and Rufous-crowned Sparrows—all year-round residents—and a number of winter-only visitors: House Wren; Ruby-crowned Kinglet; Hermit Thrush; Yellow-rumped Warbler; Green-tailed and Spotted towhees; Black-chinned, White-crowned, and Golden-crowned sparrows; Dark-eyed Junco; and Lesser Goldfinch.

Of all these birds, **White-crowned Sparrows** were most numerous, feeding on the ground near brushy areas where they could quickly find shelter if disturbed. They are among the most curious of the wintering birds, easily enticed into view with only the slightest spishing. Adults sport a bold crown of black-and-white stripes and clear whitish underparts; immatures have a brown-and-buff crown. This sparrow nests in the high mountains and northern tundra, leaving the Arizona desert by or before mid-May. However, wintering White-crowned Sparrows sometimes sing partial or full songs, especially on sunny spring mornings.

Alamo Canyon is one of the best places in the park to see Golden Eagles soaring over the high cliffs. Almost twice the size of the more common Red-tailed Hawk, adult Golden Eagles possess gold-tinted feathers on the head, evident only in the right light. Red-tails also soar over Alamo Canyon, and are readily identified by their broad wings and a brick-red tail. The common little falcon of the area is the American Kestrel. Only half the size of a Red-tail, the Kestrel has a reddish back and tail and whitish cheeks with double black stripes; the male has blue-gray wings. Both Red-tailed Hawk and American Kestrel are also common in the desert, even nesting on saguaros on occasion.

Alamo Canyon also is where the little Ferruginous Pygmy-Owl has been recorded in the past. This rare Arizona bird is an endangered species. During

White-crowned Sparrow

my visit to Alamo Canyon I encountered biologist Tim Tibbetts camping at the canyon trailhead and searching for this elusive bird. Although he did not find it that day, he told me he had recorded seven owl species at the nearby Alamo Campground: Barn, Great Horned, Long-eared, Western Screech-Owl, and Burrowing owls and the diminutive Elf Owl and Ferruginous Pygmy-Owl. He added that the Ferruginous Pygmy-Owl is "primarily a bird of the middle bajada areas with lots of large trees—ironwood, paloverde, mesquite—and of course at least some saguaros. It is also associated with large washes like Growler Wash."

My visit to Quitobaquito Springs was but one stop on the fifty-three-mile Puerto Blanco Drive. Betty and I spent most of one day along this route, stopping at the twenty-six signposts to read about each site in the interpretive guidebook. I also recorded all the birds encountered along the way. The highlights included a huge flock of more than sixty Gambel's Quail at stop six; a Greater Roadrunner singing its cuckoo song, "who, who, who, who, who," at stop seven; and six or seven White-throated Swifts flying over the high cliff to the south of stop 9. We admired a Red-tailed Hawk hovering for an extended time at stop 10; a long-tailed ground squirrel ran off as we pulled up at Bonita Well, and a male Costa's Hummingbird was feeding on chuparosa flowers in the wash at stop 14; a Green-tailed Towhee "mewed" at us along the Cristate Saguaro Trail at stop 15. Quitobaquito Oasis was stop 19.

There were not many birds about the Quitobaquito pond during our visit. A Black Phoebe was flycatching from the willows along the shore; its coal-black body, except for a white belly, was readily apparent. A pair of American Coots, black in the body and with large white bills, were feeding on water plants. And a Marsh Wren called from the cattails at the far side of the pond. The only other birds detected included a few typical desert species we had already seen in the surrounding environment.

Farther on, near stop 26, we had a superb look at a family of five **Harris's Hawks.** Four of the birds were sitting on saguaros, and one of the youngsters had just caught a fairly large mouse or rat. It was holding its prey with its claw while trying to balance itself on a skinny post. Each time it seemed steady, a gust of wind blew the bird off balance so that it spread its wings and danced around on top of the post to stay in place. It finally gave up and floated to the ground to eat. The other Harris's Hawks remained on their saguaros, allowing us wonderful views. The two adults were all dark chocolate brown in color, except for chestnut shoulder patches and a white rump patch; the three immatures were more mottled.

Harris's Hawks are highly social birds, usually found in family groups and known to hunt cooperatively. Ornithologist James Bednarz (1988) reported on "social foraging" as a common technique for this species. He found that groups of four and five Harris's Hawks pursuing prey as a relay team had considerably higher success than did birds hunting alone or in pairs. And ornithologist William Mader (1976) found that Harris's Hawks nest not only in pairs but also in trios. He found that the extra hawk, an immature bird, served as a nest helper by feeding the chicks and/or supplying prey at the nest. Harris's Hawks are one of the few cooperative-nesting raptors found in the United States.

I also drove the Camino de Dos Republicas, an unimproved road that follows the international border southeast of Highway 85 to Dos Lomitas Ranch. Park Ranger Bob Cook had told me that this route offered the best sparrow habitat on the national monument. He was correct. I added five species to my

Harris's Hawks

growing bird list, finding two Brewer's Sparrows and a single Clay-colored Sparrow (rare) with a large flock of White-crowns and then a huge flock of meadowlarks, probably Western Meadowlarks, although I was unable to detect any song; two flocks of Brewer's Blackbirds were sitting on the power lines along the roadway; and I saw a pair of Bendire's Thrashers running here and there after insects on a patch of rather barren desertscape.

The desert community changes from winter to spring almost overnight. Spring wildflowers, shrubs, and cacti come into bloom during late February and reach their peak in early April. April also is when the Neotropical birds arrive. The entire character of the desert then moves into a more urgent and exciting mood. Songs and calls of White-winged Doves, Ash-throated and Brown-crested flycatchers, Purple Martins, and Scott's Orioles mix with bird music from the many year-round resident species among the saguaros. The songs of Bell's Vireos, Lucy's Warblers, and Hooded Orioles are added to the riparian bird chorus.

Biologist Kathleen Groschupf conducted a breeding bird survey in the saguaro community on May 31, 1991, in which she recorded thirty-four species. The dozen most numerous birds in descending order of abundance were White-winged Dove, Verdin, Gila Woodpecker, House Finch, Ash-throated Flycatcher, Cactus Wren, Curve-billed Thrasher, Gambel's Quail, Black-tailed Gnatcatcher, Gilded Flicker, Mourning Dove, and Brown-headed Cowbird. Several Lucy's Warblers, Black-throated Sparrows, Phainopeplas, Lesser Nighthawks, Purple Martins, Scott's Orioles, and Northern Cardinals were recorded. Lesser numbers of Black and Turkey vultures, Red-tailed Hawks, Costa's Hummingbirds, Ladder-backed Woodpeckers, Bell's Vireos, Violet-green Swallows (transient), Common Ravens, and Northern Mockingbirds were found. And single individuals of the Harris's Hawk, American Kestrel, Brown-crested Flycatcher, and Canyon Wren were also detected. These numbers provide a good idea of the relative abundance of the breeding desert bird life.

The arrival of the **White-winged Dove** in April is a major event. Their loud and distinct songs—"who-cooks-for-you?"—suddenly blend with those of Cactus Wrens, Curve-billed Thrashers, and House Finches. This dove's large size and bold white wing patches make identification easy. Phillips and colleagues (1964, 42) point out that its nesting season may extend to as late as mid-September, and "two broods seem to be the usual number, though three might be raised where the birds are left undisturbed."

Although many desert creatures obtain sufficient water from the foods they eat, never needing to visit standing water to drink, others must drink regularly. Especially during the hot months, Quitobaquito Springs attracts many migrants and breeding birds. Ornithologist Max Hensley (1954) once counted four hundred White-winged Doves drinking at Quitobaquito in a single day in late May. From May 25 to June 7, he tallied an additional twenty species at the springs, including Great Blue Heron, Killdeer, Vermilion Fly-catcher, Crissal Thrasher, and Hooded Oriole. Quitobaquito is also where Tibbitts documented nesting Tropical Kingbirds in spring 2000. This appears to be that bird's northwesternmost nesting record.

Migrants often remain at the springs for several days, feeding on available insects, native fish, or vegetation; resting; and building up energy before they continue with the next leg of their journey. Of the 277 bird species included on Groschupf, Brown, and Johnson's annotated checklist, twenty-two are listed only for Quitobaquito as transients or migrants; twelve of these are water birds and four are warblers.

Winter birds are occasionally censused in the park as part of the nation-wide Christmas Bird Count. The most recent count was in 1983, when the Lukeville, Arizona, count tallied 641 birds of forty-three species. The dozen most numerous birds in descending order of abundance were White-throated Swift; Gambel's Quail; White-crowned Sparrow; Mourning Dove; Phainopepla and House Finch (tied); Gila Woodpecker, Cactus Wren, and Black-throated Sparrow (tied); Curve-billed Thrasher; Canyon Towhee; and Ruby-crowned Kinglet.

In summary, the park's 1988 checklist includes 277 species, of which sixty-four are known to breed. Of those sixty-four species, only two—Killdeer and American Coot—are water birds, eleven are hawks and owls, and two are warblers: Lucy's and Yellow warblers.

BIRDS OF SPECIAL INTEREST

Harris's Hawk. This is an all-dark hawk with cinnamon wing patches and a white rump; individuals are usually found in family groups.

Gambel's Quail. The park's only quail, it is a plump bird with a teardrop head plume; males sport a black face, throat, and belly and a chestnut cap.

White-winged Dove. This common summer resident is easily identified by large white wing patches and a distinct call: "who-cooks-for-you?"

Gila Woodpecker. A large woodpecker with a barred back, buff head and underparts, and a white wing spot in flight.

Verdin. This tiny bird with a yellow head and maroon shoulder patches builds softball-sized nests of thorny twigs.

Cactus Wren. One of the most common and loudest of the desert birds, it has a rollicking song and builds football-sized nests among cactus spines.

Black-tailed Gnatcatcher. This is a tiny long-tailed bird with a scratchy call; males possess a black cap and tail with white outer tail feathers.

Curve-billed Thrasher. A fairly large brownish gray bird with a decurved bill and orangish eyes, it calls loud, explosive "whit-wheet" notes at dawn and dusk.

Phainopepla. It is hard to miss this slender, crested flycatcher that frequents bunches of mistletoe; males are coal black with ruby-red eyes.

Loggerhead Shrike. This husky black-and-white bird has a black mask and preys on other birds, small mammals, and insects.

Black-throated Sparrow. One of the park's most common birds, it prefers arid areas and is best detected by its tinkling songs.

White-crowned Sparrow. This winter visitor is usually found in flocks; adults sport a boldly marked crown striped in black and white.

House Finch. One of the park's most appealing songsters; males possess a bright red throat, eyebrows, and rump and streaked underparts.

Saguaro National Park

ARIZONA

Early mornings in a saguaro forest are a one-of-a-kind adventure that everyone, even people only remotely appreciative of nature, should experience. The tall cactus forest possesses a certain calming effect that we all need in today's technological world. A principal ingredient of this forest is the bird life. The dawn chorus of birds starts each morning with vigor and excitement that makes one keenly aware of the new day. The avian chorus reverberates among the saguaros; it can be difficult to differentiate species in the clamor. Only after the initial confusion wears off can one begin to identify individuals.

Cactus Wrens, Northern Mockingbirds, Curve-billed Thrashers, Gambel's Quail, White-winged Doves, and House Finches are most evident. Cactus Wrens, for example, sing a loud, rollicking "chuh chuh chuh" song that truly can overpower the vocalizations of most of the other species. In spring, it is not unusual to find several individuals singing their songs from the very top of the saguaros. To me, their voices evoke the bass section of a choir, anchoring the rest. And if the large numbers of unruly grass nests on chollas and various thorny shrubs are any indication, these birds are among the park's most abundant species.

Curve-billed Thrashers also nest on chollas and thorny shrubs, but they build stick nests well hidden within the protective spines of their hosts. Curve-bills sing a song with loud, clear caroling similar to that of a mockingbird. Their sharp and even louder "whit-wheer" calls, given throughout the year, are enough to overpower any of the other desert sounds. This thrasher is a reasonably large bird with a subtly mottled breast, a heavy, long, and curved bill, and yellow and black eyes.

The addition of Northern Mockingbird voices to the morning chorus tends to add melody to the cacophony. And these black, white, and gray songsters are likely to continue singing even after the rest of the choir has retreated to attend to family chores. John Terres (1987, 611) reports that the Northern Mockingbird sings thirty-nine different "species songs" and fifty call notes, and "has imitated cackling of hen, barking of dog, postman's whistle, and even notes of piano." Anyone who has lived in a mockingbird's territory is well aware of the all-night serenades during the breeding season.

Gambel's Quail provide a very different perspective to the morning din, as their emphatic "cha-*ca*-go-go" calls ring out across the terrain. Males, with their black teardrop-shaped plumes, faces, throats, and bellies, and chestnut sides and caps, often perch on taller shrubs to sing their territorial songs.

Another member of the dawn chorus is the White-winged Dove. This large dove usually perches at the top of a saguaro so as to be adequately heard. Its part in the chorus is a drawled but loud cooing rendition of the somewhat redundant "who cooks for you? who cooks for you all?" Every now and then these large doves make swift courtship flights, wide circles on stiff wings, before settling back on the same cactus or an adjacent one to resume their part in the chorus.

Every choir must have its lead singer, and the saguaro chorus leader is none other than the **House Finch,** the smallest of the group but one of the most melodious. Its part consists of a joyous and warbling melody with many variations. Males possess bright red breasts, throats, and bold eyelines, and heavily striped bellies. Their spirited songs ring out even above those of the larger Cactus Wrens, thrashers, quail, and White-wings.

THE PARK ENVIRONMENT

Saguaro National Park consists of 91,446 acres of desert valley, foothills, and mountain terrain in two separate units approximately thirty miles apart. The eastern Rincon Mountains section, of which 57,930 acres were designated wilderness in 1976, ranges in elevation from 2,700 feet near the visitor center to 8,666 feet at the summit of Mica Mountain in the Rincons. The much smaller western Tucson Mountains section, adjacent to the Tucson Mountain County Park and Arizona-Sonoran Desert Museum, is situated between 2,200 and 4,687 feet elevation. Each unit has a visitor center with an information desk, exhibits, orientation programs, and a sales outlet; bird field guides and a checklist are available.

Interpretive activities vary by unit and season but include naturalist-guided walks and self-guided trails and roadways as well as environmental education programs for schoolchildren. Activity schedules are posted at each center. The park also contains more than two hundred miles of backcountry trails.

The Rincon Mountains unit of the park was established in 1933, and the Tucson Mountains unit was established in 1961 to protect lower but robust stands of saguaros. Although there has been considerable concern about and research into the long-term decline of the Rincon saguaros, Chief Park Interpreter Tom Danton explained that the reasons for the saguaro decline are complex and probably involve several factors. First, cattle were common

House Finch

within the Rincon unit until 1978, when they were finally excluded. These nonnative creatures were indiscriminate about the immature plants they stepped on, and they fed on most of the nursery shrubs that were essential for shading young saguaros. On the other hand, cattle had been excluded in the western unit since about the turn of the century. Second, the Rincon Mountains are subject to lower winter temperatures; the severe freeze of 1938 affected many plants. It often takes several years before bacterial necrosis (epidermal browning) appears and the entire plant slowly succumbs. Since 1978, nursery plants in the Rincon Mountains have begun to recover, and recent studies have shown that the saguaros are staging a slow but steady increase.

The park's often overlapping vegetation zones consist of desert scrub habitats in the lowlands, from the base of the mountains to about 5,200 feet elevation; desert grasslands from 4,000 to 5,000 feet; pine-oak-juniper woodlands and forest occur in the Rincon Mountains from 4,400 to 8,600 feet; and a mixed conifer forest exists on northern slopes and in mountain canyons from 7,000 to 8,000 feet elevation. Riparian areas occur along arroyos at all elevations.

The mixed conifer forest is dominated by Douglas-fir with lesser numbers of ponderosa and southwestern white pines, Gambel's oak, New Mexico locust, and white fir. The pine-oak forest contains many of the same species as well as Chihuahua pine, numerous oaks, alligator juniper, and Arizona madrone. And the slightly lower pine-oak-juniper woodlands, often forming a chaparral environment, are dominated by various oaks, manzanitas, Wright silktassel, Schotts yucca, and sacahuista.

Desert grasslands have stands of a variety of grasses with widely scattered trees and shrubs; most common are velvet mesquite, ocotillo, Mexican blue oak, junipers, sotol, sacahuista, agaves, and Torrey vauquelinia. Below this zone is the desert scrub, dominated by saguaro, ironwood, paloverde, catclaw acacia, velvet mesquite, and ocotillo. Common understory plants include creosote bush and numerous chollas, pricklypears, and smaller cacti.

Additional information can be obtained from the Superintendent, Saguaro National Park, 3693 S. Old Spanish Trail, Tucson, AZ 85730-5699; (602) 296-8576; Web address: www.nps.gov/sagu/.

BIRD LIFE

Few birds of the saguaro forest are as important as the Gila Woodpecker and Gilded Flicker. These two species excavate cavities within the saguaros that are utilized by an amazing variety of wildlife. The more numerous of the two is the **Gila Woodpecker,** a middle-sized woodpecker with a total range corresponding with that of the saguaro and the larger cardon, a similar tree cactus south of the border. It is next to impossible to drive or walk among the saguaros without seeing and hearing this bird. A Gila Woodpecker is easily identified by the black-and-white barring on its back, rump, and central tail feathers; gray-tan head and underparts, except for the yellowish wash on the belly; and the male's red cap. In flight the bird shows small but bright white wing patches. It calls with loud "chuur" notes.

The larger **Gilded Flicker** was once lumped with the western "red-shafted" and eastern "yellow-shafted" flickers under the single name Northern Flicker. Like the Gila Woodpecker's, this bird's range also coincides with that of the large tree cactuses. It can readily be identified as a flicker with yellow-shafted wings, a bold, black chest marking over whitish underparts that are spotted with black, a brown-barred back, and a distinct white rump.

The much smaller **Ladder-backed Woodpecker,** which also frequents this general area, has a much broader range, from central Texas to southeastern California and south into Central America. True to its name, this seven-inch

Gila Woodpecker

woodpecker sports black-and-white barring on its back and tail, spotted sides, and a black-and-white face pattern not unlike that of the Bridled Titmouse. Males possess a bright red crown. Ladder-backs excavate cavities in various trees and shrubs.

Nature has effectively provided a three-species construction crew to build apartment complexes for distinctly different-sized groups of wildlife. The builders use the cavity for only one year, pecking out a new one annually. The construction, however, is normally done in summer or fall, after the nesting season. For the saguaros, the postnesting construction of new cavities allows the cactus to form a callus over the soft tissue inside the cavity by the following season. Saguaro cavity nesters, therefore, rarely utilize nest lining.

Saguaro cavities, which are used for both nesting and roosting, have the additional feature of being cool in summer and warm in winter, varying from outside temperatures by as much as ten to fifteen degrees. They also have the advantage of holding relative humidity that is 5 to 10 percent higher than in the outside air. Ruth Kirk points out in an excellent *Audubon* article titled "Life on a Tall Cactus" (1973, 22) that "this significantly lessens the drain on birds' body moisture and is a particular advantage for nestlings."

Almost twenty species of birds are known to utilize saguaro cavities for nesting. Besides the woodpeckers, they include the American Kestrel; Western Screech-Owl, Ferruginous Pygmy-Owl, and Elf Owl; Ash-throated and Brown-crested flycatchers; Western Kingbird; Purple Martin; Violet-green Swallow; Cactus and Bewick's wrens; Bendire's Thrasher; Western Bluebird; European Starling; Lucy's Warbler; House Finch; and House Sparrow.

The largest of these is the **American Kestrel,** a small falcon with a reddish back and tail and double black stripes on its face; the male has blue-gray wings. Arizona's commonest raptor, this bird flies with fast wing beats and also hovers in the air while searching for prey. It feeds principally on grasshoppers and other insects. John Smallwood and David Bird (2002, 10) point out that throughout North America, invertebrates make up 88.7 percent of a kestrel's diet; mammals compose 6.7 percent, birds 3.3 percent, and snakes and lizards only 1.1 percent. John Terres (1987) reports kestrels can tolerate great heat and can get all the moisture they need from a carnivorous diet, freeing them from the need for drinking water.

The smallest of the cavity nesters is the four-inch **Lucy's Warbler,** tiny even by warbler standards. It is pale gray above and whitish below, the male having a red-brown rump and partially concealed cap. But in spite of its rather dull appearance, this warbler is feisty and aggressively defends its breeding territory. It is one of the earliest nonwintering warblers to appear in the spring. Throughout its nesting cycle, it sings all day through, its song a lively melody that has been described as "wee-tee wee-tee wee-tee wee-tee che." No other warbler is known to nest in desert arroyos. Lucy's Warblers also nest in mesquite thickets and in riparian areas. By late summer, however, this mite is en route south to its wintering grounds in western Mexico.

There also are a few birds that nest on the saguaros but do not use cavities:

Harris's Hawk, with its dark plumage, chestnut wing patches, and white tail with a broad black band; the common Red-tailed Hawk, which also nests on cliffs; the White-winged Dove, with its large white wing patches that are most obvious in flight; and the Mourning Dove, which sings sorrowful songs throughout the day. Great Horned Owls may build huge stick nests among the saguaro's protective arms, as may the all-black Common Raven, with its wedge-shaped tail and large head and bill. The large stick nests built on saguaros are usually those of Common Ravens and Harris's and Red-tailed hawks.

All the other desert-nesting birds at Saguaro National Park utilize shrubs or small cacti, such as the abundant chollas, or nest on the ground. The most common of these are the Greater Roadrunner, Lesser Nighthawk, Common Poorwill, Black-chinned and Costa's hummingbirds, Bell's Vireo, Verdin, Northern Mockingbird, Curve-billed Thrasher, Black-tailed Gnatcatcher, Phainopepla, Northern Cardinal, Pyrrhuloxia, Canyon Towhee, Black-throated Sparrow, Hooded Oriole, House Finch, and Lesser Goldfinch.

The tiny **Verdin** is one of the busiest and noisiest of all the desert birds. It can usually be located by its almost constant loud "chip" notes. Verdins are dull gray birds with an all-yellow head and maroon shoulder patches. They build softball-sized nests of interlaced thorny twigs, leaves, and grass, bound together with spider webs, lined with feathers and soft down from various plants, and placed among the branches of thorny shrubs or desert mistletoe. Ehrlich and colleagues (1988, 432) describe these nests as being "well protected and insulated, may last several seasons, giving the appearance of greater nesting density than is actually the case. Early season nests oriented so entrances protected from prevailing winds (to avoid cooling), late season nests oriented to face winds (to facilitate cooling)." A male builds several nests from which his mate selects her favorite in which to raise a brood. The remaining nests are maintained as dummy nests and for roosting.

The **Phainopepla** is most charismatic, a perky and lively bird with a tall crest and with a liking for trees and shrubs containing mistletoe. Males are real charmers, glossy black with blood-red eyes; their bright white wing patches are obvious only in flight. Appropriately, Phainopepla is Greek for "shining robe." Females are all grayish with white wing patches. Courting males perform fascinating displays, circling and zigzagging above their territories, sometimes to three hundred feet in the air. Nests often are built in mistletoe; the birds feed on the berries. But what makes this bird so fascinating is its habit of nesting early in spring and then moving northward to cooler habitats and nesting again. Wintering birds usually occur in small flocks, but individuals maintain separate feeding territories. For additional information about this bird, see Organ Pipe Cactus National Park.

Northern Cardinal

Eastern visitors to the Southwest are often surprised to find the **Northern Cardinal** within the cactus forest or riparian habitat of Saguaro National Park, the same species that is so common at home feeders in the East. Cardinals often visit the watering area behind the Rincon Mountain Visitor Center. The all-red male with a black bib is unmistakable. The nondescript female, however, can at first glance be mistaken for the similar Pyrrhuloxia, which is also crested. But the Pyrrhuloxia has a yellowish rather than reddish bill, and its bill is not as conical in shape as that of the cardinal. The male Pyrrhuloxia has a red face, not a black one, and a gray back and red crest, wings, and tail.

The desert grasslands contain about the same bird species as can be found in the desert scrub, with a few additions. Montezuma Quail are true grassland birds. They can be identified by their small, rounded appearance and the male's harlequin-like black-and-white head. Canyon Towhees are all brown, robin-sized birds with a single breast spot, buff throat, and rusty cap and undertail coverts. Rufous-crowned Sparrows prefer rocky areas in the grasslands and are distinguished by a rufous crown, whitish eye rings, black whisker stripes, and clear underparts. Scott's Orioles are yellow and black birds with lovely rich songs and a preference for nesting on yuccas.

The mountain woodlands and forests support a very different assortment of breeding birds. Common pine-oak-juniper birds include the Common Poorwill, a nocturnal ground-nesting species most evident by its melancholy "poor-will" calls; the Broad-tailed Hummingbird, with its green back and the males' red gorgets; and two more woodpeckers: the colorful Acorn Woodpecker, with its red, black, and yellow head patterns, and the brown-backed Strickland's (Arizona) Woodpecker. Also common are Cassin's Kingbird, its black tail tipped with white; the shy, little Hutton's Vireo, with its characteristic "sweeeet" song; the large, noncrested Mexican Jay with all-gray underparts; Bridled Titmouse, with its black-and-white head and tall crest; Bushtit, a tiny, brown-gray bird; and White-breasted Nuthatch. The long-tailed Bewick's Wren with its bold whitish eyebrows occurs here, as do the Blue-gray Gnatcatcher, black and white with a long, loose tail; Red-faced Warbler, with a red, black, and white head pattern; Painted Redstart of black, red, and white plumage; the large-billed Black-headed Grosbeak; Spotted Towhee, males having a black hood and blood-red eyes; and little Lesser Goldfinch, in which males have a blackish back and bright yellow underparts.

Of all these birds, the **Mexican Jay** is the most obvious during most of the year, although it can be surprisingly quiet and elusive when nesting. At other times, flocks of five to eighteen of these loud and aggressive birds can be expected. They are extremely curious and will investigate any unusual noise or incident. They may approach stealthily without a sound, but when discovered they fly off with great clamoring. These jays are all-blue above, except for a black bill and dark eye patches, and all-gray underneath. See Chiricahua National Monument for more about this Mexican species.

The Rincon Mountains' mixed conifer forest contains a few additional species, although many of the woodland birds can also be found there. Additional species include Band-tailed Pigeon, Flammulated Owl, Whiskered Screech-Owl, Northern Pygmy-Owl, Whip-poor-will, Hairy Woodpecker, Greater Pewee, Western Wood-Pewee, Cordilleran Flycatcher, Plumbeous and Warbling vireos, Violet-green Swallow, Steller's Jay, Mountain Chickadee, Red-breasted Nuthatch, House Wren, Hermit Thrush, American Robin, Yellow-rumped and Olive warblers, Western Tanager, and Yellow-eyed Junco.

The majority of the highland birds either migrate south for the winter months or move downslope as soon as their food supply declines. And a number of northern species arrive in late fall or early winter and stay until spring. Roy Johnson said he and Lois Haight surveyed lowland areas in the park during December and January 1990–91 and recorded twenty-seven species at five sites. The dozen most numerous species in descending order of abundance were Brewer's Sparrow, White-crowned Sparrow, Verdin, Black-throated Sparrow, Gambel's Quail, Chipping and Vesper sparrows (tied), Mourning Dove, Ruby-crowned Kinglet, Gila Woodpecker and Cactus Wren (tied), and Bewick's Wren.

In summary, the monument checklist includes 187 species, of which 123 are listed as either permanent or summer residents (and considered to nest). Of those, none are water birds, sixteen are hawks and owls, and eight are warblers.

BIRDS OF SPECIAL INTEREST

American Kestrel. This little falcon can occur anywhere in the park; it possesses a reddish back and two black stripes on its white face; the male has blue-gray wings.

Gambel's Quail. Watch for it in the lowlands; males have a tall teardrop-shaped plume, black face and throat, and chestnut cap and sides.

White-winged Dove. Common in spring and summer about the saguaros, this large dove has bold white patches on its wings.

Gila Woodpecker. This is the park's most common woodpecker, identified by its black-and-white barred back and tan-gray underparts.

Gilded Flicker. This cactus woodpecker has yellow-shafted wings, barred back, black chest stripe, and spotted underparts.

Mexican Jay. It normally occurs only in the Rincon Mountains; it is non-crested, all blue above, and grayish below.

Verdin. This is the tiny desert bird with a yellow head, maroon shoulder patches, and loud "chip" call.

Cactus Wren. Its loud, harsh "chuh chuh chuh chuh" calls, constant activity, and large size help identify this very common desert wren.

Curve-billed Thrasher. This is the large bird of dull gray-brown with a mottled breast, long curved bill, and distinct "whit-wheet" calls.

Phainopepla. Males are glossy black with a tall crest and blood-red eyes; females are dull versions of the males.

Lucy's Warbler. This is a tiny all-gray bird of the saguaro forest and riparian zones; males possess a rusty rump and concealed cap.

Northern Cardinal. Males are all red with a black bib; females are duller.

Chiricahua National Monument

ARIZONA

 The most obvious bird in the Chiricahua National Monument is undoubtedly the Mexican Jay. One cannot spend any amount of time in these mountains without getting acquainted with this charismatic creature. It is usually a bold and aggressive bird that approaches a camper or hiker with great curiosity, although at times it can be shy and elusive, especially during the nesting season. These jays usually occur in active and noisy flocks of five to eighteen individuals, moving through the forest with little heed for human beings. They can approach with great stealth, silently closing in on a point of interest. But when discovered, they may suddenly erupt out of the trees with much wing flapping and vocalization.

One morning in fall, when ripe acorns hung from the oaks and after many of the summer resident birds had already departed for warmer climes, I visited Chiricahua's Faraway Ranch. Harvest time was in full swing. The cacophony of Mexican Jays, Acorn Woodpeckers, Northern Flickers, White-breasted Nuthatches, and Bridled Titmice was audible from as far away as the parking area. As I approached the ranch buildings, I realized that the majority of birds were centered on the tall oak trees. The drum of acorns falling on the tin roofs added to the uproar.

Mexican Jays were everywhere. Two to three dozen of them had laid claim to the oak trees and seemed intent on harvesting the entire crop for themselves. They were actively searching the foliage for viable acorns, going about their investigations in a seemingly haphazard fashion, jumping from limb to limb and knocking more acorns loose than they gathered. Those were the acorns that drummed on the tin roofs. Standing beneath the trees, I watched one individual collect an acorn and hammer the prize with its large, heavy bill until it was able to retrieve the rich meat. Other Mexican Jays found acorns below the oaks, either on the bare ground or on the weedy perimeter. Perhaps their rough movement in the foliage was intentional.

At one point in my observations I noticed that many of the jays at Faraway Ranch were youngsters, evident by their yellowish bills rather than the solid black bills of adults. Nor were the young birds as brightly colored as their parents. In sunlight, the adults' deep blue upperparts contrasted with their

Mexican Jay

all-gray underparts, and their blackish ear coverts were also readily apparent. But all the jays that morning seemed intent on the acorn harvest. I was reminded of Herbert Brandt's words in *Arizona and Its Bird Life* (1951, 389) about this bird's relationship to oaks: "The jay is so closely confined to the live oak belt that it may be considered obligated to that strangely dominant tree. The latter furnishes the wily bird with acorns for a major food, twigs for the foundation of the nest, rootlets to line the cradle, . . . [and a] fork offers a proper site in which to anchor the nest. When the jaylet first opens its eyes it sees only the features and foliage of the live oak; yet evidently it is so well satisfied with its sturdy birth tree that it never leaves those evergreen mansions, but lives its whole obligate life bound to a natural economy of acorns."

THE PARK ENVIRONMENT

Arizona's Chiricahua National Monument is analogous to Big Bend National Park in Texas in that both areas represent northern extensions of Mexico's mountain provinces. Most of the range of some of the distinctive fauna and flora of the Chiricahua Mountains lies south of the border within the evergreen Madrean forest and woodland of the Sierra Madre Occidental. The Apache and Chihuahua pines, Chiricahua fox squirrel, and mountain (Yarrow's) spiny lizard are Mexican species that barely enter the United States.

Almost 12,000 acres of the Chiricahua Mountains are included within Chiricahua National Monument, established in 1924, and 87 percent of that area is designated wilderness. *Chiricahua* is said to be an Opata Indian term for "mountain of the wild turkeys." Vehicular access is limited to an eight-mile scenic drive to Massai Point and trailhead, at an elevation of 6,870 feet. The park contains seventeen miles of designated trails, part of that being the self-guided Massai Point Nature Trail.

Access to the monument is from the west, via state Highways 186 and 181. The larger portion of the Chiricahua Mountains, including Cave Creek Canyon and Rustler Park, falls under the administration of the Coronado National Forest. Access to these areas is via the Pinery Canyon gravel road that crosses the mountains between the monument entrance road and Portal, Arizona, and the Turkey Creek and Rucker Lake roads south of the monument.

The monument's visitor center is located near the west entrance at the start of the Bonita Canyon Scenic Drive. There can be found an information desk, orientation program, exhibits, and a sales outlet; bird field guides and a checklist are available. A park campground is located beyond the visitor center. Picnicking sites are available at Bonita Creek Trail, Faraway Ranch, Massai Point, Echo Canyon, and Sugarloaf parking area.

The visitor center is also the centerpiece for the area's interpretive program, which includes guided walks, talks, and evening programs, some of which address the park's rich bird life. Programs vary, and a schedule of interpretive activities is available for the asking.

Chiricahua National Monument is comprised primarily (90%) of mixed oak-conifer woodland. Dominant oaks include Arizona white, Emory, silverleaf, and netleaf oaks. Dominant conifers include Arizona cypress, alligator juniper, Mexican pinyon, Chihuahua and ponderosa pines, and Douglas-fir. Other common trees and shrubs of this environment include Schotts yucca, Wheeler sotol, bear-grass, Arizona walnut, Arizona sycamore, mountain mahogany, New Mexico locust, poison ivy, skunkbush sumac, birchleaf buckthorn, Arizona madrone, and manzanita. The park's higher and more open slopes often contain chaparral vegetation that is dominated by manzanita, Toumey oak, mountain mahogany, and buckbrush.

The lower, western edge of the park near the entrance contains riparian habitat dominated by Fremont cottonwood, willows, Arizona sycamore, Arizona cypress, pines, netleaf hackberry, and desert-willow. The adjacent arid grasslands are characterized by numerous grasses and scattered soaptree yuccas, agaves, velvet mesquite, ocotillo, and various cacti.

Additional information can be obtained from the Superintendent, Chiricahua National Monument, 13063 E. Bonita Canyon Rd., Willcox, AZ 85643; (520) 824-3560; Web address: www.nps.gov/chir.

BIRD LIFE

The **Mexican Jay** is one of the Mexican species that enter the United States only in a few mountain ranges connecting to Mexico's more massive Sierra Madre Occidental and Oriental. This species was called the "gray-breasted jay" for several years, but it is properly called Mexican Jay once again.

Chiricahua National Monument supports several other reasonably common Mexican songbirds, although none is as abundant as the Mexican Jay. The other species include the heavily streaked Sulphur-bellied Flycatcher, with its yellowish underparts and rusty tail; Mexican Chickadee, with coal-black cap and bib and dark gray flanks; and the active Bridled Titmouse, with tall crest and black-and-white head. Also common are the Red-faced Warbler, its face and throat, red, and cap, black; the Painted Redstart, all black in plumage except for a bright red belly and snow-white wing patches and outer tail feathers; and the Yellow-eyed Junco, with its rufous back and wing coverts, black tail with white outer feathers, and gray head with bright yellow eyes offset by black lores. Less common birds of Mexican affinity include the Whiskered Screech-Owl, Blue-throated and Magnificent hummingbirds, Strickland's Woodpecker, Greater Pewee, Dusky-capped Flycatcher, and Olive Warbler.

Of all these tropical birds, none possesses the appeal of the little **Red-faced Warbler.** Gale Monson described this species in Griscom and Sprunt's *The Warblers of America* (1957, 232) as "small and quick. . . . It feeds through the outer portion of the coniferous trees, with constant small jerks of the tail. Also like many other warblers, it is adept at flycatching. Close examination will show the bill to be stout at the base, the upper mandible arched like a Titmouse's."

Red-faced Warblers may return from wintering grounds in western Mexico south to Central America by early April, and males can soon be heard singing clear and penetrating whistled notes: "a tink a tink, tsee, tsee, tsee, tswee, tsweep." By May, paired birds are constructing nests of pine needles, fine bark, and soft plant materials in depressions on the ground, concealed in grasses or sheltered by rocks or logs. By early September, adults and their fledglings depart for their winter homes. This bird is a true Neotropical migrant that depends upon the long-term survival of both its breeding and wintering grounds.

One morning in May I hiked to Echo Canyon. Birdsong from the full-time residents as well as the summer-only residents was all around me. Mexican Jays were heard now and again, but their general lack of dominance that day suggested that they still were involved with nesting chores. **Acorn Woodpeckers,** however, adequately filled in for the usually noisy jays. These woodpeckers were not only vocally active but also easily observed, flying here and there and paying little attention to a hiker. Their loud calls, usually described as "jacob" or "whack-up," never ceased. I discovered a pair of these gregarious birds on a tall snag just off the trail, and I was able to examine them at leisure. The Acorn Woodpecker is a middle-sized woodpecker with an all-black back, tail, and wings, except that in flight white wing patches and a snow-white rump are obvious. Its most conspicuous feature is its contrasting black, white, red, and yellow head, almost clownlike in appearance.

The tall snag on which these woodpeckers rested when they were not cavorting about or chasing flying insects contained several dozen acorns that had been wedged into holes the previous year. Acorn Woodpeckers store acorns each fall, jamming them into holes drilled for that purpose and retrieving them to eat during the remainder of the year. There are records of old trees elsewhere in the West with fifty thousand or more storage holes, but none of the various trees I saw that morning contained more than a few dozen acorns.

The common flycatcher to be seen was the **Ash-throated Flycatcher,** most evident by its occasional "ka-brick" calls. It took me several minutes to locate one of these rather nondescript flycatchers. When I finally did find one, it was carrying a bill-full of nesting material into a cavity in an oak snag. The bird's grayish throat and breast above a yellowish belly and crissum contrasted with its reddish tail, dark wings, and slightly crested head.

Bridled Titmice were present as well, and although their vocalizations were common—very chickadee-like versions of rapid "chick-a-dee-dee" notes—they were not easily observed. After several minutes of getting only glimpses of these birds disappearing among the foliage, I made thin squeaking notes. Almost immediately, one individual approached to within fifteen or twenty feet, where I was able to observe it for several minutes, calling it back each time it seemed to lose interest. It was a lovely little bird; its bridle-

Acorn Woodpecker

like, black-and-white face pattern, tall, loose crest, and gray-green back were most appealing. In winter, this species seems to dominate bird parties; anyone searching for birds at that time of year can locate the flock by listening for these active little tits.

My squeaking also attracted two other avian members of the oak-pine community, the White-breasted Nuthatch and Black-headed Grosbeak. The White-breasted Nuthatch was walking straight down the scaly trunk of a sycamore, probing under the loose bark for insects. Its all-white underparts and face, black cap and nape, and grayish back and tail were obvious, as were the nasal "yank" notes that it made every few seconds.

The **Black-headed Grosbeak** was a beautiful male, probably nesting among the adjacent oaks. He glared at me from among the green sycamore foliage, his deep cinnamon, almost rose-red throat, flanks, and chest gleaming in the morning light, contrasting with a coal-black cap, face, and tail. The bird was close enough for me to see the large, triangular bill well through binoculars. He suddenly gave a loud "pik" call and flew away up the drainage, the bright yellow underwing coverts obvious in flight. A few seconds later I detected his distinct song, a series of rich robinlike whistles.

One of the best descriptions of this grosbeak's voice comes from Joseph Grinnell and Robert Storer's writings in Arthur C. Bent's life history series (1968, 65–66): "The black-headed grosbeak possesses a rich voluble song that forces itself upon the attention of everyone in the neighborhood. In fact at the height of the song season this is the noisiest of all the birds. The song resembles in some respect that of a robin, and novices sometimes confuse the two. The grosbeak's song is much fuller and more varied, contains many little trills, and is given in more rapid time. Now and then it bursts forth fortissimo and after several rounds of burbling, winds up with a number of 'squeals,' the last one attenuated and dying out slowly." Bent adds a description of the length of one grosbeak's song: it began fifteen minutes before sunrise, and the bird "sang from the time it began, almost without any intermission, for a period of 3 hours, each rendition of its song being followed by another with scarcely a pause between."

Spotted Towhees were also common along the canyon, preferring the dense thickets along the edge of the drainage. The Spotted Towhee male is readily identified by a coal-black hood with contrasting blood-red eyes, a black back with many white spots, whiter underparts, and rufous sides. Territorial males were extremely active along the canyon, singing songs that consisted of two sharp notes followed by a trill—"clip-clip-cheeee." Several other individuals were detected by their foraging activities among the leaves. Towhees scratch backward with both feet, raking aside the litter in their search for insects and seeds underneath. How they are able to keep their balance is a complex operation that includes excellent balance and considerable skill. The unique sound of a towhee's foraging activities can be most helpful in locating this thicket dweller.

Other resident birds found within the oak-pine woodlands during my May hike included Broad-tailed Hummingbirds, Northern Flickers, Hutton's Vireos, Mexican Chickadees, Bushtits, Canyon Wrens (in the rocky drainage),

Spotted Towhee

American Robins, Grace's Warblers, Western and Hepatic tanagers, Brown-headed Cowbirds, Yellow-eyed Juncos, and Lesser Goldfinches.

Mexican Chickadees and Yellow-eyed Juncos were present only in the higher and deeper canyons where Douglas-fir was reasonably common. Mexican Chickadees called out their rather distinct husky, buzzing "kabree, kabree, kabree, kabree" notes from the high pines and Douglas-firs. Brandt referred to this little chickadee as a "fur bird" because of the considerable amount of mammal fur used in its nest.

Yellow-eyed Juncos were present at all elevations, from ground level to the very top of the taller trees, from which they sang melodic three-part songs with contrasting pitch and rhythm, described by Terres (1987, 333) as "chi chip chip, wheedle, wheedle, wheedle, che che che che che." I located several individuals foraging over the pine needle–clad ground with a strange gait that Allan Phillips and colleagues (1964, 206) describe as "a peculiar shuffle, between a hop and a walk." This junco is very different from the wintering Dark-eyed Juncos that nest in the mountains of central Arizona and northward. Yellow-eyed Juncos, earlier known as "Mexican juncos," possess a quiet and calm demeanor, moving over the terrain with leisure, seldom in a hurry. Wintering Dark-eyes move in a jerky fashion and seem always to be in a hurry.

Lower Bonita Canyon, near Faraway Ranch, contains riparian vegetation along the creekbed and desert grasslands on the northern slope and southern flats. Common riparian birds that occur here include the Black-chinned Hummingbird, Acorn Woodpecker, Northern Flicker, Western Wood-Pewee, Ash-throated and Brown-crested flycatchers, Cassin's Kingbird, Violet-green Swallow, American Robin, Black-headed and Blue grosbeaks, and Hooded and Bullock's orioles.

The most obvious of these birds is the **Cassin's Kingbird,** a dynamic nine-inch bird that is difficult to ignore in spring and summer. Its aggressive and blustery manner, gray and yellow plumage pattern, and loud and ringing "chibew" call help to identify this hardy flycatcher. Of the several kingbirds that are known in North America, Cassin's is the only true southwesterner. The Western Kingbird is a summer resident in the Southwest, its range covering all of the western half of the United States. Only the Cassin's Kingbird is restricted to the American Southwest.

Desert grassland birds are most common along the entrance road. These include the American Kestrel, Gambel's Quail, Greater Roadrunner, Common Poorwill, Say's Phoebe, Crissal Thrasher, Phainopepla, Loggerhead Shrike, Canyon Towhee, Scott's Oriole, and four sparrow species: Cassin's (during wet years), Rufous-crowned, Black-chinned, and Black-throated sparrows.

Scott's Orioles can often be seen flying across the valley from yucca to yucca; they are especially common when yuccas and century plants are in flower. Males are gorgeous birds with a coal-black hood, back, wings (with yellow shoulder patches), and tail and bright yellow underparts and rump. Females are yellow-olive and heavily streaked with black. Their songs are lovely renditions of rich whistled phrases, somewhat like the song of a Western Meadowlark.

From any viewpoint where the open sky can be seen one is certain to find **Turkey Vultures,** with their bare red heads and great wingspan, the wings held in a shallow V pattern and flight characterized by slight tilting from side to side. These scavengers utilize thermals from the warm lowlands, riding these drafts for hours on end, rarely flapping their wings. They may begin their soaring in the lower canyons and ride thousands of feet upward as the day progresses, to a point where they can no longer be seen with the naked eye. Nesting vultures utilize the abundant rock and dirt ledges of the monument, laying two or three brownish-blotched white eggs directly on the ground; young are fledged and able to fly in seventy to eighty days.

Chiricahua National Monument is within the breeding range of the Zone-tailed Hawk, a Turkey Vulture look-alike that often soars with vultures. The Zone-tail has a feathered head and black-and-white banding on its tail but otherwise looks much like a Turkey Vulture. In flight the two species have the same bicolored wings held in a shallow V, and the Zone-tail also flies with a slight tilting from side to side. This ability to mimic Turkey Vultures provides the hawk with good cover for preying upon lizards that frequent the high cliffs.

Other soaring birds found in the Chiricahuas include Cooper's Hawks, with their short, rounded wings and long tails; Red-tailed Hawks with brick-red tails; the huge Golden Eagle, best identified by its size, flattened posture in flight, and the adult's golden head; Prairie Falcons, with pale plumage and black wingtips; and the much smaller White-throated Swifts.

White-throated Swifts are most common within the canyons, where they nest in crevices on the cliffs and chase down their insect prey with swift flights. This swift of cigar-shaped body and swept-back wings is often first detected by its loud, descending twittering calls coming from high overhead. Swifts should not be confused with summering Violet-green Swallows, which have snow-white underparts and a violet-green back. The Chiricahua Mountains are far enough south for White-throated Swifts also to spend the winter there; they summer as far north as Alberta, Canada. They congregate overnight in large overhangs and crevices on south-facing cliffs, hanging together like bees in a hive. They possess the ability to withstand occasional below freezing temperatures; semi-hibernation allows them to conserve their energy for several days until warmer temperatures prevail and insects are once more available.

During the winter months many more northern birds are present. Although no winter bird surveys have been undertaken within the national monument, Christmas Bird Counts at Portal, Arizona, provide some perspective on the bird life at that time of year. The 1999 Portal Christmas Count tallied 136 species. The dozen most numerous of those in descending order of abundance were the Red-winged Blackbird, White-crowned Sparrow, Dark-eyed Junco, Vesper Sparrow, Brewer's Sparrow, Gambel's Quail, Chipping

Sparrow, Black-throated Sparrow, Mourning Dove, Savannah Sparrow, Mexican Jay, and American Robin.

In summary, the park checklist includes 179 species, of which 112 are listed as either permanent or summer residents and are therefore assumed to nest. Of those 112 species, none are water birds, nineteen are hawks and owls, and eight are warblers.

BIRDS OF SPECIAL INTEREST

Turkey Vulture. This is the common, long-winged bird that soars with wings in a shallow V pattern and with slight tilting from side to side; it has all-dark plumage and a bare red head.

White-throated Swift. Its great speed, black-and-white plumage, swept-back wings, and constant twittering calls help identify this cliff-loving species.

Acorn Woodpecker. This gregarious woodpecker frequents snags and is rarely silent; it can be identified by its black, white, red, and yellow head pattern.

Ash-throated Flycatcher. It occurs throughout the lower, open woodlands in spring and summer and sports a grayish throat and chest, yellowish belly, and reddish tail.

Cassin's Kingbird. This is a dynamic and noisy bird that frequents open riparian habitats in the lowlands. Look for it in Lower Bonita Canyon.

Mexican Jay. One of the park's most common full-time residents, it is easily identified by its blue upperparts, dark bill and ear coverts, and all-gray underparts.

Red-faced Warbler. This beautiful bird with a red and black head pattern frequents the cooler canyons and uplands in spring and summer.

Black-headed Grosbeak. Males possess a black head, wings, and tail, white wing bars, contrasting cinnamon underparts, and a large, heavy bill.

Spotted Towhee. This bird of the thickets sports an all-black head and back, red eyes, white underparts, and chestnut sides.

Yellow-eyed Junco. It prefers the cooler canyons and uplands and is identified by its rufous back, gray head with bright yellow eyes, and black tail with white outer feathers.

Carlsbad Caverns and Guadalupe Mountains National Parks

NEW MEXICO & TEXAS

 The cave mouth was a huge gaping hole in the layered limestone terrain. The entrance trail snaked back and forth across the steep slope and disappeared into the cave's rocky gullet. Lines of visitors, enticed by the cool breeze, followed the trail and disappeared into the cavern. The only living things I detected emerging from the deep hole were Cave Swallows. Only they seemed to have conquered both the darkened cavern mouth and brilliance of day, moving freely back and forth between the two environments.

I sat near the cave entrance on a weathered block of gray limestone, observing the swallows' activities. There were at least a dozen individuals visible at any one time. Their high-pitched "weet" notes echoed from the steep slopes and from inside the cave's shadowy entrance. Six or seven individuals suddenly plummeted from the sky and dashed into the cave, close to the ceiling, en route no doubt to their mud nests and the gaping bills of their nestlings. It was impossible to distinguish individual swallows in their comings and goings, but their intent was obvious.

A Cactus Wren sang a harsh, rollicking "chuh chuh chuh chuh" song from a tall sotol stalk above the cave entrance. Through binoculars I could see its streaked breast, banded tail, bold white eyeline, and heavy bill, which firmly grasped a large insect of some sort. Then it flew to a cane cholla that held a football-sized grass nest, well protected by the numerous cactus spines. A second Cactus Wren suddenly emerged from the nest opening at the side, and the first individual, insect and all, disappeared inside. I could only imagine the eager responses of the nestlings.

Two plump all-brown birds moved to the right of the cholla, and I recognized them as Canyon Towhees. It took me several minutes to see their rusty crowns and crissums and dark chest spots. I had already seen this bird at the cavern's parking lot, where one pair had been searching for insects brought in on vehicle grills. They had also been common along the cave entrance trail, chasing one another among the desert plants, calling out loud chips, and singing songs that sounded like "chili chili chili."

The loudest songs detected, however, were those of the Northern Mockingbirds. At least three mockers were within hearing distance; each seemed intent upon outsinging the others. Their repertoire of melodies, including whistles and squeals, chucks and churrs, far surpassed the offerings of all the other songbirds that day. One individual alighted on a green-leafed ocotillo, and I could clearly see its black-and-white plumage and yellowish eyes.

It suddenly flew up after a passing insect. But just inches before it could capture the prey, a Cave Swallow, flying much faster than the mockingbird, swooped down and snatched the meal away. The mocker glided away to another perch, seemingly unperturbed, while the swallow continued into the cave and a waiting family.

THE PARK ENVIRONMENT

The Guadalupe Mountains are the southwestern portion of a huge horseshoe-shaped formation of Permian limestone that rises to 8,749 feet elevation at Guadalupe Peak. Most of the ancient reef lies below the surface of the ground, but it is exposed at three locations: for approximately thirty miles of the Guadalupe Mountains escarpment from near Carlsbad, New Mexico, to Guadalupe Peak, in Texas; the Apache Mountains, northeast of Van Horn, Texas; and the Glass Mountains, east of Alpine, Texas.

Guadalupe Mountains National Park in Texas encompasses 86,416 acres of Guadalupe Peak and its adjacent ridges, canyons, and desertscape. The north-

Cave Swallows

eastern portion of the range declines gradually in elevation and simply disappears into a matrix of rocks and gravels. Carlsbad Caverns National Park, New Mexico, with its more than seventy caves, including famous Carlsbad Caverns, covers an area of 46,755 acres at the northern end of the escarpment, directly northeast of Guadalupe Mountains National Park.

Vegetation within the two parks is primarily Chihuahuan Desert, although the deep, cool canyons and uplands of the Guadalupe Mountains contain representatives of Rocky Mountain flora. Chihuahuan Desert plants form two rather distinct associations: desert scrub and succulent desert. Creosote bush dominates the open flats and bajadas of the desert scrub, although honey mesquite, blackbrush, white-thorn acacia, ocotillo, and snakeweed are also abundant. Succulent desert vegetation forms a transition zone on the escarpment and extends from the mid-elevation slopes to near the summit. Dominant plants within this area include creosote bush, lechuguilla, sotol, bear-grass, one-seeded juniper, mariola, skeleton goldeneye, Faxon yucca, and New Mexico agave.

An evergreen woodland occurs on the cooler northern slopes and in canyonheads between approximately 4,500 and 7,000 feet elevation. Characteristic plants include two-needle pinyon, alligator juniper, gray oak, Texas madrone, and skunkbush sumac. Redberry juniper is widespread at this elevation in both parks. And above 6,000 feet is a coniferous forest that is dominated by southwestern white and ponderosa pines, Douglas-fir, and Gambel's oak. A "semi-virgin forest" occurs on about one hundred acres in the Bowl.

At springs and in moist canyons, such as Guadalupe's McKittrick Canyon, are riparian habitats where bigtooth maple, chinkapin oak, and western hornbeam are most abundant. Alligator juniper, Texas madrone, chokecherry, velvet ash, little walnut, desert-willow, littleleaf sumac, netleaf hackberry, and Apache plume are dominant in the open portions of the canyon.

National park visitor centers are located at Carlsbad Caverns, at the end of a seven-mile road beyond White's City, and in the Guadalupe Mountains at Pine Springs, off Highway 62/180, the main route between El Paso, Texas, and Carlsbad, New Mexico. Each center contains an information desk, orientation program, exhibits, and a sales outlet; field guides and area bird checklists are available. Camping is permitted at Pine Springs, and backcountry camping is available by permit.

Interpretive activities include all-year cave tours and a variety of nature walks and evening talks, including the famous bat flight talk at the cave entrance at dusk from early spring through October. Interpretive schedules are available for the asking and are posted at various bulletin boards.

Both parks possess considerable backcountry that, except for Carlsbad's Walnut Canyon Desert Drive, is accessible only by hiking trails; trails extend eighty miles in the Guadalupe Mountains and forty miles in Carlsbad Caverns National Park. More than half of the Guadalupe Mountains National Park is designated wilderness. *Trails of the Guadalupes,* a hikers' guide by Don Kurtz and William Green, contains a good overview of the park's backcountry.

Additional information can be obtained from the Superintendents: Carlsbad Caverns National Park, 3225 National Parks Highway, Carlsbad, NM 88220; (505) 785–2232; and Guadalupe Mountains National Park, HC 60, Box 400, Salt Flat, TX 79847; (915) 828-3251; Web addresses: Carlsbad Caverns— www.nps.gov/cave/; Guadalupe Mountains—www.nps.gov/gumo/.

BIRD LIFE

Cave Swallows and Carlsbad Caverns are synonymous. These swallows are among the park's most common birds and can readily be seen at the cave entrance from late February through October. But this was not always the case. Prior to the mid-1950s, Cave Swallows were Mexican breeders only and were rarely seen north of the border. Cave Swallows first appeared in the park at undeveloped caves in Slaughter Canyon in the 1950s, and two pairs finally nested just inside Carlsbad Caverns in 1966. The colony increased annually after that and, although their numbers vary from year to year, as many as four thousand birds are present some years, representing the largest colony north of Mexico. Their range has expanded eastward into much of Texas, and they also occur in Florida.

Cave Swallows are often confused with the closely related and more widespread Cliff Swallow. Both are square-tailed swallows with a dark back, whitish underparts, and buff rump. The Cliff Swallow has a dark chestnut and blackish throat and pale forehead, while the Cave Swallow has a chestnut forehead and only a tinge of buff on its throat. Cliff Swallows build enclosed mud-pellet nests on cliffs and walls of buildings, while Cave Swallows build open-topped mud-pellet nests attached to the ceilings of limestone caves and sinkholes, culverts, and similar twilight sites.

At Carlsbad Caverns, Cave Swallows are sometimes misidentified as bats because both live in or near the cave. Bats, however, are nocturnal mammals that normally spend their daylight hours far underground. Cave Swallows, on the other hand, are active during the daylight hours and roost at night in their nests or on adjacent ledges just inside the mouth of the cave.

Since 1980, local schoolteacher Steve West and a cadre of volunteers have captured and banded thousands of Cave Swallows at Carlsbad Caverns in an attempt to learn more about their life history and migration. Steve told me

September 7, 2000, that their data have shown males are primarily responsible for nest construction although females are the only ones that incubate the eggs.

The landscape of Carlsbad Caverns National Park is dominated by Chihuahuan Desert vegetation, and so the resident birds evident near the cave and along Walnut Canyon Desert Drive and the various trails are desert species. Most obvious are those already mentioned for the cave entrance and a handful of other species. One of the most widespread is the little **Black-throated Sparrow,** usually found in flocks of a few to a dozen individuals, and often detected first by its musical tinkling songs. It is easily identified by its pert manner, coal-black throat, white belly, and dark cheeks bordered by two bold white stripes. Its scientific name is *bilineata,* Latin for "two-striped." Earlier called the "desert sparrow," this bird resides in the hottest of North America's deserts, where it is able to obtain its daily supply of moisture from the desert seeds it eats. Black-throated sparrows are curious birds and can often be enticed into the open by low spishing sounds.

The common woodpecker of the desert is the little **Ladder-backed Woodpecker,** named for its black-and-white barred back. This is the only true Chihuahuan Desert woodpecker; the other woodpeckers found in the Carlsbad and Guadalupe parks prefer riparian habitats or forested areas. Ladder-backs are small enough to nest in century plant stalks. Their nest chambers are utilized by several other cavity nesters, such as Ash-throated Flycatchers, Juniper Titmice, Bewick's Wrens, and Western Bluebirds. Male Ladder-backs possess red crowns; females have all-black crowns.

The Chihuahuan Desert quail is the **Scaled Quail,** a blue-gray bird with a conspicuous white-tipped crest and breast feathers that look scalloped or scaled. It is also known as "blue quail" and "cottontop," for obvious reasons. One cannot spend much time in the desert without at least hearing this bird. Their calls consist of loud barking "kuck-yur" notes or a low whistled "pecos," and the sound can carry for a considerable distance across the desert. Harry Oberholser, author of *The Bird Life of Texas* (1974, 272), reported that "Border Mexicans translate this quail's most frequent call as 'toston' (tos-*tone*), which name they apply to the species." Flocks of a few to two dozen individuals are sometimes found running ahead of a visitor on the trail or roadway. It is considered one of the "running quail," fleeing to safety on its powerful legs and flying only when hard-pressed.

Scaled Quail have a broad range from southern Arizona to northern New Mexico and southwest Kansas, south Mexico's Jalisco, Guanajuato, and Mexico state. They seem to have a preference for desert grasslands, although they can also be found in extremely arid areas. At night they roost on the ground, employing "a clever precautionary means of self-defense against night-prowling enemies by forming a circle, tails together, head outward," notes J. Stokley Ligon (1961, 96), adding that "thus every bird represents a night sentinel on guard against surprise attack."

Other common desert birds include the Greater Roadrunner, Great Horned Owl, Lesser Nighthawk, Common Poorwill, Say's Phoebe, Verdin, Loggerhead Shrike, Pyrrhuloxia, and House Finch.

Chihuahuan Desert communities along the William's Ranch road, at

Scaled Quail

Guadalupe Mountains National Park, contain these same species. But in places where grasses are common, a few additional birds can be found: Curve-billed and Crissal thrashers, Cassin's and Rufous-crowned sparrows, Eastern and Western meadowlarks, and Scott's Orioles.

Rufous-crowned Sparrows are the most numerous of these, although they have a habit of flying into the low shrubs just when one is trying to get a good look. However, patience will prevail, and the species is best identified by its rufous crown, single black whisker stripes, and clear, grayish breast. This sparrow seems to frequent rocky places, and it is one of the most vocal of all birds; individuals call to one another continuously, even after the nesting season and in winter. They often perform a squealing duet upon greeting a mate. Their calls are clear, thin, descending notes, like "tew-tew-tew-tew." And their songs are a "staccato chittering, which changes in pitch, somewhat like a softened house wren's song," according to John Terres (1987, 346).

Rattlesnake Springs is an outstanding desert oasis located below the escarpment southeast of Carlsbad Caverns. This area of huge Fremont cottonwoods, willows, saltcedars, cattails, and other water-loving plants is considered the single best bird-finding site in the two parks. In September 2000, Steve West said that Rattlesnake Springs also is a well-known vagrant trap for birds passing through the area and that almost 90% of all the species recorded in the park have been found there.

Cave Swallows utilize the lush grounds in spring and summer for gathering insects. Then the cottonwoods ring with the calls of Mourning Doves, Ash-throated Flycatchers, Western Kingbirds, Summer Tanagers, Orchard and Bullock's orioles, and Lesser Goldfinches. And the dense undergrowth and swampy areas reverberate with the songs of Bell's Vireos, Common Yellowthroats, Yellow-breasted Chats, Northern Cardinals, Blue Grosbeaks, Painted Buntings, and Red-winged Blackbirds.

The orioles can be especially evident in spring when they are actively defending territories and courting. They seem to spend an inordinate amount of time pursuing one another among the foliage. The little Orchard Orioles, the males identifiable by a black hood, breast, and tail and chestnut back and belly, call sharp "chuck" notes at one another. Their occasional songs are loud, rapid bursts of melody that Arthur Cleveland Bent (1958, 203) described in his *Life History* series as "Look here, what cheer, what cheer, whip yo, what cheer, wee-yo." Rattlesnake Springs marks the western edge of the breeding range of this eastern oriole.

The larger **Bullock's Oriole,** distinguished by the male's black crown, orange cheeks, underparts, and rump and large white wing patches, sings a slower song with rich, whistled notes interspersed with guttural notes and

Bullock's Oriole

rattles. Oriole nests are easily identified because of their pendant character, although they are usually well hidden among the foliage. Typically a Bullock's Oriole nest is attached to twigs near the end of a branch, ten to forty feet above the ground. It consists of an oval-shaped bag approximately six inches deep woven of vegetable fibers, inner bark, and horsehair. The nest is usually lined with wool, down, hair, and mosses.

One early spring day park naturalist Brent Wauer (my brother) and I drove the Williams Ranch road, watching for wildlife along the way. Winter birds were still present. Black-throated Sparrows were most numerous; Curve-billed and Crissal thrashers were fairly numerous; and Sage Sparrows were scattered through the open desert scrub environment along the first couple miles of the roadway. Little Sage Sparrows, recognizable by a brown-gray back, bold white whisker stripe, and black breast spot, ran here and there among the shrubs, pausing only in response to loud chipping sounds made with my lips on the back of my hand.

Brushy areas in desert drainages and along the lower edge of the pinyon-juniper woodlands are the best places to find the smaller **Black-chinned Sparrow.** One September day I watched a pair of these desert shrub sparrows foraging near the Pine Springs Campground; Brent informed me that this area is the best place in the park to see this species. Both individuals were climbing about the fourwing saltbush at the edge of the parking lot. They seemed extremely active, going up and down the stems but spending equal time on the ground. Males possess a coal-black chin that contrasts with their all-gray underparts, rump, and collar and rusty wings; females are duller versions of the males.

Black-chins were also present at the mouth of McKittrick Canyon, where they sing their very distinct songs, which are reminiscent of the song of the Field Sparrow, their closest relatives. Black-chin songs begin with a series of "sweet" notes and followed by a rapid descending trill, like a bouncing ping-pong ball.

McKittrick Canyon cuts into the heart of the Guadalupes, providing access to the high cliffs and some choice riparian habitats along the way. In early spring the area can be alive with birds. Although the lower slopes are dominated by desert species, the scene changes dramatically after about one mile. Black-chinned and Rufous-crowned sparrows, Canyon Towhees, Rock Wrens, and Ash-throated Flycatchers are most numerous near the canyon mouth. Gray Vireos are also present; singing males seem to claim territories about one-quarter mile in length.

The cascading songs of **Canyon Wrens** seem to welcome visitors to the inner canyon. Their unique, descending and decelerating whistles echo across the canyon, but it takes a sharp eye to find the perpetrator. The Canyon Wren is a lovely little bird with a snow-white throat, cinnamon back and belly with numerous black-and-white flecks, and long black bill. The bill length provides a good clue to their behavior of searching for food in every crack and cranny in the rocky terrain. And every now and then they will sing their wonderful songs.

Hummingbirds can be common along the canyon, and once century plants begin to flower they provide a showplace for these brightly colored Lilliputians. One June morning I sat in the shade of a Gambel's oak and, through my binoculars, watched hummingbirds feeding on the flowers of a nearby New Mexico agave. Black-chinned Hummingbirds were most numerous,

Magnificent Hummingbird

distinguished by a purple-black chin contrasting with a white chests. Broad-tailed Hummingbirds were common as well and easy to identify by the males' trilling wing beats and rosy-red throats. Two larger hummers also put in an appearance during my hour-long vigil: Blue-throated and Magnificent.

I detected the presence of the Blue-throated Hummingbird before I actually observed it because of its loud "seep" calls made in flight. When it finally approached the yellow flowers, its size was striking in comparison with the smaller Black-chins hovering nearby. The male's bright blue throat and the white corners of his tail were also evident. But the hummingbird of the day was the equally large **Magnificent Hummingbird,** which suddenly appeared as if by magic. Its deep green back and throat patch, shiny black belly, and purple crown gleamed in the morning sunlight like a bright jewel. It stayed only a few seconds before flying off with rather loud heavy wing beats, almost directly over where I stood in admiration. Although I had seen this bird several times before in the Chisos Mountains of Big Bend National Park, the McKittrick Canyon sighting was one of the most memorable. I have seen it in McKittrick several times since then; despite being at the northern edge of its breeding range, this is the best place in Texas to find this tropical species.

The chinkapin oak groves scattered along the canyon often contain their own assortment of birds. Although several species feed among the foliage, at least one bird nests there, the Virginia's Warbler. This rather drab bird is mostly gray with yellow on its breast, rump, and crissum, and a bold white eye ring. Other birds that frequent riparian woodlands include Plumbeous Vireos, Blue-gray Gnatcatchers, Black-headed Grosbeaks, and Spotted Towhees.

McKittrick Creek is an intermittent stream that forms lush pockets of saw-grass and sedges in protected places but disappears into the gravels elsewhere.

The surface flow provides water for hundreds of birds throughout the year and is especially important during the warm summer months. Even those birds that nest on the high cliffs, such as White-throated Swifts and Violet-green Swallows, utilize the waterway to catch insects or gather nesting materials.

The little **Cordilleran Flycatcher** is one of the species that hawks insects along the creek, often from perches over the waterway. These flycatchers build their nests at the base of the cliffs in protected niches. The bird was known as "western flycatcher" until it was split from the West Coast form. It sings a very distinct two-syllable song, with the second note higher: "pit-peet!" Kenn Kaufman gives the best description of this flycatcher in his *Advanced Birding* (1990). It is identified by its yellowish underparts, greenish brown back, and almond-shaped eye ring.

Peregrine Falcons also occur in upper McKittrick Canyon, and they sometimes visit the lower canyon. Their continued survival in the Guadalupes, even during the years when DDT had eliminated all northeastern populations, attests to the canyon's relative isolation. Peregrines are among the world's most exciting birds, stooping at more than a hundred miles per hour. The watchful visitor to McKittrick Canyon may be fortunate to observe this dynamic falcon as it courts high above or hunts along the canyon. Such an observation can provide memories that will last a lifetime.

A rather extensive woodland of pinyons and junipers exists above the desert, at the base of the escarpment, as well as on the open ridges at higher elevations. Much of the pinyon-juniper bird life is similar to that which exists throughout the American Southwest, but the Juniper Titmouse is at the southeastern edge of its range in the Guadalupes. This little gray-brown bird with a short crest can best be found along the Smith Spring Trail or at Dog Canyon.

Other rather typical pinyon-juniper birds in the Guadalupe Mountains include the Common Poorwill, Broad-tailed Hummingbird, Ladder-backed Woodpecker, Western Scrub-Jay, Bushtit, Bewick's Wren, Blue-gray Gnatcatcher, Western Bluebird, Hepatic Tanager, Canyon Towhee, Chipping Sparrow, Brown-headed Cowbird, Scott's Oriole, House Finch, and Lesser Goldfinch.

One week in June I hiked the Bear Canyon Trail to the highlands and camped overnight in the Bowl. The relict forest in this high depression contains a few mountain birds that do not occur with regularity elsewhere in the park. I found several of the highland specialties reasonably common: Common Nighthawk; Whip-poor-will; Acorn Woodpecker; Western Wood-Pewee; Warbling Vireo; Steller's Jay; Mountain Chickadee; Pygmy and White-breasted nuthatches; House Wren; Hermit Thrush; Orange-crowned,

Yellow-rumped, and Grace's warblers; Western Tanager; and Dark-eyed (gray-headed) Junco. A few other species were less numerous: Band-tailed Pigeon, Western Screech-Owl, Flammulated Owl, Olive-sided Flycatcher, Brown Creeper, Pine Siskin, and Evening Grosbeak.

The most obvious of these was the **Steller's Jay,** an all-blue jay with a blackish blue crest. A pair of these birds spent considerable time watching me as I prepared my camp, and their widely varying calls were evident throughout my stay. Bent (1964a, 262) provided the best description of their vocal repertoire: They "utter low-pitched raucous squawks different from other kinds of jays; calls harsh 'weeh, waah, shaack, schaak, schaak,' and mellow 'kllok, klook, klook,' and shrill hawklike cries: 'kweesch, kweesch, kweesch,' has sweet soft song somewhat like 'whisper song' of robin; female has a rolling click call; is superb at imitating scream of Red-tailed Hawk."

Like other members of the crow (Corvidae) family, Steller's Jays are opportunists and consume a wide variety of foods. They can be extremely aggressive toward smaller birds, taking eggs and fledglings when available. And they can cache food that they often transport in their esophagus.

A survey of Guadalupe Mountain birds undertaken during the 1970s by George Newman (1975) revealed that a few other high country species also occur there at least occasionally. These include Wild Turkeys, (Mexican) Spotted Owls, Red-naped Sapsuckers, and Clark's Nutcrackers.

Wintering species within the two parks include year-round residents as well as a number of more northern breeding species. Christmas Bird Counts have been taken in both parks for several years, and these counts provide the best perspective on the wintertime populations. In 2001–2002, seventy six species were tallied at Carlsbad Caverns National Park and fifty eight species in the Guadalupe Mountains. The combined counts tallied more than a hundred species; the dozen most numerous in descending order of abundance were Dark-eyed Junco, Ruby-crowned Kinglet, Canyon Towhee, Scaled Quail, Western Scrub-Jay, House Finch, White-crowned Sparrow, White-winged Dove, House Sparrow, Mourning Dove, Pine Siskin, and Mountain Chickadee.

In summary, the two parks' checklists account for a total of 355 species, of which ninety-four are known to nest. Of those ninety-four species, only one (Killdeer) is a water bird, twelve are hawks and owls, and four are warblers.

BIRDS OF SPECIAL INTEREST

Scaled Quail. This is the bluish quail with a white topknot, most often found along the desert roadways; its call is a loud barking "kuck-yur."

Magnificent Hummingbird. One of the largest of hummingbirds, it is best found about century plants in McKittrick Canyon; males have a metallic green throat and purple crown.

Cordilleran Flycatcher. This is the little, yellowish *Empidonax* flycatcher that nests under ledges along many canyon bottoms in the Guadalupe Mountains.

Cave Swallow. It is common at Carlsbad Caverns, where it nests in the twilight area near the cave entrance and forages over the surrounding desert.

Steller's Jay. Occurring in Texas only in the Guadalupe and Davis mountains, this jay is recognized by its all-blue body and tall, blackish crest.

Canyon Wren. This is a little cinnamon bird with a snow-white throat and a beautiful descending song.

Canyon Towhee. Common throughout the parks' desert scrub environments, this towhee is all-brown with a rusty crown and crissum and a dark breast spot.

Rufous-crowned Sparrow. It is a sparrow of the rocky slopes that sports a rufous crown, black whisker stripes, and grayish breast.

Black-chinned Sparrow. This little sparrow is especially common at Pine Springs Campground; it has a black chin that contrasts with its all-gray underparts, rump, and collar.

Black-throated Sparrow. It is best identified by its coal-black throat, white belly, and dark cheeks bordered by two bold white stripes.

Bullock's Oriole. This oriole is common at Rattlesnake Springs in spring and summer; the male has orange underparts, rump, and cheeks and a black cap, throat, tail, and wings with large white patches.

White Sands National Monument

NEW MEXICO

 The loud, strident songs and rasping "creeek" calls of Cactus Wrens can hardly be ignored, especially when they are the very first creatures to greet you on your arrival at White Sands National Monument. Few species of wildlife are as dependable as the Cactus Wrens of White Sands. If at least one of these robin-sized birds is not already present when you arrive, a few squeaks or spishing sounds should immediately attract them from wherever they might be to investigate the disturbance. The visitor center parking lot, at the entrance to the park's dune drive, is lined with cane chollas, yuccas, and a few other native plant species. Almost every cholla and yucca contains an active Cactus Wren nest or the grassy remnants of earlier nests.

Cactus Wren nests are flask-shaped, football-sized structures of grasses, small sticks, strips of bark, and other debris, built among the plant's protective spines and sharp leaves. Although the nests often appear messy and poorly constructed, a second look will reveal a rather intricate pattern. Each nest is fully enclosed and waterproof; the insulated inner chamber, lined with feathers, is reached through a narrow passage built at one end near the top. A pair of wrens will build two or more nests, one of which they utilize for raising a family, and the others serve as dummy nests that one of the adults or (later) the fledged birds will use for roosting. Two or occasionally three broods are produced annually.

Cactus Wrens often sit for long periods at the very tip of a yucca stalk or other tall structure, surveying their domain and every now and then singing their unique songs: "a low, rough choo-choo-choo-choo to chug-chug-chug-chug, cora-cora-cora-cora, and other variations; all sound like a car refusing to start," according to Scott Terrill in *The Audubon Society Master Guide to Birding* (1961, 344). Then, after proclaiming their territories, they glide down to their mates and greet one another with peculiar "growls" and posturing, crouching with tails and wings extended.

I watched one individual in the parking lot searching the grills of several newly arrived vehicles for insects. It would fly up and extract a butterfly, grasshopper, or some other insect, and then fly back a few feet to consume its meal. After six or seven successful insect snacks, it flew to the ground in the adjacent planter and began to sort through the debris. I watched it lift several pieces of yucca leaves and peer underneath for prey. If nothing was found, the bird left the debris as it was, but on two occasions it threw the material aside with a quick twist of the head and grabbed up the prey found underneath. It seemed especially adept at this method of hunting.

Cactus Wren diets vary. Besides taking advantage of whatever insects they

Cactus Wren

might glean from vehicle grills, they can take advantage of a whole array of foods. See Organ Pipe Cactus National Monument for a discussion of the Cactus Wren's diet.

THE PARK ENVIRONMENT

White Sands National Monument includes the world's largest gypsum dunefield, with dunes reaching sixty feet high, numerous plants and animals that have adapted to the arid conditions, and scenery consisting of snow-white dunes that contrast sharply with the surrounding mountains and blue sky. Located at 4,000 feet elevation within the Tularosa Basin of south-central New Mexico, at the eastern base of the San Andres Mountains, the monument encompasses a total of 144,420 acres, with about half its area dominated by the graceful dunes.

Dune vegetation is limited to scattered sand verbenas, soaptree yuccas, skunkbush sumacs, and rosemary-mint on the slopes and patches of Rio Grande cottonwoods, yuccas, and grasses in depressions and along the edges. Saltbush flats, such as that along the first half of the dunes loop drive, are dominated by fourwing saltbush, yuccas, chollas, and a number of grasses. Pickleweed is common on the alkali flats and dry Lake Lucero. Honey mesquite, fourwing saltbush, and creosote bush occur on the lower mountain slopes. The Tularosa Basin is considered the northern edge of the Chihuahuan Desert.

White Sands National Monument is situated along Highway 70, between Las Cruces and Alamogordo, New Mexico, and is best viewed from the eight-mile self-guided Heart of Sands Loop Drive. The monument visitor center, located along Highway 70, contains an information desk, orientation program, exhibits, and a sales outlet; field guides and a bird checklist are available. Interpretive activities include walks, evening programs, and the self-guided Big Dune Nature Trail. Camping is not available within the park but one can camp at nearby Almagordo.

Additional information can be obtained from the Superintendent, White Sands National Monument, P.O. Box 1086, Holloman AFB, NM 88330-1086; (505) 479-6124; Web address: www.nps.gov/whsa/.

BIRD LIFE

The visitor center grounds are the park's most productive bird-viewing areas. Mourning Doves, Say's Phoebes, Western Kingbirds, Northern Mockingbirds, Bullock's and Scott's orioles, House Finches, and House Sparrows can usually be found there in spring and summer with little effort. And a dozen or more additional species can often be found with a little more time.

Say's Phoebe is a slender, brownish gray bird with buff-colored belly and black tail. Its flight is graceful, and individuals usually remain close to the buildings on which they build their nests. They often are found sitting at the edge of a building or at the tip of a tall adjacent plant, from where they search for passing insects. They fly out swiftly to snatch up their prey with a snap of the bill, and often return to the same perch, settling down with a flip of the tail. Their calls are a mournful "pee-ur" sound that can usually be heard throughout the day.

Western Kingbirds frequent the cottonwood trees behind the visitor center and can usually be located by their distinct "whit" calls or a drawn-out and harsh metallic "ker-er-ip, ker-er-ip" or "pkit-pkit-pkeetle-dot" song. Kingbirds are exquisite birds with an upright stance and pale to bright yellow underparts, a grayish throat, and a black tail with white outer edges. Unlike their Say's Phoebe cousins, which are full-time residents in the monument, Western Kingbirds spend their winters elsewhere. By September, however, the kingbird population increases substantially as southbound migrants stop over to enjoy the oasislike environment. But they soon leave for warmer climates to the south.

Scott's and Bullock's orioles also go south for the winter months. Bullock's Orioles nest among the cottonwood foliage, while the **Scott's Oriole** is a grassland species that builds suspended basket nests of grasses on yuccas. It occurs about the visitor center as well as in the dunes. The male is an extremely attractive birds with a coal-black hood, back, chest, and tail tip and yellow underparts and rump; it also has a bright yellow patch at the bend of each wing. Females are gray-green with whitish wing bars. But what is most attractive about this bird is its loud, clear whistle songs with numerous variations, sounding superficially like the Western Meadowlark's song. Echoing across the dunes, a Scott's Oriole song can be ventriloquistic and almost haunting in character.

The song of the **Northern Mockingbird** is one of the finest in the bird world. Its songs include renditions that are exact duplications of oriole songs one minute, of Cactus Wren songs the next minute, and of those belonging to several other local species after that. Mockers can carry on for hours, changing their songs continuously. If you whistle a short, catchy phrase several times, a mocker will often repeat that same phrase; hence its common name. They too are dune birds and can be expected within their rather restricted territories throughout the spring, summer, and fall months.

Besides the birds already mentioned, there are a few other residents of the visitor center grounds: Mourning Doves are common and their mournful songs can be heard throughout the year; Greater Roadrunners can sometimes be found about the parking areas running down lizards; Black-chinned Hummingbirds feed at flowering shrubs; Chihuahuan Ravens soar overhead or search the parking lot and roads for food; Brown-headed Cowbirds are social parasites that watch for opportunities to lay their eggs in other birds' nests; House Finches may be present, the males recognizable by a reddish head, streaked belly, and spirited songs; and House Sparrows are almost always searching for seeds and insects along the edges of the parking area.

Chihuahuan Ravens are all-black birds slightly larger than crows but smaller than the more heavyset Common Ravens. These birds were earlier called "white-necked ravens," because their neck feathers are white at the base, a feature evident only on a windy day. Their calls are low, drawn-out croaks, a hoarse "quark, quark." This species, like its larger cousin, is omnivorous, willing to feed on almost anything edible. Insects and a huge variety of other invertebrates, numerous vertebrates—reptiles, amphibians, and birds and their eggs and nestlings—and plant materials such as fruit and seeds are all part of their diet. And one also can expect Chihuahuan Ravens patrolling the highways during the early morning hours, looking for any roadkills from the previous night.

Gambel's Quail often occur about the visitor center grounds. Early morning is the best time of day to see this elusive bird. Then it often walks along the roadsides, and with binoculars one can see it well enough from a distance and not frighten it away. The male Gambel's Quail has a black throat, face, and teardrop-shaped plume and a chestnut cap and sides, while the female lacks the black throat and belly. Their call is a querulous "chi-*ca*-go-go," the call so often heard in western movies. Scaled Quail, a blue-gray quail with a whitish topknot, are also occasionally found at White Sands.

Another bird found along the roadway, as well as on the alkali flats, is the **Horned Lark,** a sparrow-sized bird with a black, white, and yellow head and black crescent on its chest. The "horn" refers to the tufts of black feathers that arise from the bird's crown. Initial sightings are often of birds flying up from the roadway and departing with only their blackish tail and high-pitched "tsee-ee" notes in evidence. Horned Larks are among our most widespread birds; their range includes almost all of the Americas, from the Arctic to Mexico, and much of the Old World. They prefer open areas, from coastal flats to high mountain tundra.

Of the monument's various dune birds, none is as fascinating as the **Loggerhead Shrike.** This is the black-masked, white, gray, and black bird that is sometimes called "butcher-bird," due to its predatory habit. Male Loggerheads capture insects, small rodents, birds, and reptiles and impale them on thorns or sharp yucca leaves; they even use barbed wire. The male's cache of

Horned Lark

prey decorates various plants in his territory and serves as an attractant to female shrikes.

A Loggerhead Shrike looks like a Northern Mockingbird at first glance, because individuals of both species are black and white with white wing patches. But Loggerheads are stockier birds with shorter and more powerful bills, and they fly in a straight line with faster wing beats. Shrikes lack the singing ability of mockingbirds, producing loud, harsh, almost rattling screech calls. See Death Valley National Park for more about their singing ability.

Watch, too, for the little Black-throated Sparrow on the saltbush and alkali flats. Readily identified by its coal-black throat and two white facial stripes, it is a pert and charismatic bird that is a true desert species. It is often first detected by its faint tinkling notes. Other birds of the saltbush flats and desert slopes include the Lesser and Common nighthawks, Ladder-backed Woodpecker, Chihuahuan and Common ravens, Verdin, Bewick's Wren, Crissal Thrasher, Pyrrhuloxia, and Spotted and Canyon towhees. Park naturalist John Mangimeli told me that Pyrrhuloxias are common all winter around the visitor center.

Migration time, however, can be something special at the monument, when thousands of birds stream southward across the saltbush flats. One early September morning I recorded forty-six bird species in about two hours by walking the roadway for about two miles. The most abundant species was the little Chipping Sparrow, with its reddish cap, gray underparts, and black-and-brown striped back. Other migrants found in numbers included Western Wood-Pewees; Orange-crowned, Yellow-rumped, MacGillivray's, and Wilson's warblers; Blue Grosbeaks; Green-tailed Towhees; Brewer's, Clay-colored, Vesper, Lark, and White-crowned sparrows; Lark Buntings; Red-winged, Yellow-headed, and Brewer's blackbirds; and Lesser Goldfinches. Smaller numbers of House Wrens, Sage Thrashers, Common Yellowthroats, Western Tanagers, Black-headed Grosbeaks, Lincoln's Sparrows, and Pine Siskins were recorded, as was one American Redstart.

I also watched a lone Northern Harrier hunting for prey over the flats. It slowly quartered back and forth at less than a dozen feet high, as if it had sectioned off certain portions of the flats to hunt one at a time. Every now and then it would suddenly twist in the air and drop onto the ground, as if pouncing on a prey animal. This hawk remains throughout the winter months and can usually be found hunting these fields, according to Mangimeli.

Chihuahuan Raven

During the spring and fall migration months, rain storms can create temporary pools between the dunes and at Lake Lucero. These ponds often attract significant numbers of wading birds and shorebirds. White-faced Ibis, American Avocets, and Willets can usually be found among the dunes. And grebes, ducks, and shorebirds stop off at Lake Lucero.

In addition, Mangimeli told me about an accessible artificial wetland located only three miles east of the park. Constructed by Holloman Air Force Base using treated sewage water, this site has become a mecca for migrating birds and an adequate habitat for nesting Snowy Plovers.

In summary, the park's bird checklist includes 210 species, of which seventy are listed as permanent or summer residents and breeders. Of those seventy species, only two are water birds (American Coot and Killdeer), nine are hawks and owls, and two are warblers (Lucy's Warbler and Common Yellowthroat).

BIRDS OF SPECIAL INTEREST

Gambel's Quail. This is the park's only common quail, easily identified by its teardrop-shaped topknot and its "chi-*ca*-go-go" call.

Say's Phoebe. It is especially common near the visitor center; it has gray-brown plumage with a buff-colored belly.

Western Kingbird. Watch for this flycatcher about the cottonwoods near the visitor center; its yellow belly and black tail with white outer edges are its most distinguishing features.

Chihuahuan Raven. This all-black bird is best identified by the white base of its neck feathers, seen only on windy days, and its hoarse "quark" calls.

Horned Lark. This sparrow-sized bird is often found walking along the roadway and flats about the dunes; it is best identified by its black chest crescent, yellowish throat, and black lines on its head.

Cactus Wren. The harsh, rasping songs of the monument's most obvious bird can be heard throughout the year; its nests are common on chollas and yuccas.

Northern Mockingbird. This is the black-and-white songbird with a long tail and a diversity of songs.

Loggerhead Shrike. Like a Northern Mockingbird but heavier-bodied and having more direct flight, this shrike is sometimes called the "butcherbird" because of its predatory nature.

Scott's Oriole. This is the black and yellow bird that frequents the dunes, building its pendant nests on yuccas.

Big Bend National Park

TEXAS

 I could hear the song ahead of me, to the right of the trail. There was silence for a few minutes, broken only by the almost ubiquitous calls of Bewick's Wrens and the hoarser notes of Mexican Jays. Then I heard the song again, closer now and coming from the little canyon along the trail. I stopped and waited for the little yellow and gray bird that I expected would soon move into the higher branches of an oak that grew taller than the surrounding brush. Suddenly there it was: my first Colima Warbler! I watched it work its way up and around the Emory oak, gleaning the branches and leaves for insects. It captured a long green caterpillar and for just a second or two seemed to examine its breakfast before swallowing the prize. The Colima Warbler fed there in the sunlight for several minutes, and every thirty seconds or so it would put its head back and sing, a song a little like that of a Yellow Warbler but shorter and faster and less melodic.

I fell in love with Big Bend National Park on that first visit and later had the opportunity to spend six years there as chief park naturalist.

To birders, Big Bend National Park in West Texas is America's number one national park. More species of birds have been recorded there (455) than in any other of North America's crown jewels. Several of Big Bend's 455 species are Mexican residents that barely range north of the border. The most important of these is the diminutive Colima Warbler, which breeds nowhere north of Mexico except in Big Bend.

Several other Mexican birds, including the Zone-tailed Hawk, Lucifer Hummingbird, and Varied Bunting can be found more easily in Big Bend than anywhere else. And no other national park has reported as many species of hummingbirds—fifteen occur here. In addition, the area is home to the endangered Black-capped Vireo and the Peregrine Falcon; this latter species was listed as endangered for many years but was delisted in August of 1999.

THE PARK ENVIRONMENT

Its 801,163 acres of Rio Grande floodplain, desert, and mountain habitats make Big Bend one of the largest and wildest of the U.S. national parks, besides being the best refuge representing the Chihuahuan Desert ecosystem.

Colima Warbler

The Rio Grande forms the southern boundary of the park and is contiguous with Mexico for 118 miles. This vital river, which originates in the Colorado Rockies, is usually only a trickle by the time it reaches El Paso, Texas. Most of the flow that passes through Big Bend National Park comes out of Mexico via the Rio Conchos, which enters the Rio Bravo del Norte (the Mexican name for the Rio Grande) at Presidio, southeast of El Paso.

Within the park, the lush, green floodplains are interspersed between three magnificent canyons: Santa Elena, Mariscal, and Boquillas. All contain cliffs that tower to about fifteen hundred feet above the waterway. The Rio Grande provides a popular rafting route, especially within the three canyons, and also serves as an important route for migrating birds during both spring and fall. Downstream of the park, an additional 127 miles of the Rio Grande were designated in 1978 as the Rio Grande Wild and Scenic River. The canyons along this stretch of the river are every bit as dramatic as those within the park.

The Chisos Mountains serve as a magnificent centerpiece for the park. These are the southernmost mountains in the United States, an island of greenery surrounded by arid Chihuahuan Desert. About sixteen thousand acres are above 3,700 feet elevation, the altitude of the lower edge of the woodlands. The summit of Emory Peak, the high point, is 7,825 feet in elevation, and on a clear day it affords views of much of West Texas and far into Coahuila, Mexico. The high escarpment approximately fifty miles southeast of the Chisos, the western edge of Mexico's Maderas del Carmen (the southern end of the Sierra del Carmen that forms the eastern edge of the park), rises to about 9,000 feet elevation. That area and its bird life are further discussed in my *Birder's Mexico* (1999).

The Chisos Basin, located at 5,300 feet elevation in the heart of the mountains, contains a visitor center, campground, trailheads, motel, and a restaurant and gift shop. Most people who go to the park, especially during the summer months, visit the Chisos Basin. Obtaining overnight accommodation in the motel often requires reservations far in advance, especially during holidays and weekends. The Basin's high elevation gives it pleasant temperatures in summer. Several Chisos Mountain trails originate in the Basin and provide excellent walking and hiking routes into the higher mountains and to the Window toward the west, the setting for superb sunset views.

The best time to visit Big Bend National Park is during the cooler winter months, November through March. The majority of the park's winter visitors prefer to camp in the lowlands, especially at the park's principal campground, Rio Grande Village. Situated on the eastern edge of the park along the Rio Grande, the location allows for easy day trips across the river to Boquillas, Coahuila. Boquillas Canyon and the magnificent limestone cliffs of the Sierra del Carmen provide the backdrop for Rio Grande Village. At dusk the cliffs can be a deep rose color, reflecting the sun as it sets behind the Chisos Mountains far to the west.

Cottonwood Campground, on the park's western edge, has a similar setting. Its backdrop is the fifteen-hundred-foot cliffs of the Sierra Ponce, which catch the early morning light. The tiny Mexican village of Santa Elena can be reached by fording the Rio Grande near Castolon, the historic U.S. Army compound and trading post.

Above the floodplain are six distinct vegetative zones or ecological associations (Wauer 1971). The mesquite-acacia association of the arroyos is dominated by lanceleaf cottonwood, honey and screwbean mesquites, catclaw acacia, and desert-willow. In surrounding desert lowlands is a lechuguilla–creosote bush–cactus association with ocotillo, blind pricklypear, and clavellina, dominated by creosote bush and lechuguilla. This grades into a higher sotol-grass association with tobosa and chino grama in the warmer areas and sotol, bear-grass, purple threeawn, and various grama grasses in cooler areas. The mid-elevation deciduous woodland association is dominated by Graves and Emory oaks, evergreen and littleleaf sumacs, Texas madrone, canyon maple, mountain sage, and scarlet bouvardia. In the pinyon-juniper association are Mexican pinyon; drooping, alligator and redberry junipers; gray, Emory, and Graves oaks; evergreen and littleleaf sumacs; and several grasses. The uppermost cypress-pine-oak association is dominated by Arizona cypress, Douglas-fir, ponderosa pine, Mexican pinyon, junipers, Texas madrone, birchleaf buckthorn, silktassel, mountain sage, Emory and Graves oaks, and canyon maple.

The park's principal visitor center is located at Panther Junction and houses an information desk, exhibits, and an excellent sales outlet where general field guides, a bird checklist, and the park-specific *Field Guide to Birds of the Big Bend* (Wauer 1996) are available.

Regularly scheduled talks, bird walks, and special bird seminars are available. Park interpreters give evening talks and bird walks at the Rio Grande Village and the Basin campgrounds; schedules are available on request. In addition, the Big Bend Natural History Association sponsors a Big Bend seminar program, which includes a variety of sessions on bird identification and ecology. Further details are available from the Big Bend Natural History Association, P.O. Box 86, Big Bend National Park, TX 79834; (915) 477-2251; email: BBNHA@aol.com.

Additional information on the park can be obtained from the Superintendent, Big Bend National Park, TX 79834; (915) 477-2251; Web address: www.nps.gov/bibe/.

BIRD LIFE

The **Colima Warbler** is the park's most renowned songbird, in spite of the fact that it is resident only from mid-April through September. It spends the rest of the year in Mexico's western mountains from Sinaloa to northern Oaxaca. Seeing the Colima Warbler on its U.S. breeding grounds in the Chisos Mountains is not easy, however, and requires at least a six-mile roundtrip hike

Lucifer Hummingbird

to either Pinnacles Pass or Laguna Meadows. The most reliable place to find this warbler is in Boot Canyon, which requires a nine-mile roundtrip hike.

The **Lucifer Hummingbird** is another of Big Bend's Mexican specialties. Although there have been a handful of sightings of this species in a few other localities north of the border, it occurs regularly and in numbers only at Big Bend National Park. Like the Colima Warbler, it is present only during the spring and summer months. Lucifers seem to appear mysteriously in early March with the first flowering of the acacias in the lowlands. They nest on lechuguilla stalks in spring. Ornithologist Peter Scott, while studying this bird in May and June 1982, found twenty-four nests between Panther

Junction and the Chisos Basin (Scott 1993). Another good location to find this hummingbird in spring is Blue Creek Canyon, above the old ranchhouse.

By late May, when century plants (Havard agave) begin to bloom on the slopes of the Chisos, Lucifers practically abandon the desert for the mountains. The Window Trail is a good place to find the species then. And a little later when the brilliant red flowers of the mountain sage appear at higher elevations (above approximately 6,500 feet), the birds feed almost exclusively at these beautiful shrubs.

As noted, Big Bend National Park holds the record for the greatest number of hummingbird species recorded in any of the national parks, fifteen. Besides the Lucifer, four other hummers—Broad-billed, Blue-throated, Magnificent, and White-eared—are more common in Mexico than within the United States. Although the two large hummers—Magnificent and Blue-throated—are present all summer, the White-eared and Broad-billed hummingbirds usually visit the park only for brief periods when the mountain sage is in bloom. Blue-throats are commonplace in the upper canyons, such as Boot and Pine canyons. And there are single records of Berylline and Violet-crowned hummingbirds.

The common hummingbird of the Big Bend lowlands is the little Black-chinned Hummingbird, while the Broad-tailed Hummingbird is the common species in the Chisos woodlands. Broad-tails frequent the pinyon-juniper woodlands as well as the cypress-pine-oak association in the upper canyons. Ruby-throated, Costa's, Anna's, Rufous, Allen's, and Calliope hummingbirds occur only as migrants or as occasional visitors. The Rufous Hummingbird, however, can be the single most numerous hummingbird above the desert after midsummer when these northern nesters, already on their southbound migration, reach the Chisos Mountains. There they feed on the sweet nectar of mountain sage and several other Chisos plants in preparation for the journey to their winter homes in southern Mexico and Central America.

Although the Rio Grande serves as the most important route for northbound migrants in spring, the Chisos Mountains provide an extremely valuable feeding and resting site for southbound travelers. By early August, when the desert lowlands are at their lowest ecological ebb, the flowering slopes of the Chisos are often teeming with bird life.

The **Varied Bunting** is a contender for being named the park's most beautiful bird. Although its beauty is subtle, compared with some warblers and the closely related Painted Bunting of the Rio Grande floodplain, the male Varied Bunting's purplish body, red nape and throat, and blue rump make it truly spectacular in good light. An earlier name for this bird, and well deserved, was "beautiful bunting." It is another Mexican species with U.S. occurrence only along the southern border area, where it is resident in summer; it is a sporadic winter bird as well. Varied Buntings typically frequent the brushy grasslands that occur between the desert and the Chisos woodlands. During years with heavy or average rainfall, Varied Buntings can be found in surprising abundance, but they can be uncommon during dry years. The best locations to find this bird include the Sam Nail Ranch, Blue Creek Canyon above the old ranchhouse, and along the Window Trail.

The Sam Nail Ranch is located along the roadway to Santa Elena Canyon, on the western flank of the Chisos Mountains. It is a small, quiet place with a working windmill that pumps water into a little trough, from which it overflows onto the parched ground. A bench has been placed in the shade of the huge pecan trees where one can sit in the cool stillness. It is a wonderful place to watch and listen. Sitting there one morning in early summer, I became completely mesmerized by the abundant activity around me.

Activity did not begin immediately. I must have sat there for three or four minutes. Then I was attracted to the movement of a red blotch just above me. A male Summer Tanager was searching for food in the foliage. There, too, was a Black-chinned Hummingbird, busy inspecting a spider web. The bird darted in and retrieved a tiny insect that had been detained in the web.

From the lower vegetation beyond came the short, rapid song of a **Bell's Vireo,** a nonmusical chattering, "chu-che-chu-che-chu-che-chu," ending with an upward inflection. But when the bird immediately repeated the song, it ended with a downward inflection. It is said that this songster asks a question and immediately responds. I watched this little, yellow-tinged bird, with its rather stubby bill and whitish eye rings and eyebrows, work its way to within a few feet of me, then gradually disappear into the shadows of the underbrush. But its song continued, and I heard it throughout the two hours I spent there at the old ranch. Accompanying its song was that of a Yellow-breasted Chat, which came close enough to see only briefly before moving away into the denser vegetation.

Suddenly a **Painted Bunting** appeared at the water. I had not seen it approach in spite of its bright colors. It drank its fill and then flew into the adjacent shrubbery. It sat there a moment wiping its bill, and then, as I watched through my binoculars, it sang a song of incredible sweetness, clear and musical, a song that Paul Sykes described in *The Audubon Society Master Guide to Birding* (1961) as "pew-eate, pew-eate, j-eaty-you-too." As it flew away, I was attracted to a long-tailed bird just arriving at the water: a Crissal Thrasher, named for its reddish crissum (the area under the rump).

The **Crissal Thrasher** is among Big Bend's high priority species for birders, as Big Bend is near the eastern edge of its range and it usually is elusive in its behavior. This thrasher may sit at the top of a tree or shrub at a distance, often singing its very distinct song, but as soon as it is approached, it usually drops down into the underbrush and either runs away or flies off so low down that it cannot be seen. Then it suddenly pops up on another shrub or tree a good distance away.

There were other birds at the Sam Nail Ranch that morning: Ladder-backed Woodpecker, Cactus Wren, Northern Mockingbird, Verdin, both Northern Cardinal and the look-alike Pyrrhuloxia, House Finch, and Lesser Goldfinch. I had briefly entered the birds' world, and they had ignored my presence—a wonderful sensation. Visitors to Big Bend National Park are given opportunities of this nature that few other places provide.

Pyrrhuloxias are among Big Bend's most appealing birds. At first glance they look much like the closely related cardinal, but they differ in having yellow, snubby, down-curved bills, rather than a straight-edged reddish bill, and males lack the all-red plumage of the male cardinal. Instead, the male Pyrrhuloxia is grayish with a red face and throat and red on the tip of the crest, wings, tail, and lower belly. Pyrrhuloxias are true desert birds, while cardinals prefer the heavier growth of the floodplain and at scattered oases. The songs of the two species are similar but can be separated with practice. See Amistad National Recreation Area for a description of their songs.

The steep, wooded side canyons to the north of the Window Trail provide habitat for Gray and Black-capped vireos, two birds that are becoming increasingly difficult to find. Researchers have discovered that increased numbers of Brown-headed Cowbirds have seriously affected these two vireos. Cowbirds are obligate brood parasites, species that cannot build their own nests and must take advantage of other nests and host species. Female cowbirds lay their eggs in the nests of other (usually smaller) birds, and may remove the host bird's eggs. Or the young cowbirds, which hatch in eleven or twelve days and ahead of their nestmates, may force out the natural youngsters, either physically shoving the smaller birds from the nest or outcompeting them for food. The foster parents feed whichever nestling is the most aggressive.

Female Brown-headed Cowbirds have an extremely long reproductive period, giving them the ability to "take advantage of a continuous supply of host nests for about a two-month period. An average female lays about 80 eggs; 40 per year for two years," report John Ehrlich and colleagues (1988, 621), who characterize cowbirds as "passerine chickens." These workers add: "Circumstantial evidence indicates that in some areas, at least some female cowbirds specialize in particularly vulnerable host species, to the apparent exclusion of other species nesting nearby that serve as common hosts in other parts of the cowbird's range." This may be the case for the Black-capped Vireo.

The Black-capped Vireo is a dynamic little songbird with a coal-black cap, white eye rings and lines in front of the eyes like bold white spectacles, a greenish gray back, snow-white belly, and yellowish flanks. Its song sounds a little like that of the White-eyed Vireo but is more musical. Terres (1987) describes it as "there now, wait-a-bit," or "come here, right-now-quick." The rather plain Gray Vireo sings a song that is always in three parts, "chu-weet, chee," with various inflections.

Since about 1970, the larger Bronzed Cowbird has moved into the park's lowlands and begun to impact the Orchard and Hooded orioles. Declines in both populations have occurred. Earlier increases of Brown-headed Cowbirds apparently affected Yellow Warblers during the first half of the 1900s. Early naturalists reported the Yellow Warbler to be a common nesting bird along the Rio Grande, when populations of Brown-headed Cowbirds were low. But when cowbird numbers increased during the 1940s and 1950s, there was a sharp decline in Yellow Warblers, and by the 1960s, nesting Yellow Warblers were nonexistent within the floodplain.

As many as six to ten pairs of **Peregrine Falcons** annually nest on the high cliffs of the major canyons, especially in Santa Elena and Boquillas Canyons, and an additional two to five pairs nest in the Chisos Mountains. For many years the Big Bend area was considered one of the last strongholds of the peregrine south of Alaska.

The reason that the Big Bend Peregrines were less affected was that these birds depended on a resident prey base that did not move in and out of the area, thus not coming into contact with DDT. The Big Bend Peregrines, as well as those of the adjacent Maderas del Carmen in Mexico, were dependent on resident birds such as White-winged Doves, Band-tailed Pigeons, and Mexican Jays. For additional information about this marvelous falcon, see Grand Canyon National Park.

The **Zone-tailed Hawk** is a bird of Mexican affinity that frequents open cliffs throughout the park. These hawks can be expected in the high Chisos Mountains as well as along the Rio Grande. They fly just above the cliff tops and make short dives to capture lizards off the high, open cliffs. Their appearance in flight mimics that of the Turkey Vultures that utilize the same habitats, a condition ornithologist David Ellis and colleagues (1993) term "predaceous mimicry." Both species have a bicolored pattern of black and gray in flight, fly with their wings held in a shallow **V** position, and rock slightly from side to side. However, the Zone-tail has a banded tail and feathered head, unlike the all-dark tail and bare, reddish head of the Turkey Vulture. The Zone-tail's similarity to Turkey Vultures is extremely useful in fooling their lizard prey.

Other hawks that nest in the park include the common Red-tailed Hawks at all elevations; Prairie Falcons on cliffs in the lowlands; Cooper's (some years) and Gray hawks and Common Black-Hawks on the Rio Grande flood-plain; and Golden Eagles and American Kestrels in the mountains. Occurring as migrants or casual visitors are the Osprey, Mississippi Kite, Northern Harrier, Crested Caracara, Merlin, and Harris's, Red-shouldered, Broad-winged, Swainson's, White-tailed, Rough-legged, and Ferruginous hawks.

Ten species of owls are found in the park. Barn, Burrowing, Long-eared, Short-eared, and Northern Saw-whet owls are visitors only. Five species nest at Big Bend. The most numerous of these is the Great Horned Owl, which can be found at all elevations except in the upper moist canyons and at all times of the year. Its lonesome hooting calls, "whooo, whoo, who-who," can be heard throughout the lowlands, most often during its breeding season from early winter through April and May.

The Eastern Screech-Owl's range overlaps with that of the look-alike Western Screech-Owl at Big Bend National Park. It is not unusual to hear the songs of both species during the same evening along the floodplain or in the Chisos woodlands. The Western Screech-Owl's song is described as a "bouncing ball" sound, while the Eastern Screech-Owl's song is a quavering whistle; it also sings a high whinny song on occasions. Rio Grande Village and upper Green Gulch are easy-to-reach areas to listen for the two songs. The Western Screech-Owl can usually be found at Dugout Wells. Ornithologist Joe Marshall (1967) studied these birds in the park and discovered some hybridization of the two species.

Throughout the lowlands, from late March through mid-September, the tiny **Elf Owl** can be seen after dark. This owl is common below approximately 5,500 feet elevation. Individuals can be found in the Basin Campground but are particularly numerous at Rio Grande Village. They nest in cavities in trees and utility poles in and adjacent to the campgrounds, utilizing deserted sites originally excavated by woodpeckers. Elf Owls are less than six inches in length, possess yellow eyes, and lack ear tufts. They feed on insects and other arthropods, usually captured in flight. They can often be located by their distinct call, a series of reasonably loud churp notes.

Big Bend's other small owl, the Flammulated Owl, nests only in the higher canyons of the Chisos Mountains, but it is difficult to find. Once found, however, it is easy to identify, as it is the only small owl with brown eyes. The yellow eyes and white eyebrows of the smaller Elf Owl give it a fierce countenance. The large brown eyes and tawny brown color of the Flammulated Owl make it seem more mellow than ferocious.

The most numerous bird found in the mountains is the **Bewick's Wren;** it is especially abundant within the pinyon-juniper woodlands. This bird has an incredible variety of songs and seems to imitate several other songbirds, including the Colima Warbler. Bent (1964b) gives an idea of the variety other authors have described: "the song is sweet and exquisitely tender—one of the sweetest and tenderest strains I know"; "not a voluble gobble, like the house wren's merry roundelay, but a fine, clear, bold song, uttered as the singer sits with head thrown back and long tail pendent, a song which may be heard a quarter of a mile or more"; and "in imitative ability the Bewick's wren has, apparently, no rival . . . other than the mockingbird." Its song can also be ventriloquistic in nature, making the bird's location difficult to pinpoint. Bewick's Wrens can be secretive but are readily identified by a brownish back, long tail, and bold white eyelines. Its cousin the Canyon Wren has only one song but often sings only pieces of the melody. However, its resonance makes up for its lack of variety. Its complete clear and descending whistle song cannot be mistaken for any other. This little wren is at home in the upper canyons of the Chisos as well as in the massive canyons along the Rio Grande.

The blue jay of the Chisos is the **Mexican Jay,** once called "gray-breasted jay." These large, noncrested jays frequent the woodlands, traveling in troops of five to eighteen birds. Like jays everywhere, they can be quite aggressive and loud. Although this species is commonplace in the highlands, individuals occasionally visit the lower nonforested canyons such as Blue Creek, especially during periods of drought. See Chiricahua National Monument for more about this southern jay.

Other common woodland birds not already mentioned are the "sweeet"-singing Hutton's Vireo; Black-crested Titmouse, a species earlier lumped with the Tufted Titmouse of the eastern United States; the tiny, long-tailed Bushtit; the Blue-gray Gnatcatcher, with its thin whisper call; the liver-red-colored Hepatic Tanager; and the Spotted Towhee, a ground-loving species that was known as "rufous-sided towhee" for several years.

By late summer or early fall, after the nesting season is past, it is not unusual to find eight to twelve species of warblers among the pines and oaks of the Chisos Mountains. Most numerous of these are the Orange-crowned, Nashville, Colima, Yellow, Yellow-rumped, Townsend's, and Wilson's warblers. Lesser numbers of Virginia's, Black-throated Gray, Hermit, Grace's, and Black-and-white warblers may also be found, as may the American Redstart and Northern Waterthrush. All these warblers soon move south except the Orange-crowned, which can be found in the lowlands all winter.

Winter visitors to the park usually get their introduction to Big Bend's varied bird life at the lowland campgrounds. Although many of the Mexican specialties are far south of the border at that time of year, many northern species mix with the full-time residents to delight the nature enthusiast. Probably the best example is the gorgeous **Vermilion Flycatcher,** a year-round resident. The male's brilliant red underparts and crown and contrasting black back and tail are a familiar sight around the Rio Grande Village and Cottonwood campgrounds. Their sharp "peet" or "peent" calls can be heard throughout the winter, and males begin to display as early as February. Terres (1987, 388) describes this behavior: "uttering ecstatic notes of pit-a-see!

Canyon Wren

Vermillion Flycatcher

pit-a-see! or pu-reet!, [the male] mounts upward vertically in air, red crest erected, breast feathers swollen, tail lifted; with wings vibrating rapidly, hovers in butterfly-like flight, then slowly flutters down to female."

The male House Finch also has a reddish breast, but it cannot compare with the vivid plumage of the Vermilion Flycatcher. House Finches usually appear in flocks during the winter, as do the White-crowned Sparrows that feed on the ground at the campground edges. The Vermilion Flycatcher is a loner.

The tiny, nondescript bird with white eye rings, usually seen darting around in the trees and shrubs and constantly flitting its wings, is the Ruby-crowned Kinglet. A summer resident in the high Rocky Mountains, it overwinters in the warmer southern states. And the yellow, black, and white birds seen feeding on insects among the foliage are Yellow-rumped Warblers, also visiting from summer territories among the coniferous forests in the north. Both the western "Audubon's" subspecies, with yellow throat, and the eastern "myrtle" subspecies, with white throat, occur together in winter and during migration.

Everyone's favorite avian clown, the **Greater Roadrunner,** is another common sight in the Big Bend lowlands, as engaging a character in real life as in cartoons and posters. One can watch for hours as this bird runs about on its long legs, feeding on lizards, spiders, and other creatures. Its ability to hunt down and kill rattlesnakes is probably exaggerated, though possibly true. A member of the cuckoo family, the strange-looking roadrunner would be difficult to confuse with any other species. Its tail seems too long and loose, its bill too large for its head, its body too skinny, and its long legs give it a gawky, off-balance appearance. Yet few birds are more perfectly adapted to desert conditions. Roadrunners can chase down the fastest lizard or dodge the swiftest snake, and they often nest among the long, protective spines of cholla cactus and other thorny shrubs. As a year-round resident, it is an appropriate symbol of Big Bend's desert landscape. No visitor to this great national park should be satisfied to leave without seeing the roadrunner in its desert abode or, in summer, the Colima Warbler in the Chisos highlands.

Christmas Bird Counts have been taken annually in the park for many years and provide the best perspective on the winter bird populations. A count taken on December 29, 2001, tallied seventy-one species. The dozen most numerous birds in descending order of abundance, were Ruby-crowned Kinglet; House Finch; Black-throated Sparrow; Rock Wren; Common Raven, White-winged Dove, and Yellow-rumped Warbler (tied); White-crowned Sparrow; Black-tailed Gnatcatcher; Black Phoebe; Ladder-backed Woodpecker; and Mallard.

In summary, the 1999 revision of Big Bend's checklist of birds includes 446 species. Seventy-four of those are present throughout the year, and 111 species are known to nest; seven of those are water birds, sixteen are hawks and owls, and five are warblers.

BIRDS OF SPECIAL INTEREST

Zone-tailed Hawk. A migrant and summer resident in the Chisos Mountains and along the Rio Grande canyons, it looks very much like the common Turkey Vulture.

Peregrine Falcon. It is present all year and nests on cliffs in the Chisos and along the river. It is most numerous in migration from early March to early May along the Rio Grande.

Greater Roadrunner. This long-legged character is most common in the lowlands, along the roadways, and in the campgrounds.

Elf Owl. Fairly common in summer below the mountain woodlands, it can best be found at nest sites in cottonwoods and utility poles at Rio Grande Village.

Lucifer Hummingbird. Present in the park from March through September, it utilizes flowering acacias in spring, century plants in early summer, and mountain sage in late summer.

Vermilion Flycatcher. The male's brilliant red plumage is unmistakable; this flycatcher is common at the Rio Grande Village and Cottonwood camp-grounds all year.

Bell's Vireo. This tiny bird is common in summer along the floodplain and at scattered wet areas below the woodlands; it is best located by its rapid song.

Mexican Jay. Troops of five to eighteen of these noncrested blue and gray jays are fairly common within the Chisos woodlands.

Bewick's Wren. This most numerous summer resident in the mountains has a confusingly large repertoire of songs.

Crissal Thrasher. Look for this long-tailed, long-billed bird in brushy areas, such as along the Window Trail and in Blue Creek Canyon, during the spring and summer months.

Colima Warbler. Big Bend's most famous bird, it nests in the Chisos Mountains and can best be found at Laguna Meadow and Boot Canyon.

Pyrrhuloxia. This desert bird looks a little like a cardinal but has a red stripe down its chest, on its wings and tail, and a yellowish rather than reddish bill.

Painted Bunting. This is the almost gaudy rose-red, blue, and greenish bunting of the floodplain; females are greenish.

Varied Bunting. Males of this bunting are purplish with a red nape and throat and blue rump; these birds summer in brushy areas between the desert and pinyon-juniper woodland.

Amistad National Recreation Area

TEXAS

 The dawn literally exploded with birdsong. Northern Cardinals, Yellow-breasted Chats, Northern Mockingbirds, and Painted Buntings were the earliest birds to the songfest. Chats and mockingbirds had sung their territorial songs throughout much of the night. But with the dawn, other nesters joined the choir. As daylight began to spread, a dozen or more Lesser Nighthawks dominated the air, swooping and circling with fluttering wing beats. Their low, purring trills filled the air.

From where the Spur 406 roadway reaches the reservoir, I walked slowly up the road through the campground and surrounding vegetation. The mournful calls of Mourning Doves were detected next. Then Bewick's Wrens and Bell's Vireos added their voices to the concert. Bewick's Wrens sang rather complex songs of variable notes ending with musical trills. Bell's Vireos' songs were distinct because of their habit of asking then quickly answering questions. A House Finch joined in. Red-winged Blackbirds called "konk-a-ree" from the adjacent shoreline. And from far across the little bay, I detected the distinct gobbling of a Wild Turkey. But still only the nighthawks were visible.

Suddenly, a Yellow-breasted Chat arose from a nearby acacia. I watched as it flew forty or fifty feet into the air, and then, with wings flapping like a huge butterfly, it fluttered downward. Its descending display included an amazing series of whistles, mews, grunts, and groans. When it alighted on a secluded perch, it continued its barrage of calls. I moved to the far side of the road, where I could clearly see this highly vocal warbler. Its bright yellow breast and throat contrasted with its olive-green back and bold white spectacles.

By now birds were moving over the water. Three Great Egrets flew by, their long white wings beating slowly. A Great Blue Heron, with its even slower wing beats, passed over in the opposite direction. Five Blue-winged Teal zoomed across the water and landed among the snags on the far shore. Through binoculars I could see the males' distinct white crescent patch in front of each eye. Nearby was a pair of Pied-billed Grebes, and farther to the right was a flock of American Coots. These plump, all-black water birds with white bills were bathing and preening, preparing for the new day. Coots are

Yellow-breasted Chat

members of the rail family (Rallidae), not ducks. They can be extremely aggressive with each other. One may grab a neighbor with a clawed foot, slap with the other foot, and jab with its heavy bill. Coots are among the reservoir's most visible and abundant residents, especially during the winter months from October to May. But they have a bad reputation; see Lake Mead National Recreation Area for more about their aggressive behavior.

On the near shore was a pair of Mallard-like ducks. I studied these two carefully because Mallards are winter residents at Amistad only; they should be far north by now, in late April. Neither had the typical green head of a Mallard drake, and both showed dark blue speculums bordered with white on their wings. Then I realized that they were Mexican Ducks, a subspecies of Mallard that was once considered a separate species. These birds apparently had not interbred with the dominant Mallard. They exhibited true Mexican Duck traits: both sexes were heavily streaked above and spotted below, the male had a yellow-orange bill with a dark ridge, and the female possessed an unmarked yellow-green bill. My identification was confirmed when I discovered three more Mexican Duck pairs that morning.

Altogether, I found fifty-two species from the roadway in about three hours. Most interesting was the diversity of species within that patch of riparian habitat. For instance, both the western Bullock's Oriole and the eastern Orchard Oriole were present; individuals were chasing one another about the mesquite and huisache in typical oriole courting fashion. Northern Bobwhites, apparently at the western edge of their range, were common there too, delivering their loud "bob-white" calls with great vigor. I also discovered a few Brown-crested Flycatchers and Long-billed Thrashers and numerous Olive Sparrows. These three are Mexican birds that range north only to South Texas and westward along the Rio Grande only as far, apparently, as Amistad.

THE PARK ENVIRONMENT

Amistad National Recreation Area is best known as a boating and fishing reservoir that extends from Del Rio, Texas, up the Rio Grande for seventy-four miles above the dam. Elevations range from 900 to 1,500 feet above sea level. When full, Amistad Reservoir with its 850 miles of shoreline backs up into the Devil's River for twenty-five miles and the Pecos River for fourteen miles. The nonflooded riparian zones and a few side canyons contain remnants of the original environment. The riparian zones comprise scattered stands of giant and common reeds and cattail, honey mesquite, willows, seepwillow, tree tobacco, and saltcedar, with an understory dominated by skeleton goldeneye. Drainages that flow into the reservoir are often narrow and insignificant, but a few, such as lower California Creek (on Spur 406) and Lowry Spring, possess a luxuriant growth of trees and shrubs. Most common species in this habitat are honey mesquite, blackbrush acacia, huisache, cat-claw guajillo, little walnut, Texas mountain laurel, Texas persimmon, little-leaf leadtree, and seepwillow.

The open, drier flats above the reservoir are influenced by Chihuahuan Desert flora to the west and Tamaulipan Scrub flora to the southeast. Indicator species of the Chihuahuan Desert region include lechuguilla, candelilla, creosote bush, tarbush, ocotillo, and mariola. Indicator plants of the Tamaulipan Scrub region include blackbrush acacia, cenizo, desert yaupon, and Texas mountain laurel. Common widespread species include guayacan, wolfberry, sacahuista, sotol, and yuccas.

The headquarters of the national recreation area, located on Highway 90 just north of Del Rio, has an information desk and a sales outlet; bird guides and a checklist are available. In addition, a National Park Service exhibit on the U.S. side of Amistad Dam contains interpretive exhibits on the dam and recreation area.

Interpretive activities during the winter months include weekly evening programs and coffees with a ranger and monthly bird walks. Details on times and locations are available at headquarters as well as being posted on various bulletin boards.

Additional information can be obtained from the Superintendent, Amistad National Recreation Area, HCR 3, Box 5J, Del Rio, TX 78840; (830) 775-7491; Web address: www.nps.gov/amis/.

BIRD LIFE

Amistad's riparian vegetation, like that at Spur 406 Campground, supports the most birds in spring and summer. Besides the birds mentioned, this is where you are most likely to find the outstanding **Vermilion Flycatcher.** Males sport a bright red crown and underparts, which contrast with their deep brown back, tail, wings, and cheeks; females are duller versions of the males. Because of the male's fiery plumage, in Latin America it is known as *la brasita de fuego,* or "little coal of fire." During the breeding season, males perform amazing aerial displays much like those of the neighboring chats. They fly high in the air and descend with wings pumping, singing a tinkling "pit-a-see pit-a-see."

Two *Myiarchus* flycatchers can be found in this habitat, the Brown-crested Flycatcher and the slightly smaller and more common Ash-throated Flycatcher. But neither can match the Vermilion Flycatcher in dress and personality. Brown-crested and Ash-throated flycatchers are brownish above and possess a gray to ashy throat, yellowish belly, and buff tail and wings that show a reddish tinge. They can be difficult to tell apart, but the Brown-crested Flycatcher is a bulkier bird with a heavier bill and a distinctly yellow belly. In addition, Brown-crested Flycatchers produce sharp "whit" or "queet" calls, while the Ash-throated Flycatchers call is a two-syllable "ka-brick" or "ka-wheer." Both are cavity nesters that utilize vacant woodpecker nests and natural holes in trees and shrubs. Vermilion Flycatchers construct small grass and twig nests on the lower branches of woody plants; they usually are fairly easy to locate.

Two additional flycatchers frequent these areas. Scissor-tailed Flycatchers with their long, deeply forked tails can often be found perched on wires, tall poles, or trees in the open. The smaller Black Phoebe usually perches on snags over the water. Its all-black body and snow-white belly make identification easy.

I also spent several hours at Lowry Spring, located along a paved but poorly maintained roadway northeast of Rough Canyon. Betty and I had the place all to ourselves; apparently it is remote enough to receive little use. The bird life almost duplicated what I had found at the Spur 406 Campground area, with a few additions. Several tall Vasey shin oaks in the rocky drainage apparently enhanced the habitat enough to attract White-eyed Vireos, Black-crested Titmice, Blue-gray Gnatcatchers, and Summer Tanagers.

Painted Buntings were abundant along the drainage, singing their spirited songs from various shrubs. I recorded it that day as clear musical couplets, like "pew-eate, pew-eata, j-eata, you-too." Males perched in full view so that their contrasting, almost gaudy plumage was obvious: the bright blue head, red underparts, and greenish yellow back stood out. Through binoculars I could also see the red eye rings and short, conical bill. A truly gorgeous creature! Females possess a lime green back and duller underparts.

Also along the drainage I discovered a **Great Horned Owl** perched on a branch. It watched me intently but remained still as I approached. Partly concealed by foliage, it apparently did not feel threatened. A large owl with ear tufts and yellow eyes, it is sometimes seen perched on utility poles along highways at dusk and dawn. Its loud song, a deep "whooo whoo who-who," can usually be heard throughout the night.

The Great Horned Owl is one of several birds that nest on the high limestone cliffs along the canyons, even the deep canyons of the Rio Grande, Pecos, and Devil's rivers. Also nesting there are Great Blue Herons, Black and Turkey vultures, Red-tailed Hawks, Rock and Canyon wrens, and Cliff, Cave, and Barn swallows.

When nesting, **Great Blue Herons** can usually be detected from a considerable distance. They emit terrible grunts and groans that echo off the cliffs and seem to permeate the entire area. They select small, secure ledges, often with small shrubs, where they build bulky stick nests. Several nests were visible on the cliff ledges across the river from the Pecos River Picnic Site overlook one spring day.

Tall, skinny birds with long legs and neck, a huge yellow bill, and black-and-white plumage, Great Blue Herons fish the shoreline of the reservoir year-round. Although they are most active during the morning and evening hours, they can be busy all day and, when feeding young, all night as well. They usually fish by standing perfectly still over shallow water, beak poised for an instant thrust at passing prey. They capture small fish in their bill sidewise, but they actually spear larger fish. Like most predators, they are opportunists that will take a wide variety of prey, ranging from insects to other birds, reptiles, amphibians, and even mammals like mice and rats.

The open shoreline of the reservoir is seldom without the constant "killdee" calls of the **Killdeer,** another common year-round resident. If disturbed, this shorebird can cause a tremendous fuss, especially when nesting. Then it may pretend injury by dragging a wing, as if the wing is broken, as it runs in the opposite direction from its nest. Thus a predator like a coyote or badger may be enticed away from the nest. But just when the predator is about to close in, the Killdeer will "recover" and fly off to safety. Although the Killdeer is most numerous along the moist shoreline of the reservoir, individuals occasionally are found in drier sites some distance from the water. Even there, they may fly up with great agitation, loudly calling their piercing "kill-dee" or "dee-dee-dee" cries.

To the inexperienced eye, the drier shoreline beyond is an uninviting desertscape devoid of wildlife, where the dominant vegetation consists of thorny or armored shrubs. But anyone who takes time to walk out into the desert scrub will find this habitat alive with birds. Especially in spring, when nesting birds are most active in their territorial defense, a short walk can easily produce a dozen or more species.

Cactus Wrens and Northern Mockingbirds are likely to be detected first, primarily due to their loud singing and habit of perching on top of the tallest shrubs. The **Cactus Wren** sings a rollicking, throaty "chug-chug-chug-chug" or "cora cora cora cora" song that is more a series of grunts than a melodic aria. Its song is usually delivered with so much enthusiasm that it can hardly be ignored. See White Sands National Monument for details about its nest construction and behavior.

The Cactus Wren is a robin-sized, chunky bird with a heavy bill, dark brown spots on its whitish underparts, a streaked back, rusty crown, and bold, whitish eyebrows. Its behavior also helps with identification. Besides singing from the tops of shrubs, it exhibits fascinating feeding behavior, pry-

Great Blue Heron

ing up pieces of debris to search underneath for insects. But its diet is not limited to insects. This aggressive wren captures small lizards and frogs, and when cactus fruit is ripe it takes advantage of those delicacies as well.

It seems as if there is unending competition between the Cactus Wren and the **Northern Mockingbird** during the nesting season as to which is the more voluble. The mockingbird, true to its name, often mimics Cactus Wren songs. Then suddenly it switches to a totally different song, often one with various phrases and a melody. Besides being just as loud as the neighboring Cactus Wrens, the mockingbird often sings off and on throughout the night, after the Cactus Wren has retired. In his classic *Guide to Bird Songs* (1951, 128), Aretas Saunders wrote that the mockingbird's "song is made up of imitations of other birds, and not only these, but of other kinds of animal life and of inanimate sounds. These are interpolated into the middle of the song, and sometimes songs are largely made up of imitations. The bird often sings in flight, and commonly does this on moonlight nights, at times apparently singing almost all night long." It has been called our "national songbird." In Texas it is the official state bird.

The Northern Mockingbird is one of our most recognized birds, slim, gray and white, and with a long tail. Often found in gardens and fields, it is also a common bird of the southwestern deserts. There it feeds on a wide variety of foods, from insects to fruit. When searching for insects, it often uses its contrasting plumage to advantage. "Wing flashing," or quickly opening and closing its wings while perched on a shrub or on the ground, tends to flush insects. This behavior may also be used to distract predators.

There are several other common desert birds at Amistad. The smallest is the Verdin, with gray body, yellow head, and maroon wing patches. One of the largest is the Curve-billed Thrasher, brownish gray with lightly spotted underparts and yellow-orange eyes. The Black-throated Sparrow possesses a black throat and white stripes above and below the eyes; it seems to prefer the most arid habitats. Conversely, the nondescript Cassin's Sparrow appears only after high to moderate rainfall; it is best detected by its constant singing from a perch or while "sky larking," flying high in the air and descending with wing speed and singing. The Rufous-crowned Sparrow may be one of the shyest of sparrows. This bird sings a song of jumbled whistle notes and prefers rocky terrain. And the Lark Sparrow can be abundant in spring and summer; this large sparrow is easy to identify by its chestnut, white, and black head, white underparts with a central breast spot, and black tail with conspicuous white corners.

Another common arid land bird is the **Pyrrhuloxia,** a species that closely resembles the Northern Cardinal but lacks the all-red body and bill. Both sexes of Pyrrhuloxia have yellow bills. Males are a subtle buff color with a red face and throat and red on the tip of the crest, belly, and tail. Females are duller. Pyrrhuloxias also sing a song very much like that of cardinals, but there is a difference. Pyrrhuloxias sing a clear "quink quink quink" song, all on the same pitch, while cardinals sing with slurred whistles, like "cheer cheer cheer," diminishing in pitch. Both also sing "what-cheer" notes; those of the Pyrrhuloxia are thinner and shorter.

Amistad's desert quail is the **Scaled Quail,** sometimes called "cottontop" because of its whitish crest, which looks like a tuft of cotton. It also is known as "blue quail" because of its overall bluish color. However, seen up close, its breast feathers appear scaled, the reason for its name. In spite of its relative abundance, this bird is more often heard than seen. It has a loud, nasal, intrusive "pe-cos" call, unlike the clear "bob-white" call of that quail.

Scaled Quail are true southwesterners; their range is limited to the Chihuahuan Desert region from northern New Mexico through West Texas, reaching westward only to southeastern Arizona and southward into Mexico. They are most often seen along the roadsides during the morning hours or along brushy arroyos. They may run away or, when startled, fly off with quick wing beats.

Most of Amistad's dry land birds are full-time residents, remaining on preferred territories year-round. Fall migrants and wintering species often add substantially to the bird life in areas with abundant seeds and fruit. And by late fall, northern water birds begin to arrive. Many remain all winter, while others continue south to favored sites in Mexico. Various species of ducks stay until spring, feeding around the lake and flocking in deeper water overnight. The most common species include the Mallard, Northern Pintail, American Wigeon, and Ring-necked Duck. Smaller numbers of Blue-winged Teal, Northern Shovelers, Gadwalls, Redheads, Common Goldeneyes, Buffleheads, and Ruddy Ducks can also be expected. American White Pelicans fish the reservoir in winter; they are most common at Pecos River, Upper Rio Grande, Cow Creek, and San Pedro Canyon.

Winter bird populations are censused each year in Christmas Bird Counts. The Del Rio Count includes only a portion of the national recreation area but provides the best indication of species abundance. For example, the January 5, 2002, count produced 109 species. The dozen most numerous species in descending order of abundance were American Coot, Great-tailed Grackle, Northern Shoveler, Red-winged Blackbird, Common Grackle, House Sparrow, Redhead, Wild Turkey, Mallard and Green-winged Teal (tied), Blue-winged Teal, and Yellow-rumped Warbler.

In summary, the park checklist of birds includes 204 species. Ninety-six of those are listed for summer and presumably nest. Of those ninety-six species, fourteen are water birds, seven are hawks and owls, and three are warblers.

BIRDS OF SPECIAL INTEREST

Great Blue Heron. This tall, long-legged wader with a six-foot wingspan can be expected anywhere in the park; it nests on high cliffs.

American Coot. Small to huge flocks of these chubby all-black birds with white bills occur along the shore and in secluded bays of the reservoir year-round.

Killdeer. This shorebird is best recognized by its loud "kill-dee" calls; it is a year-round resident that frequents moist areas surrounding the reservoir.

Scaled Quail. Locally called "blue quail" because of its overall bluish appearance, it has a whitish crest and a loud, strident call: "pe-cos."

Great Horned Owl. This large "horned" owl is often seen perched on high posts or heard calling deep "whooo whoo who-who" notes after dark.

Vermilion Flycatcher. With the male's fiery red underparts and dark brown back, this little songbird cannot be mistaken for any other species.

Cactus Wren. This is the plump, all-brown bird of arid landscapes; its song is a distinct, rollicking "chug chug chug chug" or "chur chur chur chur."

Northern Mockingbird. Widespread and familiar from home gardens, the mockingbird is also common throughout Amistad's arid landscapes; it can imitate almost any bird or sound.

Yellow-breasted Chat. A common summer resident at riparian areas, it sings a wild assortment of notes and has all-yellow underparts, olive-green back, and white spectacles.

Pyrrhuloxia. This is the cardinal look-alike without the all-red plumage; it is tan overall with a red chest, crest, and tail and a yellowish (not red) bill.

Painted Bunting. The male is a gorgeous little bird with a bright blue hood, rose-red underparts and rump, and a yellow-green back.

Common and Scientific Plant Names

Abrojo, gray-leaved. *Zizyphus obtusifolia.*

Acacia, blackbrush. *Acacia rigidula.*

Acacia, catclaw. *Acacia constricta.*

Acacia, white-thorn. *Acacia constricta.*

Agave, Havard. *Agave havardiana.*

Agave, New Mexico. *Agave neomexicana.*

Agave, Utah. *Agave utahensis.*

Alumroot. *Heuchera rubescens.*

Apace plume. *Fallugia paradoxa.*

Arrowweed. *Tessaria sericea.*

Aster. *Aster* sp.

Ash, fragrant. *Fraxinus cuspidata.*

Ash, velvet. *Fraxinus velutina.*

Aspen. *Populus tremuloides.*

Baccharis, Arizona. *Baccharis thesioides.*

Barberry, Fremont. *Berberis fremontii.*

Beargrass. *Xerophyllum tenax.*

Bear-grass. *Nolina erumpens.*

Birch, water. *Betula papyrifera.*

Blackbrush. *Coleogyne ramosissima.*

Bladdersage. *Salazaria mexicana.*

Bouvardia, scarlet. *Bouvardia ternifolia.*

Boxelder. *Acer negundo.*

Brickellia, Mohave. *Brickellia oblongifolia.*

Brittlebush. *Encelia farinosa.*

Buckbrush. *Symphoricarpos occidentalis.*

Buckthorn, birchleaf.
  Rhamnus betulaefolia.

Buckthorn, hollyleaf. *Rhamnus crocea.*

Bulrush. *Scirpus olneyi.*

Bursage. *Franseria dumosa.*

Cactus, acuna.
  Echinomastis erectocentrus acunensis.

Cactus, beavertail. *Opuntia basilaris.*

Cactus, Bigelow. *Opuntia bigelovii.*

Cactus, dahlia-rooted. *Cereus striatus.*

Cactus, organ pipe. *Stenocereus thurberi.*

Cactus, senita. *Cereus schottii.*

Candelilla. *Euphorbia antisyphilitica.*

Catclaw. *Acacia greggii.*

Cattail. *Typhs latifolia.*

Ceniza. *Leucophyllum frutescens.*

Century plant. *Agave* sp.

Cheese-bush. *Hymenoclea salsola.*

Chokecherry. *Prunus melanocarpa.*

Cholla, cane. *Opuntia imbricata.*

Chuparosa. *Beloperone californica.*

Clavellina. *Opuntia schotti.*

Cliffrose. *Cowania stansburiana.*

Cottonthorn. *Tetradymia spinosa.*

Cottonwood. *Populus* sp.

Cottonwood, Fremont. *Populus fremontii.*

Cottonwood, lanceleaf.
  Populus acuminata.

Cottonwood, narrowleaf.
  Populus angustifolia.

Cottonwood, Rio Grande.
  Populus deltoides wislizenii.

Creosote bush. *Larrea tridentata.*

Cypress, Arizona. *Cupressus arizonica.*

Dalea. *Parosela* sp.

Datura, sacred. *Datura discolor.*

Desert holly. *Atriplex hymenelytra.*

Desert-fir. *Peucephyllus schottii.*

Desert-willow. *Chilopsis linearis.*

Douglas-fir. *Pseudotsuga menziesii.*

Elephant tree. *Bursera microphylla.*

Fendlerbush. *Fendlera rupicola.*

Fernbush. *Chamaebatiaria millefolium.*

Fir, white. *Abies concolor.*

Goldeneye, skeleton. *Viguiera stenoloba.*

Gooseberry. *Ribes* sp.

Gooseberry, oak-belt. *Ribes quercetorum.*

Grama, chino. *Bouteloua ramosa.*

Grape. *Vitis* sp.

Grape, desert. *Vitis girdiana.*

Grass, sacaton. *Sporobolus airoides.*

Greenmolly. *Kochia americana.*

Guajillo, catclaw. *Acacia berlandieri.*

Guayacan. *Guaiacum angustifolium.*

Hackberry, netleaf. *Celtis reticulata.*

Hawksbeard. *Crepis nama.*

Honeysweet. *Tidestromia oblongifolia.*

Hopsage, spiny. *Grayia spinosa.*

Hoptree, common. *Ptelea angustifolia.*

Hornbeam, western. *Ostrya knowltonii.*

Huisache. *Acacia smallii.*

Iodine-bush. *Suaeda suffrutescens.*

Ironwood. *Olneaya tesota.*

Jojoba. *Simmondsia chinensis.*

Joshua tree. *Yucca brevifolia.*

Juniper, alligator. *Juniperus deppeana.*

Juniper, California. *Juniperus californica.*

Juniper, drooping. *Juniperus flaccida.*

Juniper, one-seeded.

   Juniperus monosperma.

Juniper, redberry. *Juniperus pinchoti.*

Juniper, Utah. *Juniperus osteosperma.*

Leadtree, little-leaf. *Leucaena retusa.*

Lechuguilla. *Agave lechuguilla.*

Locust, New Mexico.

   Robinia neomexicana.

Lupine. *Lupine* sp.

Madrone, Arizona. *Arbutus arizonica.*

Madrone, Texas. *Arbutus texana.*

Mallow, desert. *Sphaeralcea* sp.

Manzanita. *Archostaphylos* sp.

Maple, bigtooth. *Acer grandidentatum.*

Maple, western mountain. *Acer glabrum.*

Mariola. *Parthenium incanum.*

Mesquite, honey. *Prosopis glandulosa.*

Mesquite, screwbean. *Prosopis pubescens.*

Mesquite, velvet. *Prosopis velutina.*

Mormon tea. *Ephedra viridis.*

Mountain laurel, Texas.

   Sophora secondiflora.

Mountain mahogany.

   Cerocarpus montanus.

Ninebark. *Physocarpus alternans.*

Nolina, Parry. *Nolina parryi.*

Oak, Ajo. *Quercus ajoensis.*

Oak, Arizona white. *Quercus arizonica.*

Oak, chinkapin. *Quercus muhlenbergi.*

Oak, Emory. *Quercus emoryi.*

Oak, Gambel. *Quercus gambelii.*

Oak, Graves. *Quercus gravesii.*

Oak, gray. *Quercus grisei.*

Oak, Mexican blue. *Quercus oblongifolia.*

Oak, netleaf. *Quercus rugosa.*

Oak, scrub. *Quercus pungens.*

Oak, silverleaf. *Quercus hypoleucoides.*

Oak, Toumey. *Quercus toumeyi.*

Oak, wavyleaf. *Quercus pauciloba.*

Ocotillo. *Fouquieria splendens.*

Olive, desert. *Forestiera phillyreoides.*

Paintbrush, Indian. *Castilleja* sp.

Palm, California fan.

   Washingtonia filifera.

Palm, date. *Phoenix* sp.

Paloverde. *Parkinsonia* sp.

Persimmon, Texas. *Diospyros texana.*

Pickleweed. *Allenrolfea occidentalis.*

Pine, Apache. *Pinus engelmanii.*

Pine, bristlecone. *Pinus aristata.*

Pine, Chihuahua. *Pinus leiophylla.*

Pine, limber. *Pinus flexilis.*

Pine, pinyon. *Pinus edulis.*

Pine, ponderosa. *Pinus ponderosa.*

Pine, southwestern white.

   Pinus strobiformis.

Pinyon. *Pinus edulis.*

Pinyon, Mexican. *Pinus cembroides.*

Pinyon, singleleaf. *Pinus monophylla.*

Pinyon, two-needle. *Pinus edulis.*

Poison-ivy. *Toxicodendron radicans.*

Pricklypear, blind. *Opuntia rufida.*

Pussy-willow. *Salix discolor.*

Rabbitbrush. *Chrysothamnus* sp.

Rabbitbrush, rubber. *Chrysothamnus nauseosus.*

Reed, common. *Phragmites communis.*

Reed, giant. *Arundo donax.*

Rock nettle. *Eucnides urens.*

Rosemary-mint. *Poliomintha incana.*

Sacahuista. *Nolina texana.*

Sagebrush, big. *Artemisia tridentata.*

Sagebrush, sand. *Artemesia filifolia.*

Sage, desert. *Salvia dorrii.*

Sage, fringed. *Artemisia frigida.*

Sage, mountain. *Salvia regla.*

Saguaro. *Carnegiea giganteus.*

Saltbush, fourwing. *Atriplex canescens.*

Saltcedar. *Tamarix* sp.

Saltgrass. *Distichlis stricta.*

Sand verbena. *Abronia* sp.

Sawgrass. *Cladium jamaicense.*

Seepwillow. *Baccharis glutinosa.*

Senecio, creek. *Senecio douglasii.*

Serviceberry. *Amelanchier alnifolia.*

Shadscale. *Atriplex confertifolia.*

Silktassel. *Garrya lindheimeri.*

Silktassel, Wright. *Garrya wrightii.*

Skunkbush. *Rhus trilobata.*

Smoke tree. *Parosela spinosa.*

Snakeweed, broom. *Gutierrezia sarothrae.*

Snowberry. *Symphoricarpos* sp.

Sotol. *Dasylirion leiophyllum.*

Sotol, Wheeler. *Dasylirion wheeleri.*

Spruce, blue. *Picea pungens.*

Spruce, Engelmann. *Picea engelmannii.*

Squawbush. *Rhus trilobata.*

Sumac, evergreen. *Rhus virens.*

Sumac, littleleaf. *Rhus trilobata.*

Sumac, skunkbush. *Rhus aromatica.*

Sycamore. *Platanus occidentalis.*

Sycamore, Arizona. *Platanus wrightii.*

Tamarisk. *Tamarix* sp.

Tansy. *Tanacetum canum.*

Tansy bush. *Chamaebatiaria millefolium.*

Tarbush. *Flourensia cernua.*

Thistle. *Cirsium* sp.

Thistle, Russian. *Salsola iberica.*

Threeawn, purple. *Aristida purpurea.*

Tobacco, tree. *Nicotiana glauca.*

Tobosa. *Hilaria mutica.*

Tomatillo. *Lycium pallidum.*

Vauquelinia, Torrey. *Vauquelinia torreyii.*

Walnut, Arizona. *Juglans arizonica.*

Walnut, black. *Juglans niger.*

Walnut, little. *Juglans microcarpa.*

Water molly. *Baccharis glutinosa.*

Willow. *Salix gracilis.*

Willow, Goodding. *Salix gooddingii.*

Willow, slender. *Salix gracilis.*

Winterfat. *Ceratoides lanata.*

Wolfberry. *Lycium andersonii.*

Yaupon, desert. *Schaefferia cuneifolia.*

Yucca, banana. *Yucca baccata.*

Yucca, Faxon. *Yucca faxoniana.*

Yucca, Mohave. *Yucca schidigera.*

Yucca, Schotts. *Yucca schottii.*

Yucca, soaptree. *Yucca elata.*

References

American Ornithologists' Union (AOU). 1983. *Check-list of North American Birds.*
6th ed. Washington, D.C.: American Ornithologists' Union.

———. 1998. *Check-list of North American Birds.* 7th ed. Washington, D.C.: American
Ornithologists' Union.

———. 2000. Forty-second supplement to the American Ornithologists' Union
Check-list of North American Birds. *Auk* 117:847–58.

Bednarz, J. C. 1988. Cooperative hunting in Harris' hawks (*Parabuteo unicinctus*).
Science 239:1525–27.

Bellrose, Frank C. 1976. *Ducks, Geese and Swans of North America.* Harrisburg, Pa.:
Stackpole Books.

Bent, Arthur Cleveland. 1958. *Life Histories of North American Blackbirds, Orioles,
Tanagers and Allies.* Washington, D.C.: Smithsonian Institution Press.

———. 1963. *Life Histories of North American Flycatchers, Larks, Swallows, and Their
Allies.* New York: Dover Publications.

———. 1964a. *Life Histories of North American Jays, Crows and Titmice.* New York:
Dover Publications.

———. 1964b. *Life Histories of North American Nuthatches, Wrens, Thrashers, and Their
Allies.* New York: Dover Publications.

———. 1968. *Life Histories of North American Cardinals, Grosbeaks, Buntings, Towhees,
Finches, Sparrows, and Allies.* Washington, D.C.: Smithsonian Institution Press.

Brandt, Herbert. 1951. *Arizona and Its Bird Life.* Cleveland, Ohio: Bird Research
Foundation.

Brockman, C. Frank. 1968. *Trees of North America.* New York: Golden Press.

Brooks, Paul. 1980. *Speaking for Nature.* San Francisco: Sierra Club Books.

Brown, Bryan T., Steven W. Carothers, Stephen W. Hoffman, and Richard L. Glimski.
1990. Abundance of peregrine falcons in Grand Canyon National Park has
implications of region-wide recovery. *Park Science* Spring: 7.

Brown, Bryan T., Steven W. Carothers, and R. Roy Johnson. 1987. *Grand Canyon Birds.*
Tucson: University of Arizona Press.

Carothers, Steven W., and H. H. Goldberg. 1976. Life after the rain of fire. *Plateau*
49(2):14–22.

Chapman, Frank M. 1966. *Handbook of Birds of Eastern North America.* New York:
Dover Publications.

Clark, William S., and Brian K. Wheeler. 1987. *A Field Guide to Hawks of North America.*
Boston: Houghton Mifflin.

Collins, Henry H., Jr. 1951. *Birds of Montezuma and Tuzigoot.* Globe, Ariz.:
Southwestern Monuments Association.

Council on Environmental Quality and Department of State. 1980. *The Global 2000 Report to the President*. Washington, D.C.: Government Printing Office.

Ehrlich, Paul R., David S. Dobkin, and Darryl Wheye. 1988. *The Birder's Handbook*. New York: Simon and Schuster.

Ellis, David H., James C. Bednarz, Dwight G. Smith, and Stephen P. Flemming. 1993. Social foraging classes in raptorial birds. *BioScience* 43:14–20.

Griscom, Ludlow, and Alexander Sprunt, Jr. 1957. *The Warblers of America*. New York: Devin-Adair Company.

Groschupf, Kathleen D., Bryan T. Brown, and R. Roy Johnson. 1988. *An Annotated Checklist of the Birds of Organ Pipe Cactus National Monument, Arizona*. Tucson: National Park Service and University of Arizona.

Halle, Louis J. 1947. *Spring in Washington*. New York: Harper and Brothers.

Hensley, M. Max. 1954. Ecological relations of the breeding bird population of the desert biome in Arizona. *Ecological Monographs* 28(2):185–207.

Hoose, Phillip M. 1981. *Building an Ark*. Covelo, Calif.: Island Press.

Howe, Steve. 1992. Raptor redux. *National Parks* July–August: 28–33.

Jackson, Betty. 1941. *Birds of Montezuma Castle*. Special report no. 28. Globe, Ariz.: Southwestern National Monuments Association.

Kaufman, Kenn. 1990. *Advanced Birding*. Boston: Houghton Mifflin.

Kirk, Ruth. 1973. Life on a tall cactus. *Audubon* July: 12–23.

Kurtz, Don, and William D. Goran. 1992. *Trails of the Guadalupes*. Champaign, Ill.: Environmental Associates.

Ligon, J. Stokley. 1961. *New Mexico Birds and Where to Find Them*. Albuquerque: University of New Mexico Press.

Lockwood, Mark, James Paton, Barry R. Zimmer, and William B. McKinney. 1999. *A Birder's Guide to Rio Grande Valley*. Colorado Springs: American Birding Association.

Mader, William J. 1976. Biology of the Harris' hawk in southern Arizona. *Living Bird* 14:59–85.

Marshall, Joe T., Jr. 1967. *Parallel Variation in North and Middle American Screech-Owls*. Monograph no. 1. Los Angeles: Western Foundation for Vertebrate Zoology.

Miller, Alden H., and Robert C. Stebbins. 1964. *The Lives of Desert Animals in Joshua Tree National Monument*. Berkeley: University of California Press.

Mayfield, Harold F. 1960. *The Kirkland's Warbler*. Bloomfield Hills, Mich.: Cranbrook Institute of Science.

National Audubon Society. 1983. The eighty-ninth Christmas Bird Count. *American Birds*. New York: National Audubon Society.

———. 1999. One-hundredth Christmas Bird Count. *American Birds*. New York: National Audubon Society.

National Fish and Wildlife Foundation. 1990. Proposal for a Neotropical migratory bird conservation program. Photocopied report.

National Geographic Society. 2002. *Field Guide to the Birds of North America*. 4th ed. Washington, D.C.: National Geographic Society.

National Park Service. 1980. State of the Park—1980. USDI National Park Service.

———. 1981. State of the Parks: A Report to the Congress on a Service-wide Strategy for Prevention and Mitigation of Natural and Cultural Resources Management Problems. U.S.D.I. National Park Service.

Newman, George A. 1975. Compositional aspects of breeding avifaunas in selected woodlands of the southern Guadalupe Mountains, Texas. In *Biological Investigations in the Guadalupe Mountain National Park, Texas.* (H.H. Genoways and R. J. Bokey, Eds.). Proceedings and Transactions Series, No. 4. Washington, D.C.: National Park Service.

Nice, Margaret Morse. 1964. *Studies in the Life History of the Song Sparrow.* New York: Dover Publications.

Oberholser, Harry C. 1974. *The Bird Life of Texas.* Austin: University of Texas Press.

Peterson, Roger Tory. 1990. *A Field Guide to Western Birds.* Boston: Houghton Mifflin.

Robins, Chandler S., Bertel Bruun, and Herbert S. Zim. 1966. *A Golden Guide to Field Identification: Birds of North America.* Racine, Wis.: Western Publishing Company.

Phillips, Allan, Joe Marshall, and Gale Monson. 1964. *The Birds of Arizona.* Tucson: University of Arizona Press.

Rich, Terry. 1989. Forest, fire and the future. *Birder's World* June: 10–14.

Saunders, Aretas A. 1951. *A Guide to Bird Songs.* Garden City, N.Y.: Doubleday.

Scott, Peter E. 1993. A closer look: Lucifer hummingbird. *Birding* 25(4):245–51.

Sibley, David Allen. 2000. *National Audubon Society: The Sibley Guide to Birds.* New York: Alfred A. Knopf.

———. 2000. *National Audubon Society: The Sibley Guide to Bird Life and Behavior.* New York: Alfred A. Knopf.

Smallwood, John A., and David M. Bird. 2002. American Kestrel. No. 602 in *The Birds of North America.* Ed. A. Poole and F. Gill. Philadelphia, Pa.: Birds of North America, Inc.

Spangle, Paul, and Elsie Spangle. (undated). *Birds of Walnut Canyon.* Globe, Ariz.: Southwestern Monuments Association.

Sykes, Paul. 1961. Painted Bunting. In *The Audubon Society Master Guide to Birding.* Ed. John C. Farrand, Jr. New York: Alfred A. Knopf.

Taylor, Richard Cachor. 1995. *A Birder's Guide to Southeastern Arizona.* Colorado Springs: American Birding Association.

Terrill, Scott. 1961. Cactus Wren; Abert's Towhee. In *The Aududon Society Master Guide to Birding.* Ed. John C. Farrand, Jr. New York: Alfred A. Knopf.

Terborgh, John. 1992. Why American songbirds are vanishing. *Scientific American* May: 98–104.

Terres, John K. 1987. *The Audubon Society Encyclopedia of North American Birds.* New York: Alfred A. Knopf.

Trimble, Stephen. 1979. *Joshua Tree desert reflections.* Twentynine Palms, Calif.: Joshua Tree National History Association.

Wauer, Roland H. 1962. A survey of the birds of Death Valley. *Condor* 64:220–33.

———. 1964. Ecological distribution of the birds of the Panamint Mountains, California. *Condor* 66:287–301.

———. 1971. Ecological distribution of birds of the Chisos Mountains, Texas. *The Southwestern Naturalist* 16(1):1–29.

———. 1996. *A Field Guide to Birds of the Big Bend*. Houston: Gulf Publishing Company.

———. 1999. *Birder's Mexico*. College Station: Texas A&M University Press.

———. 2001. Breeding Avifaunal Baseline for Big Bend National Park, Texas. Occasional Publication of the Texas Ornithology Society 3:1–31.

Wauer, Roland H., and Terrell Johnson. La Mesa fire effects on avifauna: Changes in avian populations and biomass. 1981. In *La Mesa Fire Symposium, Los Alamos, New Mexico, October 6 and 7, 1981*. Los Alamos: Los Alamos National Laboratory.

Williamson, Sheri L. 2002. *Peterson Field Guides: Hummingbirds of North America*. Boston: Houghton Mifflin.

Youth, Howard. Birds fast disappearing. In *Vital Signs 1992*. Worldwatch Institute. New York: W. W. Norton.

Zimmer, Kevin J. 1985. *The Western Bird Watcher: An Introduction to Birding in the American West*. Englewood Cliffs, N.J.: Prentice-Hall.

Index

Pages with illustrations are indicated in **boldface** type.